ROLLING BACK R

ROLLING BACK REVOLUTION
The Emergence of Low Intensity Conflict

IVAN MOLLOY

Pluto  Press

LONDON • STERLING, VIRGINIA

First published 2001
by PLUTO PRESS
345 Archway Road, London N6 5AA
and 22883 Quicksilver Drive,
Sterling, VA 20166–2012, USA

www.plutobooks.com

British Library Cataloguing in Publication Data
A catalogue record for this book is available from
the British Library

Library of Congress Cataloging in Publication Data
Molloy, Ivan.
 Rolling back revolution : the emergence of low intensity conflict/
Ivan Molloy.
   p. cm.
Includes bibliographical references (p.) and index.
 ISBN 0–7453–1707–3 (hbk.) — ISBN 0–7453–1706–5 (pbk.)
 1. United States—Foreign relations—1981–1989. 2. United States—
Foreign relations—1989– 3. United States—Military policy. 4.
Low-intensity conflicts (Military science)—United States. I. Title.
 E876 .M65 2001
 327.1'17'0973—dc21

00–012925

ISBN 0 7453 1707 3 hardback
ISBN 0 7453 1706 5 paperback

10 09 08 07 06 05 04 03 02 01
10   9   8   7   6   5   4   3   2   1

Designed and produced for Pluto Press by
Chase Publishing Services, Fortescue, Sidmouth EX10 9QG
Typeset from disk by Stanford DTP Services, Northampton
Printed in the European Union by Antony Rowe, Chippenham, England

CONTENTS

LIST OF ABBREVIATIONS

AAFLI	Asian American Free Labor Institute
AFL-CIO	American Federation of Labor – Congress of Industrial Organizations
AFP	Armed Forces of the Philippines
AIFLD	American Institute for Free Labor Development
ARDE	Alianza Revolucionaria Democratica (Democratic Revolutionary Alliance)
ARVN	Army of Republic of Vietnam (South Vietnamese Army)
ASC	American Security Council
ASD[SO/LIC]	Assistant Secretary of Defense for Special Operations and Low Intensity Conflict
ASEAN	Association of Southeast Asian Nations
ATC	Rural Workers' Association(s)
BAYAN	New Patriotic Alliance
CANF	Cuban American National Foundation
CAUSA	Confederation of the Associations for the Unity of the Societies of the Americas
CBN	Christian Broadcasting Network
CDA	Cuban Democracy Act
CDS	Sandinista Defense Committee(s)
CENCOM	Central Mindanao Command
CER	Centro de Estudios Religiosos
CHDF	Civilian Home Defense Forces
CHR	Commission on Human Rights
CIA	Central Intelligence Agency
CINCPAC	Commander-In-Chief of the Pacific
CMA	Civilian Military Assistance
COPROSA	Comision de Promocion Social Arquidiocesana (Commission of Archdiocesan Social Promotion)
COSEP	Nicaraguan Business Association (Nicaraguan Democratic Front)
CPD	Committee on the Present Danger
CPP	Communist Party of the Philippines
CPS	Coalition for Peace through Strength
CRMA	Civilian Refugee Military Assistance

DCI	Director of Central Intelligence
DCSOPS	Deputy Chief of Staff for Operations
DOD	Department of Defense
DPA	Deep Penetration Agent
EMJP	Ecumenical Movement for Justice and Peace
ENVIO	the publication of Instituto Historico Centroamericano
EPIC	Ecumenical Partnership for International Concerns
EPS	Sandinista People's Army
ESF	Economic Support Funds
FDN	Frente Democratico Nicaraguense
FID	Foreign Internal Defense
FMLN	Farabundo Marti National Liberation Front
FOA	Friends of Americares
FSLN	Frente Sandinista de Liberación Nacional
GHQ	General Headquarters
ICFTU	International Confederation of Free Trade Unions
IDB	Inter-American Development Bank
IMET	International Military Education and Training
IMF	International Monetary Fund
INP	Integrated National Police
IRD	Institute for Religion and Democracy
ISA	Intelligence Support Activity
JCS	Joint Chiefs of Staff
JGRN	Government Junta of National Reconstruction
JSOA	Joint Special Operations Agency
JSOC	Joint Special Operations Command
JUSMAG	Joint United States Military Advisory Group
KMP	Philippine Peasant Movement (Kilusang Magbubukid ng Pilipinas)
KMV	May First Movement
LIC	Low Intensity Conflict
LIW	Low Intensity Warfare
MAA	Military Assistance Agreement
MAP	Military Assistance Program
MDB	Multilateral Development Bank
MDB	Mutual Defense Board
MDN	Nicaraguan Democratic Movement
MEDCAP	Medical aid programmes
METROCOM	Metropolitan Command
METRODISCOM	Metropolitan District Command
MNLF	Moro National Liberation Front
MTTs	Military/Mobile Training Teams
NAFP	New Armed Forces of the Philippines
NDC	National Defence Council
NDF	National Democratic Front

NED	National Endowment for Democracy
NEPL	National Endowment for the Preservation of Liberty
NICA	National Intelligence Co-ordinating Authority
NISA	National Intelligence and Security Agency
NPA	New People's Army
NSC	National Security Council
NSC-68	National Security Council Directive 68
NSDD	National Security Decision Directive
NSPG	National Security Planning Group
NSSD	National Security Study Directive
OSS	Office of Strategic Services
PAHRA	Philippine Alliance of Human Rights Advocates
PC	Philippine Constabulary
PCHR	Presidential Committee on Human Rights
PNF	Philippine News and Features
PRODEMCA	Friends of the Democratic Center in Central America
PSC	Presidential Security Command
PSYOPS	Political/Psychological Operations
RAM	Reform the Armed Forces Movement
RDF	Rapid Deployment Force
RIG	Restricted Interagency Group
RP	Republic of the Philippines
SOCOM	Special Operations Command
SOFs	Special Operations Forces
SOTs	Special Operations Teams
SOUTHCOM	Southern Command
SWAG	Special Warfare Advisory Group
TRADOC	US Army Training and Doctrine Command
TUCP	Trade Union Congress of the Philippines
UCLAs	Unilaterally Controlled Latino Assets
UNO	United National Opposition
US	United States
USAF	United States Air Force
USAID	United States Agency for International Development
USCWF	United States Council for World Freedom
USIA	United States Information Agency
USIS	United States Information Service
USMC	United States Marine Corps
USSR	Union of Soviet Socialist Republics
VC	Viet Cong
VOA	Voice of America
WACL	World Anti-Communist League
WB	World Bank

ACKNOWLEDGEMENTS

My sincere gratitude is due to many individuals and organisations who have in some way contributed to the completion of this book. Most particularly I wish to thank the Department of Politics, La Trobe University for financing much of this research.

In the United States I received much kind assistance from many individuals and organisations but in particular I would like to thank Mr John Veach for his advice, the staff of the Center for Defense Information, the State Department, the Defense Department and the many individuals who assisted me at the Library of Congress and elsewhere. In Nicaragua I would like to thank many individuals and organisations who also assisted me, most particularly those representatives of the Nicaraguan Government who allowed me access to areas of the country I otherwise would not have been able to visit. I would also like to give special thanks to Daniel Knott for acting as my interpreter on many occasions. While in the Philippines I received much kind assistance from many sources and so I wish to acknowledge the help of the staff of the Dansalan Research Center, Marawi City, and the staff of the Third World Studies Center, University of the Philippines for access to and assistance with their research materials. I also wish to thank Mrs Mendoza and family, the staff of Kahayag, Davao City, Datu Tahir Lidasan and family for their kindness of heart and wonderful accommodation, and similarly Mrs Lita Lorenzo and Dr Bob McAmis of Mindanao State University.

I would also like to extend my thanks to the many combatants and supporters of both the government and insurgent movements in Nicaragua and the Philippines who assisted me, some even at great risk to themselves. While the sheer number of these people prohibits me from listing them individually here, I must also point out that in many cases the nature of their involvement in the conflicts I investigated during the course of my research prevents me from publicly revealing their true identities.

Finally, I wish to thank my family, particularly Cate and my three daughters, Honorlee, Melanie and Bonnie, and my mother and father, for their support and for putting up with me during the long time I have been locked away working on this project.

SOURCES

This study relied on a wide range of first-hand accounts, including interviews with insurgents from the New People's Army and the Contras, members of the Philippine armed forces, ex-US servicemen and Philippine and Nicaraguan government sources. Other primary sources include official US and Philippine government documents. I gathered much of this material in the course of extensive fieldwork in the Philippines, the United States, Nicaragua and Cuba between 1983 and 1995. In pursuing this work I received invaluable assistance from such institutions and organisations as the University of the Philippines, the Philippine Alliance of Human Rights Associations (PAHRA) in Manila, the Philippine military, the New People's Army and members of the National Democratic Front (NDF). In the United States, I consulted and was assisted by the Library of Congress, the State Department, the United States Information Agency (USIA), the United States Agency for International Development (USAID), the Heritage Foundation, the Institute for Religion and Democracy (IRD), and the Center for Defense Information in Washington DC. In Nicaragua, the University of Central America was most helpful as was the Instituto Historico Centroamericano (the publishers of *ENVIO*), and the Sandinista People's Army (EPS) which allowed me to visit a number of war zones and interview Contra prisoners. Secondary source materials in the form of articles and works by other theorists were also extensively consulted. It should be stressed that the difficulties and personal dangers involved in undertaking some aspects of this research made the gathering of certain primary source material virtually impossible. To fill these gaps, it was often necessary to rely upon secondary sources.

INTRODUCTION

Since the end of the Cold War, the 'New World Order' President Bush once described so glowingly during the West's crushing of Iraq continues to be racked by countless nationalist struggles, many led by guerrilla movements. The world community continues in disorder evident in many crises such as in the former Yugoslavia, East Timor, Chechenya and elsewhere with dire possible consequences for regional and even world peace. As a result some argue we have entered an age of competing 'nationalisms'. But this phenomenon is not new. Throughout the Cold War, many revolutionary nationalist struggles ensued in the Third World albeit most were presented as expressions of the greater superpower rivalry with their true nature diminished or distorted. However, in the post-Cold War era their true nature can no longer be obscured.

Also apparent in these post-Cold War years has been the continued use of a very effective *de facto* US strategy designed to combat those Third World revolutionary and post-revolutionary forces that are deemed threatening to Western interests. This strategy is best described as 'Low Intensity Conflict' (LIC). Originating during the Reagan era and used with great effect in the waning Cold War of the 1980s, LIC remains the foremost and most effective means by which the United States can combat threatening revolutionary nationalism when direct intervention is not an option. Or alternatively, it remains the pre-eminent strategy for preparing the ground for direct and 'just' US military intervention in foreign target states. As such, this most effective strategy has continued to be used either fully or partially by the United States, and indeed other countries, since the 1980s and its original emergence in the Philippines and Central America. Used to fight wars when 'it is not fighting wars', LIC remains one of the most enduring legacies of the Reagan era. Just as LIC was most effective in rolling back revolution and forcing the end of the Cold War, at the beginning of the twenty-first century the effectiveness of this strategy continues to be seen in many conflict situations around the world. It is indeed one of Reagan's success stories, one however that has been relatively neglected or little told. This book aims to tell part of that story by investigating LIC's emergence and outlining the part-overt, part-covert 'profile' of what has proven to be a very effective *de facto* US national security strategy. In so doing this book also aims to assist the identification of LIC's 'footprint' wherever it may appear in revolutionary conflicts around the globe today.

A FRESH PERSPECTIVE

Some may ask what is so special about LIC when many activities associated with this strategy have been around for years? The answer is in the uniqueness of the entire multidimensional LIC package as it emerged during the Reagan years. In the 1980s, hostile public opinion at home in the wake of Vietnam actually forced the Reagan Administration to grope towards a different philosophy and approach for fighting revolutionary nationalist struggles in the Third World. The result was the emergence of a new strategy package – LIC. Again there is still nothing new in such an observation. However there is something very special about the nature of the package itself, and this is the fresh perspective I bring to the study of LIC. As I demonstrate in this book, LIC is not primarily a military doctrine for use against target movements and/or governments. In pursuing this strategy, US intervention is continually masked to avoid potential US domestic opposition by deliberately 'privatising' and 'civilianising' US actions. As a result actual US intervention in, or orchestration of, a foreign conflict renders it purely local and domestic in appearance with only peripheral American involvement. Finally, like other strategies LIC relies heavily on psychological operations or 'psyops'; however, in waging LIC, the American people themselves are a major target of this strategy in order to win support for the foreign policy objective sought.

When the use of LIC is identified in any astute analysis of post-Reagan US foreign policy, a fresh perspective emerges as to the respective successes and failures of the different forms of US intervention during the Bush and Clinton Administrations in places like Panama, Haiti, Somalia, Bosnia, Kosovo, Cambodia and even Cuba. On the surface these might seem very different from the Nicaraguan and Philippine experiences in the 1980s, but are they? Do these overseas commitments/interventions represent even more of a downgrading of the military side of US security strategy or were, and are, they simply LIC by other means? This is a very important question not just political observers but the American public should be asking when considering post-Cold War US security policy. As I demonstrate in this book, the operation of LIC involves by necessity intense pysops operations including misinformation programs aimed in part at the US people themselves with obvious implications for rational public debate and even democracy itself. By tracing LIC's emergence in the 1980s and identifying its nature, this book thus goes some way towards addressing this question.

THE ARGUMENT IN A NUTSHELL

In the latter half of the 1970s, the United States lacked an effective national security strategy to combat Marxist revolutionary nationalism it considered antagonistic to its interests in the Third World. The former US national security strategy of military containment had collapsed with the US defeat in Vietnam: the strategy had proved incompatible with the predominantly political nature of Third World revolutionary conflict best described and from here on identified as 'low intensity warfare' (LIW). A strong anti-interventionist sentiment known as the 'Vietnam Syndrome' soon permeated the American public psyche and acted as a powerful domestic constraint on future interventionist foreign policy in the Third World.[1] Enshrined in the Clarke Amendment and the War Powers Act of November 1973,[2] it prohibited direct US involvement in the Angolan conflict in 1975 where 'democratic' resistance forces were attempting to overthrow a Soviet-backed Marxist regime. Ensuing US administrations eschewed direct military intervention in revolutionary conflicts for the rest of the decade. The US military returned to more traditional preoccupations: containing the Soviet threat in the European theatre and defending the West's oil supplies in the Middle East. Meanwhile, in accordance with the Nixon Doctrine, the responsibility of maintaining US economic and strategic interests in the Third World lay with strong allies bolstered with American military and economic aid. Between 1974 and 1980, however, the Third World was swept by a 'wave of revolution': many pro-US regimes serving as American regional 'pillars of power' collapsed and the Nixon Doctrine lost its viability.[3] This wave of what was for the most part Marxist revolutionary nationalism subsequently fed a 'militarist' backlash within the United States that led to the election of the Reagan Administration.

Promising to make the United States 'stand tall' again, the Reagan Administration pledged to reverse the gains it considered the Soviets had made in the Third World often using Marxist revolutionary nationalist movements as proxies. The Administration perceived that these movements (and the 'ambiguous' nature of the low intensity warfare they waged) posed the greatest threat to US strategic interests in the Third World (particularly military bases and facilities), and US economic interests by denying access to valuable resources and markets, thereby hindering the free operation of US capital. Moreover, the Administration considered LIW the most probable form of conflict the US would be involved in at least until the end of the century.[4] The strategic stalemate in Europe between the two superpowers at that time had rendered the Third World the most likely arena for US involvement in conflicts over access to valuable markets and resources. The Reagan Administration thus sought a means of combating Third World revolutionary nationalist movements, which could also accommodate domestic opposition and other constraints on an interventionist foreign policy.

By the end of 1987 the Reagan Administration had developed a multidimensional foreign policy approach that could achieve these objectives. Identified as low intensity conflict, this *de facto* national security strategy, while depending on a number of important conditions, nevertheless allowed America to intervene to combat revolutionary nationalism in select target states while circumventing domestic and international constraints on such a policy. As such, LIC emerged as a low-cost, low-risk, low-profile means of engaging in low intensity warfare to 'roll back' Marxist revolutionary nationalist forces without direct 'conventional' US military intervention.

To demonstrate the above, I first examine the changing assumptions present in US policy during the Reagan era and the theoretical formulation of LIC as a coherent strategy with which to combat revolutionary nationalism. I then explore the development and nature of LIC as it emerged in Nicaragua and the Philippines in the 1980s as two major case studies.

Although LIC boasted universal application, its relevance seems to have been, and still is, 'situation-specific', hence my selection of Nicaragua and the Philippines as case studies. Both were important in the 1980s in terms of US strategic and other interests in Central America and Southeast Asia respectively. Though both lay within the US's sphere of influence, in Nicaragua a revolutionary nationalist movement had captured power; while in the Philippines a similar movement challenged a US-supported regime. As such, both countries soon emerged as 'target states' for some form of active US intervention.

I also selected Nicaragua and the Philippines because by 1987 each exhibited the full conflict profile of the strategy, thus enhancing a comparative analysis of LIC's revolutionary and counter-revolutionary forms. Low intensity conflict, as partly a covert instrument of US foreign policy, was developed and used to varying extents according to a wide ranging spectrum of 'applicability'. However, with the exception of El Salvador and perhaps Afghanistan in the 1980s, only Nicaragua and the Philippines provide the most readily identifiable examples of LIC's full operation and its 'profile'. This is because the strategy's complete development at that time depended on a number of preconditions and/or determinants. These included: the existence of US strategic, economic and/or other interests in a target state and the perception that these were threatened by Marxist revolutionary nationalism; a history of close economic and military ties (including aid) with the US; the viability of different forms of intervention also determined by favourable location and geography; the strength of likely international and US domestic opposition to direct military intervention, and, finally the existence, or the potential for, local opposition groups to assist with the implementation of this strategy. In both Nicaragua and the Philippines the full range of these necessary conditions existed.

One should not assume, however, that LIC was waged elsewhere in the Third World in the 1980s, or even now, simply because of the existence of similar circumstances and activities associated with LIC that I outline in this book. Many activities associated with this strategy are congruent with long-held practices of many Third World militaries and police. Moreover, it should not be assumed that low intensity conflict was, or is, always an external imposition on an essentially passive or archaic security apparatus in any given target state. LIC grew out of the actions of the Reagan Administration, the US military, private agencies and allied forces in the Third World over time. As a *de facto* national security strategy, low intensity conflict gradually gained conceptual coherence and legitimacy with US policy makers only after an effective and recognisable pattern of responses, which were its essence, emerged from many *ad hoc* attempts to combat revolutionary nationalism. One would be mistaken therefore to perceive LIC to be everywhere, when closer scrutiny reveals this is simply not the case. Though universal in theory, in practice the operation of low intensity conflict, as its rationale suggests, will probably always remain difficult to identify. As noted, there were many Third World states in the 1980s and later where it can be argued that elements of LIC existed such as in Afghanistan and Cambodia, and yet the strategy did not fully emerge. Only by recognising LIC's preconditions or determinants, the existence of its agencies, and all of the dimensions of either its revolutionary or counter-revolutionary conflict profile, can the full operation of the strategy, or its 'footprint', be positively detected.

A number of key propositions are central to this book. Collectively they reflect both the determination of the Reagan Administration to roll back anti-US forces in the Third World, and the strong constraints on the US's ability to achieve this objective in the 1980s – constraints that still exist today.

First, I argue that low intensity conflict achieved conceptual and operational coherence as a de facto national security strategy by the end of 1987 – this coherence was measured by LIC's ability to achieve stated national objectives by ideologically legitimate means closely linking foreign policy with operational doctrine.[5]

Second, I argue that LIC was and is more suited than conventional military force to combat the predominant Maoist or 'people's war' strategy of revolutionary warfare as waged in the Third World since the Second World War. While military action is important, people's war emphasises the political objective of gaining the support of the local, or 'target', population. It thus involves 'total' conflict between two different political systems wherein the 'hearts and minds' of target populations are deemed more important than military victories.

My third argument is that low intensity conflict embraces a strong political/psychological theme and a heavy reliance on psychological operations, or 'psyops', and hence covert action. It seeks to replicate people's war, indicating that the Reagan Administration eventually recognised the primacy of the political objective in such conflicts. Accordingly, various US foreign policy agencies pursued political, economic and civic action as a priority to win the support of target populations, or at least deprive the revolutionary nationalist forces of their popular base.

Fourth, I argue that during the Reagan era the American public was, and still remains today, also a target of LIC psyops, indicating that the strategy developed partially as a response to the lingering Vietnam Syndrome. Low intensity conflict involves obscuring the level of US intervention in target Third World states by 'civilianising' and 'privatising' these conflicts. More than just merely militarising conflicts without uniforms, the strategy involves politicising and mobilising target populations behind US objectives, as well as enlisting private US groups and agencies to not only support but also implement (often covertly) American foreign policy. This process serves to circumvent US domestic opposition to an interventionist foreign policy and generate political and other support for the US-sponsored 'agencies of democracy', as well as opposition to Marxist revolutionary movements or regimes. Civilianising conflicts in target states also lessens the degree to which local nationalist sentiments are antagonised. Private US organisations and individuals therefore can play an important part in this process. During the Reagan era they assisted the Administration's military and civilian (hence official) agencies in creating and supporting insurgent movements against revolutionary nationalist forces which had assumed power, as in Nicaragua; on the other hand they assisted local paramilitary groups, such as the 'vigilantes' in the Philippines who at that time supported the counter-revolutionary programmes of pro-US governments. In both cases, these local elements were presented for US and international consumption as expressions of a popular struggle for democracy that was sweeping the Third World.

Fifth, I suggest that the Reagan Doctrine was itself a psyops tool and an expression of LIC. The Doctrine sought to further overcome the Vietnam Syndrome by generating US public support for the Administration's backing of opposition groups in target states. This was particularly so in the case of Nicaragua after continual press exposure of US covert operations in support of the Contras resulted in Congressional constraints being placed on the activities of the Central Intelligence Agency (CIA). The Doctrine rationalised the operation of those 'exposed' facets of LIC by placing them firmly into an East–West perspective which claimed that the US-supported forces were struggling for 'democracy' and 'freedom' against Soviet-backed, totalitarian Marxist aggression. Unlike other US national security dogmas, the Reagan Doctrine was not focused on major European theatres of conflict or on direct confrontation with the Soviet Union. Instead, it proclaimed Washington's intention to reassert US power and influence in the Third World at the expense of communism. Indicating that the Administration perceived that 'pro-Soviet' revolutionary nationalist forces posed the greatest threat to US interests, the Reagan Doctrine pledged Washington's support for indigenous 'democratic' forces struggling against Marxist aggression, without committing US troops directly. In so doing, the Reagan Doctrine blurred the North–South dimension of regional Third World conflicts by implying that many primarily nationalist movements struggling against corrupt dictatorships or neo-colonial regimes were actually communist, or at least Soviet-backed, and hence were to be combated.

Sixth, I argue that low intensity conflict as a means of achieving stated national objectives only gained coherence gradually and has never been explicitly articulated as a national security strategy. It emerged instead as a function of the Reagan Administration's fumbling, and often *ad hoc*, attempts to deal with low intensity warfare in lieu of a 'popularly' accepted and ideologically legitimate strategy for direct US military intervention post-Vietnam. However, LIC did achieve *de facto* national security status by the end of 1987 for two reasons: first, because it emerged ostensibly as a global approach applicable against revolutionary nationalist regimes or movements in such regionally diverse states as the Philippines, El Salvador, Nicaragua and Angola. Second, the articulation of the Reagan Doctrine actually supplied many LIC activities, initially pursued covertly, with some sense of ideological legitimacy.

LIC IN CONTEXT

Many covert activities associated with LIC have underpinned previous US national security doctrines including those of Presidents Kennedy, Nixon and Carter. Apart from Carter's Rapid Deployment Forces (RDF) to be used against direct Soviet aggression, the trend inherent in these doctrines indicates a drift in US foreign policy down the conflict scale from an emphasis on conventional forms of direct military intervention to less direct forms of intervention in the Third World. The emergence of low intensity conflict in the mid-1980s continued this trend. The novelty of LIC's emergence, however, is that it is a low-cost national security strategy that goes one step beyond conventional forms of containment/intervention. US foreign policy goals were now to be pursued with an increasing emphasis on psyops and civilianising and privatising conflicts in target countries.

The emergence of this strategy, nevertheless, also reflects the severe constraints on an interventionist US foreign policy in the 1980s. The risk of Soviet retaliation in regions outside the US's sphere of influence was always a factor constraining an interventionist foreign policy. As a constant factor in US policy making, however, Washington accommodated this constraint by various mechanisms including 'brinkmanship' diplomacy and a massive military build-up. This allowed the US to maintain its sphere of influence in the Third World within which it could pursue its objectives relatively unhindered by Soviet military opposition. The economic cost of intervention was, and still is, another obvious constraint. Corresponding to its defeat in Vietnam, the United States suffered a continuing loss in economic power that directly influenced the limits of its military power. By the early 1970s, the US had lost its strategic monopoly due both to the rise of Japanese and European economic power and the decline of the US dollar.[6] In what emerged as a historic reality that no future American administration could ignore, the US's capacity to intervene in the Third World to protect and further its interests was reduced to such an extent that the strategy of military containment was rendered much too costly in simple economic terms, regardless of other concerns. However, as the Grenada operation in 1983, the Gulf War in 1991 and interventions via NATO in the former Yugoslavia in the late 1990s demonstrate, the economic cost factor constraining US military intervention should not be overstated where popular domestic and international support exists for such intervention. This suggests, therefore, that in the 1980s the lingering Vietnam Syndrome was relatively the most powerful constraint on an interventionist US foreign policy. Together with potential international political opposition, this continuing domestic factor represented then, as it does today, a significant loss of power for the US to project its will in the Third World.

The strategy of low intensity conflict as it emerged in the Reagan years aimed to maintain and protect, as well as project, US strategic, economic and political interests in target states in the Third World. In this sense it was no different than the earlier US Doctrine of Containment. LIC, however, is a multidimensional but primarily political strategy. It seeks to achieve its objectives by avoiding direct military intervention, pursuing instead a varying combination of political, economic and psychological initiatives, and some covert military involvement by 'official' and 'private' US agencies. In practice, the emergence of LIC in the 1980s represented an increasing US concern with North–South conflicts that often involved issues of nationalism and self-determination. This contrasted significantly with the stridently anti-communist and anti-Soviet rhetoric of the Reagan Administration that portrayed many of these conflicts, including those in Nicaragua and the Philippines, in East–West terms. As I demonstrate in this book, though LIC ostensibly addressed the threat of communism in target states, it was aimed primarily at combating Third World revolutionary nationalism which was perceived to be just as threatening to US interests, although ideologically more difficult to discredit.[7]

A NEW PERSPECTIVE

In the late 1980s, much was written about the nature of low intensity conflict from which three mainstream views emerged. First, a number of specialists argued that low intensity conflict is nothing more than a reappli-cation of traditional counterinsurgency tactics, largely developed during the Kennedy years.[8] However, others argued that it is a new 'first-stage' strategy on the conflict escalation table designed purely to soften up anti-US forces before the US initiated direct military intervention.[9] In both these cases, low intensity conflict is perceived primarily as a military strategy, occupying a broad area of the conflict spectrum outside conventional and nuclear war that the United States could use to combat potential threats to its interests.[10] The third view, however, with which I largely agree, argues that LIC is not fundamentally a military strategy at all. Though LIC embraces many counterinsurgency tactics formerly used by the United States in the Third World, it is a multidimensional approach that subordinates military to political activities. Moreover, the level of official US military and political involvement in this approach is obscured by the extensive degree to which it is privatised and civilianised.

While this latter school of thought accepts that LIC's emergence in a target state could be a forerunner to direct US intervention and even conventional war, should the necessary preconditions for such escalation develop, LIC was considered, nevertheless, to be an alternative strategy in the Reagan years. It became an end in itself with victory redefined in political terms. Establishing the 'third way', or the 'democratic alternative' government in the target state, and popular acceptance of it, was one acceptable goal. If the revolutionary nationalist force could not be defeated, a more limited goal of preventing it from taking power was another acceptable objective. Other limited goals could include imposing such high costs on target regimes that the nationalist and often Marxist alternative would prove unpalatable to regional audiences; and to cause the regime's benefactors, particularly the Soviet Union, to be severely strained socially, economically and militarily.

While my position is largely consistent with the third interpretation of the role of LIC as more a political than military strategy, in this book I bring a new perspective to the table by more deeply analysing the strategy's conceptual and practical development to flesh out further its nature and 'conflict profile'. By so doing, the application and continued use of LIC in conflict situations by the US and indeed now other powers, not only in the 1990s but also in the years to come, becomes much more readily identifiable.

My argument diverges most from the mainstream in my analysis of the formulation of LIC. Much LIC literature reflects considerable agreement over the origins and implementation of the strategy. The generally accepted position argues that LIC's theoretical assumptions were derived, in large part, from the lessons learnt from the American defeat in Vietnam, earlier US experiences in the Philippines, and the experiences of the European colonial powers in combating revolutionary nationalism.[11] More importantly, it is commonly accepted that low intensity conflict was intentionally formulated and applied in the Central American 'testing ground' or LIC 'laboratory' before being applied elsewhere in the Third World according to some hidden timetable or foreign policy agenda. In contrast, however, I argue that low intensity conflict was not intentionally formulated as an alternative strategy or prior stage to conventional military intervention. Instead, it evolved from the convergence of many factors (including the neo-conservative current that achieved dominance within the Reagan Administration) and primarily from the Administration's uncertain attempts at that time to engage in low intensity warfare in different Third World locations. LIC broadly encompasses many counterinsurgency and unconventional warfare tactics, as well as diplomatic, political, economic and other initiatives. The pursuit of these activities by agencies of the Reagan Administration steadily formed a common pattern, or conflict profile, which, by the end of 1987, had assumed the form of a coherent strategy which appeared applicable to target states either threatened by revolution or already experiencing revolutionary transformation. Hence, the appearance of this strategy in the 1980s masked its reality. LIC actually emerged in practice before its conceptual formulation and was the product of a number of identifiable preconditions that limited its 'applicability' in the Third World.

Most LIC theorists at the time of its emergence tended to confine their observations to Central America, or in some cases to the Philippines with only fleeting references to other locations. Within this book, by focusing on Nicaragua and the Philippines, I identify and compare (in terms of establishing parallels) the operation of LIC in revolutionary and post-revolutionary, as well as differing geopolitical, contexts. Rather than being LIC's testing ground, Central America was only one of many regions in which elements of this strategy were waged. Other 'laboratories' included Afghanistan, Angola and the Philippines, in each of which LIC was developed to very different extents. However, the operation of this strategy achieved much of its recognition, and hence scholarly attention, in Central America because of the extreme importance attached by the Reagan Administration to maintaining US hegemony in the region and the related Congressional and domestic constraints hampering attempts to do so. The Reagan Doctrine intensified this attention by bestowing LIC with ideological legitimacy while generating US public support for an interventionist foreign policy. As this book demonstrates, however, LIC achieved the status of a *de facto* security strategy not merely because of its emergence in Central America, but also because of its development elsewhere. More than that, I suggest that LIC proved so effective in the late 1980s that the US has continued to apply elements, if not the full 'formula' of this part-covert, part-overt strategy wherever applicable to achieve its national security ends against opposing forces, particularly, but not exclusively, to revolutionary movements and post-revolutionary governments.

THE APPROACH

In this book I adopt a two-part approach to analysing the nature and emergence of low intensity conflict in the Reagan years. I adopt a chronological approach in order to trace LIC's origins and emergence. However, to identify the strategy's conflict profile in terms of its major dimensions and most salient features, a thematic approach is more appropriate because it allows comparative analysis of the two case studies.

To demonstrate that LIC did finally emerge as an accepted strategy, and not merely as a series of unconnected responses with merely a coincidental or, at best, assumed interrelation, in Chapter 1 I discuss the nature of LIC and its identifiable conflict profile as it emerged in the 1980s. I show the differences between low intensity warfare which is a 'conflict' or 'warfare environment' and LIC, which is a strategy for engaging in this form of warfare. I then analyse the distinctive elements comprising LIC's conflict profile by establishing a conceptual model based on the common understanding of this strategy by LIC theorists. I use this theoretical model later as a reference plane for investigating and comparing practical applications of LIC by the Reagan Administration in the Philippines and Nicaragua. This model also provides a tool for identifying other cases of LIC's operation in the 1990s and beyond.

In Chapter 2, I place the strategy in its historical and political context to demonstrate that LIC was indeed a mixture of both old and new, that it derived from earlier foreign interventionist experiences and that it emerged as a result of the militarist persuasion regaining dominance in Washington. This enables some measurement of the degree of continuity and discontinuity that LIC's emergence poses in the evolution of US foreign policy.

By the end of 1987 LIC had gained conceptual coherence and acceptance as a foreign policy strategy – in Chapter 3 I trace the debate over its nature and conceptual formulation within the Reagan Administration and the US military in the 1980s. I also explore the restructuring of the US armed services and the expansion of the capabilities of many of the Administration's official foreign policy agencies to pursue this form of conflict.

In Chapter 4, I analyse the Reagan Doctrine in some detail to demonstrate that it had elevated LIC to the status of a *de facto* national security strategy. I explore the outline of LIC implicit within the Doctrine in terms of its nature, conflict profile, aims and objectives, and selective application. With this strategy so defined, the Reagan Doctrine's role in providing LIC with ideological legitimacy and doctrinal coherence is more than apparent.

Chapters 5 and 6 are devoted to an analysis of LIC's emergence in practice in Nicaragua. In Chapter 5 I trace the Reagan Administration's desire to crush revolutionary nationalism in Central America, and outline the constraints that forced the Administration to rely on covert and often 'illegal' activities, ultimately leading to the development of LIC in the Nicaraguan context. In Chapter 6 I demonstrate how the conflict profile in practice in Nicaragua replicated that of LIC. This readily identifiable 'application' of LIC in Nicaragua, along with El Salvador, led many observers at the time to consider Central America to be the testing ground of low intensity conflict and, in Nicaragua's case, the revolutionary form of the strategy.

Though LIC was and is selective in operation, the Philippines case in the 1980s is examined in Chapters 7 and 8 to demonstrate how LIC emerged as a global strategy in terms of its possible application in a number of revolutionary and counter-revolutionary locations. In the Philippines the counter-revolutionary form of LIC was evident as the US and both the Marcos and Aquino governments attempted to combat the insurgency waged by the Communist Party of the Philippines (CPP) and its military arm, the New People's Army (NPA). Significantly, in Chapter 7 the determinants and the agencies of the Reagan response to the CPP/NPA insurgency are examined both to illustrate the strong parallels with what occurred in Nicaragua and to demonstrate how the Philippines was a highly suitable target for the development of LIC. In Chapter 8, the profile of the counter-revolutionary conflict in the Philippines is compared to the conceptual model to show the extent the strategy did emerge in practice by the end of 1987. Many LIC characteristics are revealed, including the most important themes of total war and the civilianising and privatising of the conflict. As such, LIC was fully developed in the Philippines, as it was in Nicaragua, by agencies of the Reagan Administration to combat the threat to US interests posed by revolutionary nationalism. This phenomenon underlines the fact that by the end of 1987 a coherent, part-covert part-overt national security strategy had emerged for the US to use against revolutionary nationalism in appropriate circumstances. In the case of Nicaragua and the Philippines it was used with great success and evidence suggests it has been used since then in varying forms and varying locations with similar success.

In concluding this book, in Chapter 9 I briefly outline some of the early successes of LIC in the 1990s. I also suggest that LIC is just as relevant now at the beginning of the twenty-first century as a US security strategy as it was in the Reagan years. In the post-Cold War years, LIW environments have proliferated and the LIC footprint is identifiable in many cases as governments attempt to manufacture or create the appearance of a total war against revolutionary nationalist opponents. I suggest that this approach remains a standard formula for US interventionist action when more direct military and other forms of intervention, and even 'containment', in the Third World proves inappropriate to achieve US foreign policy ends. While LIC's full profile remains hard to identify given its seemingly unrelated elements and its heavy reliance on psyops and covert action, Cuba remains an ongoing example of the continued use of this strategy and a case study worthy of much more research.

THE SCOPE

While many have claimed that LIC addresses a range of threats to US national security, including drug trafficking and terrorism, in this study I deal only with the threat posed to the United States by revolutionary nationalism. Drug trafficking and terrorism clearly do not constitute separate scenarios equivalent to the status of either the revolutionary or counter-revolutionary strand of LIC. Attempts by others to perceive such activities as separate strands within the scope of this strategy indicate some misunderstanding of LIC's nature.[12]

Confusion over the status of terrorism and drug trafficking originates from the fact that the Reagan Administration identified these 'anti'-US activities in the 1980s with the struggles of many revolutionary nationalist movements in an effort to discredit them politically. Accusations of pursuing 'irrational' terrorist activities often obscured these movements' ideological motivations and justifications for existence, thus rendering them illegitimate in the minds of regional and international audiences. To interpret these activities as separate strands of LIC is therefore to fall victim to LIC itself.

I also maintain that 1987 was the end point of the evolution of LIC as a *de facto* US national security strategy, symbolised by the creation of an Assistant Secretary of Defense for Low Intensity Conflict within the National Security Council and the publication of the major overt features of LIC strategy in the

January 1988 White House publication: *National Security Strategy of the United States.*[13] Respective US administrations have since appeared to embrace a new form of US intervention in the Third World, with often devastating impact at least in the short term for those revolutionary nationalist movements and governments the US could target with this form of warfare.

TERMINOLOGY

The terms used in this book to describe collective activities, schools of thought or ideological persuasions are in no sense intended to be pejorative. The term 'militarists' is used loosely and simply to describe advocates of US direct military intervention to achieve American foreign policy goals in the Third World. These advocates were strong supporters of the Reagan presidential campaign and a range of positions exists within this general persuasion, from supporting military containment to different forms of roll-back, and then to the more 'complex' ideological positions inhabited by 'realists' and 'neo-conservatives'. For my purposes, however, the term 'neo-conservative' is loosely equated with the neo-internationalist position, which originated from the split in the liberal internationalism school that dominated US foreign policy from Roosevelt to Johnson. This position, defined by Charles Krauthammer, insists:

... that the end of American foreign policy is not just the security of the United States, but what John Kennedy called 'the success of liberty'. That means, first, defending the community of democratic nations (the repository of the liberal idea), and second, encouraging the establishment of new liberal polities at the frontier, most especially in the Third World. Both missions require for their success an assertive, activist, interventionist foreign policy.[14]

This contrasts with those realists who advocate intervention purely for the sake of US power and the defence of its interests, thus favouring a selective interventionist foreign policy devoid of ideology.

I use 'revolutionary nationalism' to refer broadly to forces or movements that agitate for power by revolutionary means. Such movements generally justify their actions with a nationalist ideological rationale, charging that the forces they oppose are a vestige of Western imperialism. These forces most often are influenced by Marxism, though Marxism's impact differs in each case, as any comparison of the strongly communist New People's Army in the Philippines and the predominantly nationalist and socialist 'Sandinismo' of the Sandinistas in Nicaragua reveals.

'Conflict environment' broadly refers to the political, economic, cultural, military and historical environment within which a conflict is located. The nature of the conflict environment can be determined by the predominance of any one element, or combination of these elements, influencing a transformation of the prevailing status quo.

Finally, the differences between low intensity conflict and low intensity warfare need to be clearly stated. Theorists often mistakenly use the terms LIC and LIW interchangeably, partly because no universally accepted definition of the terms or any satisfactory convention for using them exists. This leads to confusion when examining LIC literature. The term 'low intensity' derives from the military level of weaponry used in small-scale conflicts outside of conventional and nuclear war. Because low intensity conflict, as a strategy of warfare that emphasises political over military action, has been so often associated with conflicts of 'lower-level' intensity, it is often loosely labelled low intensity 'warfare'. For clarity's sake, I refer to LIC as the US *strategy* for both creating and engaging in a low intensity warfare environment. The latter is regarded as a distinct conflict environment outside of nuclear and conventional war within which the military dimension is subordinate to the political. Since the Second World War, this has been a major and common form of conflict environment created by the total warfare strategy waged by revolutionary nationalist movements in the Third World where it was particularly popularised by the Chinese communists and the Viet Cong. LIW has also been more simply described as revolutionary and counter-revolutionary warfare embracing the total mobilisation of target populations.[15]

In the 1980s, the emergence of LIC indicated that the United States had finally reached an understanding of the realities and nature of low intensity warfare and in response it had developed a strategy that could both accommodate and create such a warfare environment. The following is a detailed analysis of that strategy.

1 WHAT IS LIC?

What exactly is LIC? Before investigating this strategy's emergence during the Reagan era, both its nature and the context of its evolution needs to be understood. In this chapter, I define this strategy in terms of its objectives and applications (or more precisely its likely environment for full operation), and construct a conceptual model of its 'conflict profile' to support my analysis of LIC's major forms and dimensions. In addition I discuss the ideological rationale that grew around its operation and the nature and activities of the major 'agencies' that implemented LIC in the 1980s. All the above is essential to fully understanding this strategy.

THE STRATEGY'S BROAD THRUST

As with low intensity warfare, LIC is multidimensional and predominantly political/psychological in nature. It emerged in the 1980s as the collective result of the Reagan Administration's efforts to develop a common response to revolutionary nationalist movements in a variety of target states. Basically, LIC served two purposes during the Reagan years: it enabled the United States and allied Third World governments to engage in low intensity warfare environments created by revolutionary nationalist movements, and it enabled the US to create its own LIW environment in target states. Within such an environment, the US could wage 'revolution' against revolutionary nationalist governments antagonistic to its interests, and thereby circumvent domestic constraints that a more direct form of US intervention might provoke.

General agreement exists between political and military analysts that low intensity conflict emerged with specific goals, targets and applications. LIC's minimum objective during the Reagan era was to maintain US economic, strategic and other interests loosely defined as vital to national security. Its maximum objective was to expand US power and influence in the Third World at the expense of the Soviet Union, its proxies and anti-US revolutionary nationalist forces without the United States again becoming directly involved in a protracted and costly military conflict. Although LIC's operation depended entirely on circumstance and opportunity, the overriding consideration was that any operation should remain a low-cost, low-profile and low-risk one. If these conditions were fulfilled, LIC would effectively enable the US to create and engage in protracted low intensity warfare in the Third World.

LIC's specific targets in the 1980s included movements struggling for power such as the New People's Army in the Philippines, or those having already seized it as in the case of the Sandinistas in Nicaragua. However, its operation depended on the existence of 'windows of opportunity' in the target state. LIC also targeted the United States in terms of attempting to generate domestic support for US foreign policy and eradicating the Vietnam Syndrome that severely constrained the Reagan Administration's military options.

A DEFINITION OF LOW INTENSITY CONFLICT

Although the broad thrust of LIC is widely described and documented, low intensity conflict lacks an agreed and common definition. The broad range of activities LIC encompasses produced considerable confusion and debate within the Reagan Administration and US military about the nature of LIC and its operational parameters, to such an extent that it was rumoured to have sometimes blocked implementation of actual policy.[1] General Paul F. Gorman US Army (Ret.), a chairman of the Reagan Administration's Regional Conflict Working Group Commission on Integrated Long Term Strategy, noted that even the bombing of Libya and the invasion of Grenada were considered by some within the US defence establishment to be within the range of LIC activities. Gorman rejected this position himself, however, as he regarded any use of conventional forces for fire support or manoeuvre as 'mid-intensity conflict'.[2] Each branch of the US military exacerbated this doctrinal confusion, not only defining LIC differently but also having a different concept of its role in the pursuit of this strategy. As Colonel Kenneth Alnwick (USAF) noted, each service branch tended to consider itself the major vehicle for waging low intensity conflict, thus obstructing the emergence of any joint service doctrine for LIC operations.[3]

Nevertheless, an important step towards a joint services doctrine was eventually taken by the Joint Chiefs of Staff (JCS), who, on the direction of the Army Chief of Staff on 1 July 1985, formulated a definition of LIC in a joint-low intensity conflict project:

... a limited politico-military struggle to achieve political, social, economic, or psycho-logical objectives. It is often protracted and ranges from diplomatic, economic, and psychological pressures through terrorism and insurgency. Low-intensity conflict is generally confined to a geographic area and is often characterized by constraints on the weaponry, tactics, and level of violence.[4]

Though seemingly similar to LIW, LIC in fact is a strategy for action within a particular warfare environment – that environment being LIW.

The JCS project also found that low intensity conflict entailed a range of civil-political activities that no single service or department of the Reagan Administration could conduct alone. Further, while from a purely military perspective the term 'low intensity conflict' appeared ambiguous, the many activities associated with this approach were not. They generally shared a common operational environment outside the range of conventional combat. The JCS project defined LIC as embracing activities that could be divided into four categories: insurgency/counterinsurgency, terrorism counteraction, peacetime contingency and peacekeeping operations. Through these categories the United States could provide:

... diplomatic, economic, and military support for either a government under attack by insurgents or an insurgent force seeking freedom from an adversary government; in cooperation with our allies, protection of personnel, property, and institutions from terrorism; military presence, humanitarian assistance, noncombatant emergency evacuation, limited strike, and similar operations; and support or participation in peacekeeping operations.[5]

However, Colonel Harry G. Summers, a noted strategist upon whose work many elements of the Reagan Administration's response to revolutionary nationalism were based, argued that such a definition made no distinction between peacetime and wartime activities in support of an ally without committing US combat forces, and supporting an ally through the direct commitment of such forces. Instead, he defined appropriate LIC parameters of operation as: 'Non-nuclear situations ranging from terrorism and crisis to revolutions and counterrevolutions, requiring tailored mixed political-economic-military and other US responses in support of allies; but not involving direct commitment of US combat forces.'[6]

Summers also substituted the term 'collective security' for LIC, believing that this more accurately described US intentions and attempts to secure its own security by supporting those of its allies threatened by insurgency.

The emergence of low intensity conflict therefore inspired a number of definitions; however, most were too narrow as they failed to account for the many different dimensions of activity that can be associated with the strategy and what fundamentally links these activities.

This common shortcoming derived from the predominantly political/ psychological nature of low intensity conflict. Above all, LIC emerged as a strategy that involves no mobilisation of the US economy, few if any troops and few admitted casualties because military victory, though welcomed, is not its primary objective. LIC is instead distinctive because its major priority is to discredit politically the target revolutionary nationalist movement or government. When viewed from other perspectives, LIC's many elements appear *ad hoc* and unrelated. Only when viewed from this political/psycho-logical perspective does the strategy assume a degree of coherence. As a major priority LIC seeks to deny popular support (within the target country and from sympathetic sources in the United States and internationally) for either anti-US regimes or anti-US forces in the Third World. Once this political/psychological objective is achieved, 'military victory' follows. Relying heavily on psychological warfare to win the 'hearts and minds' of the target population, LIC redefines victory in terms of gaining popular support for US foreign policy objectives. Victory in LIC terms is thus essentially political and can vary in its application from place to place and time to time. It can simply mean producing a change of 'attitude' or 'political allegiance' in the target population, or alternatively it can mean avoiding undesired outcomes such as the nationalisation or confiscation of American interests, or, for example as in the case of the Philippines in the 1980s, the possible expulsion of US military bases.

Low intensity conflict is a multidimensional strategy involving both covert and overt means. Theoretically LIC can be an alternative when direct intervention appears precluded by a lack of domestic and international support for such action, and when the risk of military confrontation with another major power, such as the then Soviet Union in the 1980s, is high. On the other hand, the strategy can be a forerunner to 'conventional' intervention where its operation sufficiently destroys the political support base of the opposition while generating sufficient support from the US public for direct military intervention to compel victory on the battlefield (thereby formalising and consolidating the political victory already achieved).[7] Further, LIC might also be followed by direct military intervention if the situation in the target state deteriorates to the point where the United States has no option but to intervene directly to protect its interests, regardless of domestic and international constraints, for example, the US intervention into Panama (and perhaps later in Iraq).

To adopt this latter perception, however, risks confusing LIC's potential with its operation in practice. The most compelling explanation for LIC's emergence in the Third World in the 1980s was the need for an alternative strategy to direct US intervention.

LIC as Defined by the Reagan Administration

Since low intensity conflict emerged as a multifaceted strategy, it is not surprising that no commonly accepted, concise definition should exist. Nevertheless, in the January 1988 White House publication, *National Security Strategy of the United States*, the Reagan Administration did broadly outline the nature and parameters of US actions which broadly constitute the essence of this strategy.[8]

According to the Administration, low intensity conflict embraced the main principles of waging revolutionary and counter-revolutionary warfare in a low intensity environment. These principles included: the provision of security assistance to allied governments for the development of their economies and armed forces as a 'bargain-priced' means of ensuring the protection of US security interests;[9] to conduct covert action to deal with 'developing threats to our [US] security before the employment of US military power or other actions entailing higher costs and risks are required';[10] efforts to 'ameliorate the underlying causes of conflict in the Third World by promoting economic development and the growth of democratic political institutions'; support for selected resistance movements 'opposing oppressive regimes working against US interests'; use of 'instruments of US power' to help friendly nations under internal or external threat; and 'steps to discourage Soviet and other state-sponsored adventurism, and increase the costs to those who use proxies or terrorist and subversive forces to exploit instability'.[11] In the above document the Reagan Administration thus outlined all the elements in its foreign policy arsenal with which it attempted to combat revolutionary nationalism, particularly in Central America.

What is especially distinctive about this account is the implicit avoidance of direct military intervention and the emphasis placed on covert action and other measures that would obviate such intervention. Equally distinctive is the omission of any reference to the political/psychological objective, which locates all these elements within the LIC framework. This indicates: first, the Reagan Administration apparently assumed that US-backed forces in the Third World were morally superior to their opponents; second, it assumed a relative weakness in the US's capacity to pursue direct military intervention to secure foreign policy objectives, and third, in lieu of such intervention the US relied heavily on psyops to achieve its objectives. Finally, such an omission indicates the Administration's increasing emphasis on dubious means, and indeed agencies, the operations of which might not have been sanctioned by Congress, or even fully understood by the Administration itself.

THE LIC CONFLICT PROFILE

While most observers readily agree on LIC's parameters, none have articulated a fully-fledged conceptual model of LIC's conflict profile to aid its identification in practice, which in turn reflects the lack of an adequate definition of the strategy. To construct such a model, the nature, extent and interrelationship of LIC's agencies and its full operational dimensions (hence its 'profile') need to be outlined and analysed.

Sketching a conceptual profile of LIC based on what most agree is its nature and the range of activities it encompassed in the Third World in the 1980s provides a useful analytical tool for identifying LIC in operation (that is, its 'footprint').[12] However to do this, LIC's central theme must first be understood, as should its major forms in terms of the distinctive configurations LIC activities can assume, and the ideological rationale used to justify and legitimise such activities.

The Theme: Civilianising Conflict

In the Reagan era, the imperative of pursuing low intensity *conflict* was for the US to avoid direct 'high intensity' conventional military intervention into LIW environments, as this sort of intervention was incompatible with the primarily political nature of low intensity *warfare*.[13] Reflecting this central precept, the major theme of LIC became one of 'civilianising' conflicts as much as possible in target states.

One of the most basic and widely accepted premises underpinning LIC is that the civilian population is the most critical factor in low intensity warfare.[14] Civilianising conflicts blurs the distinction between civilian and military involvement thus obscuring the nature of such conflicts while embedding them in the social fabric of target states. This avoids antagonising nationalist sentiments among the local people, which often militated against US military intervention in the past. Civilians can be used in a number of ways in this civilianising process. They can be used as sources of intelligence. They can be armed to attack the target government as were the Contras in Nicaragua. Or they can be armed and mobilised to protect villages and government installations against insurgent attacks, as were the Civilian Home Defence Forces (CHDFs) and the vigilantes in the Philippines in the 1980s. Either way, during the Reagan years the civilianising of a revolutionary or counter-revolutionary conflict in a target state enabled the US to pursue military and other interventionist objectives by proxy.

LIC's characteristic emphasis on civilianising conflicts further indicates the essentially political nature of this strategy and its replication of some tactics of Mao's 'people's war'.[15] People's war seeks the total mobilisation of the local civilian population by political indoctrination and other means to support and pursue revolutionary warfare. In other words, the strategy (pursued so effectively by the Chinese communists) involves waging 'total war' wherein the enemy is deprived of a mass support base, which then leads to the eventual defeat of the opposing forces – militarily and otherwise. In this sense, LIC seeks to turn a popular Third World revolutionary insurgent strategy back against its proponents. Also, civilianising conflicts was and is far cheaper than conventional military intervention: the crucial lesson from Vietnam was that in low intensity warfare, conventional military forces are not only counterproductive but also very costly.

LIC's Major Forms: Its Revolutionary and Counter-Revolutionary Strands

Low intensity conflict consists of two major forms or strands: the revolutionary strand often termed 'unconventional war' by the US military, and the counter-revolutionary strand alternatively labelled 'Foreign Internal Defense' (FID).[16] In the former, the Reagan Administration sought to create its own LIW environments wherein its 'agencies' could wage revolution against revolutionary nationalist governments (as in the Nicaraguan and Angolan contexts), or regimes considered to be Soviet proxies (as in Afghanistan). In the latter strand, the US used intensified counterinsurgency psyops, among other operations, to wage protracted political warfare campaigns in support of friendly Third World governments combating revolutionary nationalist movements (as in El Salvador and the Philippines).

In both revolutionary and counter-revolutionary LIC,[17] the Reagan Administration civilianised its approach to gain maximum political advantage by organising pro-US forces locally at the grassroots level to create total war. In both strands, political/psychological operations were supported by economic and military pressure to achieve the political objective of winning popular local support for either the 'democratic' insurgents, or US-supported government. The *U.S. Army Field Manual 31–16*, 'The Counterguerrilla Operations Handbook', first published in 1986, stated for example: 'The enemy of the guerrilla is the government ... which may not be popularly supported by the majority of the people ... The essence of the counterguerrilla campaign is to win back the support of the people for the established government.'[18] From the US Army's perspective, this clearly articulated the military's acceptance of LIC's relative priority on achieving the political objective of creating popular support while engaging in low intensity warfare. Moreover, it also indicated the significant extent to which the US military had absorbed the logic of LIC by 1986.

The Ideological Rationale: The Democratic Revolutionary Alternative – Constructing the 'Third Way'

Integral to both forms of low intensity conflict is the concept of the 'third way', the political model around which popular allegiance and support is to be generated. During the Reagan era the third way was presented as the democratic alternative to the ideology of the revolutionary nationalist forces (usually Marxist in nature) and, on the other hand, the extreme right often represented by forces in many of the Third World states that the US had formerly supported via the Nixon Doctrine, the latter including the Marcos regime in the Philippines and Somoza in Nicaragua.

In promoting the third way, the Reagan Administration claimed to be exporting 'democratic revolution' (as articulated in the Reagan Doctrine) to the Third World, and was considered to be synonymous with 'nation building', the process of establishing democratic institutions, functions and safeguards, and a free market economy. This perception was an integral component of LIC's political/psychological dimension which sought to portray pro-US forces as striving to build a revolutionary new democratic society, which forces of both the extreme right and left were attempting to destroy.

Nation building involves civilianising the government at the national level, while simultaneously militarising civilian life at the grassroots. In the revolutionary case, the legitimacy of the regime's claims to represent the aspirations of the people is challenged, as is the legitimacy of the revolution in the counter-revolutionary case. In both situations, the strategy's objective is to rally the population to support the democratic alternative. In seizing the initiative, LIC therefore attempts to take the 'revolution out of the hands of the revolutionaries', a strategy which Sarkesian claims is the most effective for defeating revolutionary forces.[19]

In the process of 'building' the democratic state, complete with democratic institutions, a multiparty system and electoral processes, the third way's viability as an alternative to the revolution must be validated. A democratic government, as an integral part of an economically and politically stable community, must be created. Similarly, in opposing Marxist regimes, the democratic revolution must offer a legitimate and convincing alternative social system.[20] This is the long-term challenge for the strategy, and in this respect an analysis of the long-term viability, if not durability of the third way after the initial victory, lies largely outside the scope of this book, although LIC's apparent continued use post-Reagan indicates it has been achieving some success.

Essential to the Reagan Administration's attempts to create the third way in low intensity warfare environments was the avoidance of direct, or at least overt, involvement of US combat troops.[21] Direct intervention was thought to be counterproductive and inconsistent with the civilianising theme of low intensity conflict. Apart from escalation to conventional warfare, direct military involvement promoted nationalist sympathies for the revolution. Mass-scale US involvement also tended to 'Americanise' the conflict and thus delegitimise the regime the United States supported. Instead, the Administration came to rely on covert US military involvement with US Special Operations Forces (SOFs), the CIA and other agencies playing a central role.

The Agencies of Low Intensity Conflict

Several of the American agencies responsible for the emergence of LIC in the 1980s were civilian, reflecting LIC's predominantly non-military nature. These agencies included the National Security Council (NSC), the State Department, the United States Agency for International Development (USAID), the United States Information Service (USIS), its domestic counterpart the United States Information Agency (USIA), the CIA and the Peace Corps, which was often used by the US as an instrument for anti-communist propaganda in the Third World.[22] Within the target state, other agencies included the civilian government and aid agencies. At this level, LIC's military agencies consisted of the local 'defence forces' (including the national guard and police) and paramilitary groups. In revolutionary LIC, military agencies obviously included the insurgent movement while US military agencies, though including all armed service branches, usually consisted more of Special Operations Forces including the Marines, and service intelligence organisations.

Each 'official' US Administration agency had its own charter, with the overall programme guided in Washington by a multi-agency task force and an embassy-based country team or mission council which directed it in the field.[23] However, the activities of 'non-official' agencies such as private business and relief organisations and political cause-oriented groups and individuals were also included. While these latter agencies generally pursued their own political agenda independent of the Reagan Administration, they nevertheless shared similar objectives. Because of the special relationship of many of these 'private' elements to the Administration and their involvement in the emergence of low intensity conflict, they shall be dealt with separately in this chapter.

The Profile's Major Dimensions

LIC's conflict profile consists of many overlapping dimensions covering a wide range of activities, all of which are aimed at achieving the political/ psychological objective of undercutting a target government or movement's support base, destroying its legitimacy and influencing support for US objectives. In this respect all LIC activities constitute political/psychological operations, or 'psyops', which form an integral part of every dimension of low intensity conflict and are not a separate activity as such.

All LIC activities thus constitute either explicit or 'initiated' psyops in which LIC agencies directly use psychological warfare to achieve immediate psychological outcomes, or implicit or 'self-initiating' psyops in which the operations of the various agencies also produce a desired psychological effect upon target populations. In both cases this is usually popular support for the 'democratic' forces. As Sarkesian noted, the centre of gravity in revolutionary war is the political-social system and 'its psychological coherency [sic]', therefore in LIW '... political cadre and psychological instruments are most important in determining the outcome of such conflicts'.[24]

The Political/Psychological Dimension

In accordance with the nineteenth-century military theorist Carl von Clausewitz's axiom that '... war is simply a continuation of political intercourse, with the addition of other means',[25] the primary dimension of low intensity conflict is political.

Using initiated psyops, LIC accommodates threats in low intensity warfare environments on a number of different political levels simultaneously. Internationally during the Reagan era support for Third World 'democratic' forces was justified by the State Department, USIA and other agencies by arguing that their struggle was part of the greater East versus West showdown. It was important for both US domestic and international consumption that the Third World conflict in question be perceived as essentially a regional manifestation of the greater Cold War superpower confrontation, or more simply as a struggle between communism and democracy, and even more simplistically as a struggle against terrorism. Diplomatic pressure in such forums as the United Nations was also used to isolate the revolutionary regime or movement. In this context, international negotiations with the target government played an important role, not as an alternative to waging low intensity conflict but instead as an integral part of the same process.[26] The isolation of the target government or movement from its regional neighbours was deemed essential, as the revolutionary strand of LIC requires neighbouring countries that can supply bases and staging areas, or alternatively lend assistance to pro-US governments.

Domestically, the American people were, and are, also a target of LIC. As Secretary of Defense Caspar Weinberger noted during the Reagan era, this was to ensure that before the United States committed combat forces abroad, the Reagan Administration would have some 'reasonable assurance' of both public and Congressional support.[27] Essentially the Administration desired to eliminate the lingering legacy of Vietnam and thereby free itself from the constraint this imposed on US foreign policy. The Reagan Administration argued that in the final analysis the 'balanced application' of the various elements of national power in low intensity warfare was of 'little use' without US domestic support that was both 'determined' and resilient in the face of what could develop into direct US military involvement in 'protracted struggles'.[28] Psyops in the form of propaganda campaigns were thus pursued domestically. The Administration claimed that it was 'fighting a war' of ideas to protect US national security and to 'help support the political infrastructure of world democracies'. It argued that 'informational aspects of our diplomatic power' had to be used to build a 'domestic constituency for America's foreign policy' as no natural one existed. To build this 'domestic constituency' an 'understanding' of US objectives had to be propagated using the full range of US 'informational programmes'.[29] Mrs Jean Kirkpatrick, former US ambassador to the United Nations and an architect and staunch supporter of the Reagan Doctrine, noted that the biggest problem in implementing the Reagan Administration's foreign policy was 'sustaining the popular support and discipline for the necessary expenditures'. This, she argued, required that the public understood the 'policies of the Soviet Union and its associated states'. Without this understanding there would be no popular support for the Administration to deal with the 'military problem' nor for 'appropriate policies of trade, aid, and support for resistance movements'.[30]

The tools of this 'perception management' campaign included disinformation activities, a selective use of facts and information leaks designed to spread alarm about 'Soviet aggression' and often, as Noam Chomsky noted, the 'misimpression that it is the Soviet Union that [we] are fighting'.[31] The essential message of such psyops was that revolutionary nationalist struggles in Third World LIW environments were reducible to conflicts between Soviet-inspired 'terrorist' forces committing aggression against forces of democracy. The alarm such a message caused was intended to mobilise the American people in fear and render them willing to 'pay the costs' of US foreign policy.[32]

During the Reagan era, LIC thus redefined the nature of the conflict and the enemy in target states. Though generally placed within an East–West framework, by often portraying Marxist movements as irrational terrorist organisations the Reagan Administration sometimes also rendered the ideological motivations of these movements less discernible. The conflicts in which these movements were involved were reduced to simplistic equations of good versus evil, which made them more easily understandable to the American public.[33] Moreover, the US Congress was much more willing to support aid to military dictatorships when these regimes were portrayed as combating terrorists. In the wake of many terrorist attacks on American citizens in the 1980s,[34] this process contributed effectively to a personalisation of these conflicts within America's political culture and consequently generated political support for anti-terrorist action across the board. As a result, the real issues involved in many low intensity warfare environments were often obscured from the American people.[35]

In this dimension of activity, the Reagan Administration exploited and manipulated the dominant religious values of America's political culture so as to influence public and Congressional opinion. Similar to using the fear of terrorism, the Administration exploited the public's predominantly Christian values with propaganda campaigns that reduced Third World conflicts to struggles between Christianity and the 'evil Soviet empire',[36] harnessing the support of evangelical and staunchly anti-communist religious groups in the United States, particularly those in the strongly religious Midwest, behind US foreign policy. Moreover, it undermined the activities of those domestic religious organisations and communities, which because of their opposition to US foreign policy appeared by implication to be pro-communist and 'un-Christian'. Liberation theology in Latin America, for example, proved a particular target of such propaganda.[37] In this context, the crusade-like energy of the Reagan Doctrine enhanced the Administration's ability to establish strong links with conservative religious groups.

Within LIC's counter-revolutionary strand at the level of the target state, the Reagan Administration urged reform of unpopular governments to defuse political opposition. If these regimes could not be reformed or if they proved intransigent, the US would distance itself and promote a more palatable, popular 'democratic alternative' headed, for example, by an Aquino or Duarte figure. The United States would then manipulate, sponsor, or at least urge, elections within which 'the democratic alternative' could be presented as the political expression of the 'third way' that would redress such internal grievances that spawned revolution.[38] In this way the US, while appearing an impartial observer of democracy in action, could influence elections in target states and maintain leverage over elected governments. At the same time it could co-opt some of the opposition into the electoral process, thereby undermining support for the revolution.

Using initiated psyops, US agencies also projected a non-interventionist, goodwill image for regionally based US conventional military forces. The US military, in conjunction with host governments,[39] often participated in medical aid programmes (MEDCAP) and other missions designed to enhance its local popularity. For example, the military would often distribute medical aid and other relief to civilians in select areas of insurgent activity. The US Agency for International Development was often involved in this 'internal development' process, which it claimed helped developing countries become more self-sufficient and cost-effective in providing health services for their people.[40] USAID regularly acted as a conduit for health care commodities and assisted in establishing a medical infrastructure for the health care of target populations. However, much of USAID's work was usually contracted out to private organisations as it lacked the staff to fully implement its programmes.[41]

In revolutionary LIC at this level, the forces the Reagan Administration supported were also trained to wage direct psychological warfare against target governments. Local religious beliefs were similarly manipulated and terror tactics often used against the population. Alternatively, in counter-revolutionary responses, LIC agencies capitalised on local superstitions wherever possible, spreading rumours that could in turn spread fear and panic among the revolutionary forces and thereby disrupt their operational effectiveness. This manipulation of local belief systems (such as portraying the opposition as 'godless' in character) was an especially effective tool for gathering important local intelligence, as well as undertaking psyops campaigns at the grassroots level. As Sarah Miles, one noted LIC theorist observed, this was in apparent recognition that many revolutionary nationalist forces were 'ideologically shaped as much by religious values as by Marxist theory'.[42] Former US Captain John Zindar also claimed:

> Well, religion is important in LIC. It is a main element in the development of the psychological campaign – it is the broadening of the civilianising of the conflict ... It means getting the local priest to spy on the people for you ... to get the trust of the Church hierarchy. To get them to galvanize support for your objectives ... Religion is one of the most perfect ways to manipulate people ... This is recognised in LIC doctrine.[43]

Gathering local intelligence was critically important in pursuing psyops at the grassroots level. It involved obtaining knowledge of local political and religious belief systems, dominant social structures, superstitions, culture, local history and the identities of important figures and potential leaders within the population, as well as knowledge of the local terrain. LIC agencies emphasised a heavy reliance on human intelligence, a high level of civilian involvement, and the use of high technology in propaganda and surveillance operations. In these initiated psyops programmes, the US Information Agency played a major role in propaganda and psychological campaigns to combat those waged by the target movement or government.

Psyops can be many and diverse, including, for example, shows of massed military force and other 'sabre-rattling exercises' such as the staging of wargames and threatening manoeuvres in neighbouring states to exploit local fears of a US invasion. While not overtly intervening in target states, in this sense US conventional forces can play a 'muscle-flexing' role in LIC operations.[44] Major Andrew Pratt, USMC, argued: 'In a low-intensity scenario, shows of force demonstrate a US commitment to friendly nations linked by alliances and understandings. An appropriate show of force can assist a US diplomatic effort by expressing resolve to use force if negotiations fail.'[45] These exercises sap the morale of both the target regime and the population as well as having the potential to force the regime into mobilising its forces and population needlessly, thus disrupting the country's economy and everyday life.

The Economic Dimension

Economic action is an important component of low intensity conflict and a critical activity underpinning its political/psychological dimension; particularly when used coercively not only to hurt economically but also politically discredit target governments. The Reagan Administration confirmed this aspect of its strategy when it claimed in its 1988 National Security Strategy Report that there are times 'when we must restrict economic relations between the United States and other countries not only for reasons of national security, but to protest odious national behaviour'. Its suggested targets were regimes with 'unacceptable' behaviour. Included in this category at that time were Cuba, Libya and Nicaragua, against which the US applied economic leverage because these states 'threatened regional stability or support international terrorism'.[46]

When opposing a revolutionary regime, economic pressures are imposed to render the target government unable to meet the basic needs of its people, thereby damaging the regime's political credibility among its domestic and international support base. During the Reagan era, these pressures included US-sponsored aid and trade embargoes and the denial of financial assistance from such bodies as the World Bank and the International Monetary Fund (IMF). By economically strangling target regimes and rendering their economic reform programmes unworkable, not only can the credibility of these governments be damaged but also their ideological legitimacy, while enhancing the appeal of the alternative US-supported socioeconomic system. Within the target state, the 'democratic' forces can be supplied with the wherewithal to mount alternative economic and assistance programmes in controlled areas so these forces can demonstrate the efficacy and legitimacy of the democratic alternative.

Within LIC's counter-revolutionary strand, economic assistance is seen as an important component of the psychological concept of 'nation building'. US-supported regimes launch economic reform programmes to undermine the support of the revolutionary forces, particularly in the area of land reform. In the 1980s many revolutionary nationalist forces targeted the need for land reform in such states as El Salvador and the Philippines where large-scale peasant landlessness was a fact of life due to intensive cash cropping and the operation of local and multinational agribusiness corporations on plantations or haciendas. To undercut support for the opposition, land reform programmes were often promised and even implemented. Employment and retraining schemes were also initiated. USAID, the World Bank and other Western aid and development organisations assisted in such 'modernisation' and development programmes. In secure areas, for example, schools and hospitals and other institutions critical in the nation-building process were built with USAID funds. In contested areas that civilian agencies could not reach, the local armed forces using 'tactical civic action' often also attempted to win the support of the population by sometimes participating in construction and harvesting projects.

In the 1980s US economic aid (particularly 'humanitarian' aid consisting of food and medicine) to pro-US revolutionary movements and governments was hard to discredit when presented as promoting Western models of economic development and nation building, or as relief projects for 'needy refugees'. Similarly, American aid programmes were difficult to discredit when presented as political, and not military, solutions to a particular conflict.

The Military Dimension

Military action does not constitute LIC's primary dimension, but is subordinate to other activities. During the Reagan era, the Administration did not intervene directly in low intensity warfare environments with combat troops on anything above the overt level of advisers. It was apparent that as soon as US forces became directly and conventionally involved, the conflict environment would change to one less appropriate for achieving US political objectives – as had occurred in Vietnam.[47] Nevertheless, US Special Forces, CIA operatives and others covertly assisted local forces in battlefield operations, for example, by fighting as mercenaries or flying helicopters.[48] To camouflage this form of involvement the process of 'sheep dipping' was used, that is, CIA or Special Forces personnel would 'leave' the service for a short period during which, in the capacity of civilians, they would aid the pro-US forces before returning to active service. These SOFs and other LIC agencies, including the US Light Infantry, could undertake many functions in counter-revolutionary LIC, including psyops and intelligence gathering, logistics operations and other 'security assistance' programmes. For example, General Duane Cassidy, USAF Commander-in-Chief of the Military Airlift Command, which was responsible for the transport of SOFs, testified that US Special Forces were 'trained, equipped, and organized to conduct unique operations in pursuit of national military, political, economic, or psychological objectives'. He argued that 'special operations' were conducted across the spectrum of conflict, 'from counterterrorism to global war' and included 'unconventional warfare, counterterrorism, collective security, psychological operations, deception, direct action missions, and intelligence collection and reporting'.[49] These agencies could supply 'mobile/military training teams' (MTTs), to train, equip, support and advise the local army, national guard, military reserve and police,[50] as well as organising paramilitary organisations and thereby civilianising actual military operations against the revolutionary movement. Selective operations such as labour union breaking and terror campaigns, psyops and assassinations of members of politically suspect civilian organisations could also take place.[51]

Within this dimension of LIC's profile as it emerged during the 1980s, the local military and police would induce and train civilians to assume greater responsibility for carrying out some military activities. Moreover, the local police assumed a greater role in counter-revolutionary activities, particularly in intelligence gathering. Extensive communications systems and intelligence networks would be installed to gather and analyse intelligence about the opposition. An important LIC task was to separate and eliminate the 'insurgent' from the civilian population, thus disrupting the movement's attempts to build a popular support base.

In the revolutionary case, US Special Forces and the CIA could arm, train, direct and sometimes form local insurgent movements or 'freedom fighters' to combat target regimes. These groups would undermine the government's reform programmes, and in secure areas politically validate the cause of the US-supported revolution by implementing the 'democratic alternative's' own civic action campaigns, including health and education programmes.

From a purely military perspective, aiding indigenous groups is an effective method of inflicting high costs on the incumbent regime. As William Bode observed: '... government troops are more costly to train, equip and maintain than are guerrilla forces, and the regime under attack bears the additional burden of maintaining and guarding the nation's economic infrastructure, part of which is exploited by the guerrillas'.[52] This 'offensive' tactic is beneficial both militarily and economically as the widely accepted cost ratio in terms of manpower needed by a regime to combat guerrilla warfare is 10:1 in favour of the insurgency.[53]

The Civic Dimension

Similar to military and economic activities associated with low intensity conflict, this strategy's 'civic' dimension activities underpin the primary political objective of destroying support for the revolutionary nationalist movement. To popularise their own image, the local military in counter-revolutionary operations can be encouraged to pursue psyops in the form of humanitarian aid and relocation projects such as distributing medicine and assisting in harvesting and building programmes. Military spokespeople also learn to approach the local and international media from a more 'political' perspective in order to enhance the local military's image as an expression of the people's will.

The Private and International Dimension of LIC

LIC as it emerged during the Reagan era also possessed another dimension, which involved the activities of private American and even international political, corporate business, paramilitary, and other organisations including religious and labour groups that were supportive of the Reagan Administration's foreign policy objectives.

Generally operating autonomously from the Administration, though at times encouraged and even assisted by it, the 'private war' waged by these organisations became however somewhat characteristic of the Reagan Administration's approach to low intensity warfare. Moreover, since a fundamental aspect of LIC in the 1980s was the attempt to create people's war, these private campaigns (though often including ex-Administration and military figures) should be assessed as an expression of LIC. Indeed the involvement of many private organisations represented a further element of the civilianising of the Reagan Administration's foreign policy, to such an extent that it ultimately became significantly privatised in itself. In January 1988, the Administration stated that it had 'encouraged the American private sector to become a key element in the projection of US foreign policy goals' during the previous seven years, that these 'leading private citizens and groups' had a 'direct stake in our nation's relations with the rest of the world' and that these organisations were doing 'an indispensable job of public education' which it strongly encouraged and supported,[54] indicating the role these groups played in psyops directly targeting the US public.

In both LIC's revolutionary and counter-revolutionary strands, the Reagan Administration sought to privatise and indeed even 'internation-alise' the pursuit of its foreign policy. Quite apart from its normal diplomatic and military channels (aid and other agreements), it used the CIA and other covert channels, in collaboration with a number of US private and international organisations, to achieve its goals in target countries. These organisations included the American Institute for Free Labor Development (AIFLD) of the American Federation of Labor – Congress of Industrial Organizations (AFL-CIO), and the IMF, the World Bank (WB) and other multilateral funding bodies wherein the United States could exert considerable power. By privatising foreign policy, Congressional constraints could be circumvented and the conflict 'localised' in the respect that private group involvement tended to make US foreign policy more relevant to domestic political opinion, hence facilitating the American people's acceptance of US involvement in low intensity wars. With the shadow of Vietnam continuing to constrain interventionist policy, the more public support that could be demonstrated for such policy the less resistance the Administration was likely to encounter within Congress.[55]

Private organisations can undertake multiple activities (often coordinated with official agencies) in all dimensions of low intensity conflict. For example, during the Reagan era, conservative religious groups often attacked American church groups opposing the Administration's foreign policy by portraying the forces the US opposed in the target state as terrorist, godless and even totalitarian. In what was a 'hearts and minds' campaign within the United States, the Reagan Administration characteristically courted such conservative groups to help generate domestic support for its foreign policy. The involvement of private relief organisations, churches and businesses helped generate an image of public consensus and the necessary psychological conditions for it to strengthen. In terms of the ideological battle within America, such private support counterbalanced the arguments of Reagan's opposition by helping the Administration present its foreign policy objectives as a worthy moral crusade. Within a target state itself, private groups were also involved in many functions, including covert military operations and providing an alternative source of funding for the democratic forces when the Reagan Administration was constrained from doing so.[56] Also, the armed services and intelligence organisations of third-country governments often assisted the US to channel advisers and aid (including arms), and helped in intelligence operations, embargoes and other activities.[57]

THE NEED FOR CONTEXT?

LIC is a multidimensional US strategy to combat revolutionary nationalism in the Third World. However, understanding its conflict profile has little use unless we also understand the political and historical factors that led to its emergence. Only then can we appreciate why it assumed the nature it did, both the continuity and discontinuity it represents in the evolution of US foreign policy, and the strategy's apparent selectivity in 'application' despite appearing global in character. In the next two chapters I examine the historical and political context of LIC's emergence in the 1980s.

2 AN INEVITABLE STRATEGY: LIC'S EMERGENCE IN CONTEXT

It is important to examine the political and historical context of LIC's emergence so one can understand that its development in the 1980s was perhaps inevitable. In this chapter I examine the origins of the broad ideological persuasion loosely termed 'militarist' within the United States, which dominated the Reagan Administration and demanded the development of such an interventionist strategy. I also review the important foreign policy debates within the US since the 1950s that spawned this persuasion and contributed to its ascendancy in the late 1970s.

CONTINUITY AND DISCONTINUITY

Though appearing initially as a piecemeal foreign policy approach, LIC's development actually established further continuity in the evolution of postwar US foreign policy. For example, evident in the strategy's emergence were recurrent foreign policy themes and influences as well as familiar actors who had helped shape American foreign policy since 1945. However, while establishing continuity in theme, LIC's emergence represented discontinuity in practice or, in other words, the way in which foreign policy objectives were actually achieved. A review of these recurrent themes, influences and actors is therefore useful as it demonstrates more clearly this strategy's continuities and discontinuities with previous forms of US 'coercive diplomacy' pursued in the Third World.

The Postwar Character of US Foreign Policy

Until the end of the Cold War, the nature of postwar US foreign policy was broadly consistent in character: the US regularly pursued a global policy of active intervention in the affairs of other states to achieve its required objectives. Underpinned by massive military power, from 1945 onwards this interventionist approach was a defining feature of US foreign policy.

Many long-held assumptions and goals underpinned the theme of US Cold War policy, which was one of strident anti-communism and opposition to the Soviet Union which, as the world's strongest communist power, was consistently perceived as posing a 'threat' to the United States. In the postwar years, virtually every US administration maintained this theme in foreign policy action and to differing extents rejected isolationism in favour of 'containing' Soviet 'expansionism'. After Carter's somewhat wavering and confused foreign policy posture, in the 1980s the Reagan Administration reasserted this strident foreign policy theme. While LIC was only one manifestation of such coercive diplomacy, its development clearly reflects familiar influences maintaining this continuity in American foreign policy.

Influences

Many interrelated influences shape US foreign policy: using Kegley and Wittkopf's analysis for example, these can range from the external (global) environment, the nation's societal environment, the 'governmental setting', the roles played by central decision makers and even the very nature of the individuals making up the US foreign policy-making elite.[1] These influences differ in potency and, while acknowledging that they exist, it is virtually impossible to identify which ones predominate at any given time or under what circumstances. It is also not my task to undertake that sort of inquiry here.

What is important to note, however, is that LIC's emergence resulted from a combination of many of the above influences and in this sense its development represents continuity in US foreign policy. Moreover, some influences did appear, perhaps, to be more powerful than others in shaping the eventual nature of LIC. As my following analysis shows, these influences were mainly domestically derived, stemming from societal sources. They are also important to note because they represent possible discontinuity in the 'means' used to achieve what have been otherwise rather consistent goals in US foreign policy since the Second World War.

Additional influences include the force of public opinion, religious sentiment to some extent, and pressure exerted by cause-orientated movements and business interests. All play a role in formulating and justifying US foreign policy conduct, and, in the case of private cause-orientated groups and business interests in the 1980s, even implementing US foreign policy. As I demonstrate later, the operation of these 'societal influences', which unlike other variables are clearly evident in LIC's emergence, forged a strategy consistent with the prevailing trend in postwar US foreign policy, at least in theme. This was the pursuit of interventionism, fuelled largely by competing strains of 'liberalism' and 'realism' within both the Reagan Administration and American society at large.

Competing Tendencies

For the last century or more, there has been a continuing tension in US foreign policy formulation, the result of conflicting perceptions as to the nature of the world and the role of the United States within it. As a consequence, a number of competing tendencies have been clearly manifest in the nature of US foreign policy. These have been interventionism (usually equated with internationalism) as opposed to isolationism, and idealism (moralism) versus realism (often labelled as pragmatism), with the latter two tendencies both motivating the pursuit of coercive diplomacy, albeit for different reasons.

Both isolationism and internationalism are long-established foreign policy traditions, which the United States fluctuated between before the Second World War.[2] However, since the Second World War America has firmly embraced an interventionist policy. This is generally perceived as the consequence of its assuming superpower status and adopting a global stance against what many US administrations perceived was communist expansionism sponsored and supported by the Soviet Union.

US interventionist policy has also been influenced, if not driven, by competing tendencies in the predominant value systems of US decision makers, which I describe herein as realism as opposed to moralism. Also known as liberalism, moralism as a diverse philosophical position basically assumes that human beings are essentially good and capable of altruism and cooperation and that bad behaviour is basically the result of 'bad institutions' which breed this behaviour. Consequently, moralists believe that undesirable political events can be avoided by appropriate international, national and domestic reforms. Moreover, moralism as a prescription for action in foreign policy is concerned with what ought to prevail in international affairs. As such, moralism in US foreign policy has been an ingredient in both isolationism and internationalism. As a persuasion, at different times it has both urged the withdrawal of the US from an immoral world or, on the other hand, demanded that America should reform it. In this sense moralism has added to the cyclical swings between isolation and globalism in US foreign policy.[3]

Political realism (or *realpolitik*), however, focuses largely on such concerns as national interest and power, arguing that the basic motivating factor in international politics is a quest by nation states to acquire power to achieve and maintain their national interests. Nations ought to pursue these interests rather than abstract moral or legal principles, and the reality of world politics is that all states ultimately behave this way – only in this manner can the affairs of international politics best be understood.[4] Similar to internationalism, the realist persuasion or 'balance of power' politics has dominated US foreign policy since 1945, with many presidents regarding themselves as realists and rationalising their foreign policy decisions using such vocabulary. However, moralism still bears considerable influence in policy formulation, as was evident during the Carter presidency and the Reagan Administration's pronouncements and actions, particularly with regard to the 'Project Democracy' initiative.[5]

Regardless of the rhetoric, however, postwar US foreign policy has been mainly interventionist in nature, albeit driven at times by either one or sometimes both of these competing tendencies even while they operate from different premises about reality. As I later demonstrate, the Reagan Administration pursued an interventionist foreign policy motivated in part by both realist and moralist tendencies. In this sense, LIC further continued the foreign policy pattern wherein most administrations exhibited these different tendencies to varying degrees, at different times and over different issues.

The US Foreign Policy Continuum

As an element of foreign policy continuum, LIC has diverse origins as deeply embedded in early US Cold War 'containment' thinking dating back to 1946 and Kennan's long telegram as they are in the 1970s when US policy makers, also loosely described here as 'militarists', perceived the Soviets to be expanding unchallenged throughout the Third World. As an interventionist approach, LIC emerged from the long debate within the US over the Soviet Union's true nature and the most appropriate means of dealing with it. LIC was also a product of the US 'national security state', the loose combination of the White House, the State Department, the Defense Department and other government agencies – the state within a state forged to combat communist expansionism in the early 1950s.[6] As I demonstrate later, LIC grew out of the doctrine of containment (or the strategy of 'containment militarism' as it was also known), the cornerstone of American Cold War interventionist foreign policy until it was discredited in the Vietnam War.

Military Containment

Containment as it emerged in 1950 was embodied in National Security Council Directive 68 (NSC-68). This realist directive mandated the worldwide military containment of communism by a vastly rearmed United States and its allies to prevent more territory, labour and markets from falling under perceived Soviet control.[7] The inherent assumption underpinning NSC-68 was that the US was morally obligated and able to undertake this global responsibility. In adopting this policy, the Truman Administration appeared motivated by moralist concerns; however, NSC-68 represented more the globalisation of the 'militarist' strategy enunciated earlier in 1947 by President Truman. NSC-68 departed significantly from the original conviction, held by Kennan and others, that the Soviet challenge to US interests could be restricted by diplomatic and economic means in certain parts of the world, including Western Europe. In fact, by seeking the global containment of communism principally by force of arms, NSC-68 was inherently realist in nature.

With the adoption of NSC-68 at the outbreak of the Korean War in June 1950, military containment was firmly established as the centrepiece of US foreign policy strategy for at least the next 20 years.[8] Much of Reagan's approach to combating revolutionary nationalism originated from within this realist worldview; LIC is a further manifestation of containment in the Third World, albeit in a very different form. Further, many militarists who had originally lobbied for the acceptance of military containment as US foreign policy, later re-emerged in the 1970s to lobby for the resurrection of interventionism and the election of President Reagan.

The Militarists

The Committee on the Present Danger (CPD) was perhaps the primary and most powerful militarist lobby group, listing prominent academics, businessmen, politicians, scientists, technocrats and ex-military personnel among its members.[9] In foreign policy debate, it was opposed primarily by the 'isolationists' of the conservative 'right' within the United States who preferred containment, with an 'Asia before Europe' emphasis. The CPD's objective was to turn this focus around. The Truman Doctrine had generated an ongoing debate within the United States and demands from the most fervent anti-communists for far more than merely containing 'Soviet-backed' communism. These people regarded NSC-68 as not interventionist enough, and instead demanded a more aggressive approach. None the less, extensively sponsored by the CPD, NSC-68 was adopted and, with the completion of its objective, the original CPD disbanded in 1953.[10]

Much of Reagan's interventionist foreign policy is traceable to the Cold War years of the late 1940s and the prevailing perception at that time that the Soviets were bent on global expansion, either directly or through proxies. As a measure of the increasing domestic support this persuasion gained through the early 1950s, a period encompassing Mao's victory in China, the Korean War and perceived Soviet-backed communist expansionism in Indochina, Eisenhower came to power in 1952 promising to 'roll back' communism using the threat of 'massive retaliation'.[11] However, succumbing to the geopolitical and economic realities of such a strategy, Eisenhower ultimately could do little more than continue military containment as it had already developed in Europe and Asia.[12] Nevertheless, the Eisenhower Administration did manage to sell this 'reduced' strategy to all but the most extreme anti-communists of the American 'right' by maintaining that military containment actually entailed forcing back Soviet influence.

Resurgent Anti-Interventionism

In the 1950s two other factors helped forge the nature of Reagan's later response to Marxist revolutionary nationalism. The first was the growth within the US of an anti-interventionist sentiment in the wake of the Korean War, a forerunner to the Vietnam Syndrome in the 1970s. The second was Eisenhower's heavy reliance on the Central Intelligence Agency to covertly implement foreign policy and thereby avoid growing US domestic opposition to military intervention in the Third World. This occurred, for example, in 1954 in Guatemala where the US has a long tradition of intervention, as it does in the rest of Central America and the Caribbean.[13] After the Korean conflict in the 1950s, it was increasingly difficult to mobilise public support for direct military intervention against 'communist aggression', just as it had been against the nationalism of the Mossadeq Government in Iran. In both Iran and Guatemala, national governments were perceived as threatening US business interests and thereby US national security. Washington responded in both cases by working to overthrow these governments. This reinforced, if not set, the precedent for following US administrations in alliance with American business and interest groups to use covert action to achieve foreign policy objectives when faced by potentially significant US domestic opposition to direct military intervention.[14]

The growth of Marxist revolutionary nationalism in the 1950s was also an important factor in the eventual emergence of LIC. Militarists then, as they did later in the 1980s, perceived revolutionary movements and governments as posing the greatest threat to US economic and strategic interests in the Third World. In 1959, Castro's victory in Cuba alarmed those in Washington already shaken by the 'loss' of China. It was seen as a clear case of revolutionary nationalism openly confronting US hegemony in the Caribbean, and as such, would set a dangerous precedent for the rest of Latin America. Moreover, it was also considered further evidence of Soviet expansionism occurring elsewhere at that time, particularly in the growing Vietnam conflict. Nevertheless, Eisenhower was constrained from directly intervening in Cuba. The Cold War was thawing, the Administration was under pressure to reduce military spending and support for another Korea-like conflict was hard to generate. Eisenhower therefore sought to topple Castro using alternative means, namely economic pressure and military intervention waged by Cuban exiles, which resulted however in the failed 'Bay of Pigs' operation. From these and other significant containment 'innovations', later pursued by Kennedy, grew much of LIC's framework.[15]

Alarmed by the Cuban disaster, the Kennedy Administration responded vigorously in this era of 'resurgent communist expansionism'. For example, it rapidly increased US involvement in Vietnam, signalling a recommitment to the principles of NSC-68 and strong 'leadership'. However in a more innovative approach to this new era of insurgency, President Kennedy, in keeping with the doctrine of 'flexible response', placed considerable emphasis on waging counterinsurgency campaigns against 'wars of liberation' in both Latin America and Asia.

Assuming that communism and revolt grew out of poverty, Kennedy grafted both development and counterinsurgency activities into what basically remained a militarised approach. Vietnam thus became the testing ground for an emerging US national security strategy that exhibited an element of political and economic flexibility borne out of the lessons from Korea and Castro's success in Cuba. If the US could prove victorious in Vietnam with this approach, revolutionary nationalism could be defeated elsewhere. For the next decade, this expression of containment, often known as the 'doctrine of limited wars' appeared effective in containing revolutionary activity.[16] In the nearly twelve years that followed there was only one successful seizure of power by revolutionaries in the Third World and that was in South Yemen.

From Containment to Managerialism

Over time, however, the strategy of flexible response increasingly relied on conventional military power and with the US defeat in Vietnam, military containment (and in essence the precepts of NSC-68) was discredited, as was the militarist persuasion within Washington's foreign policy circles.[17] Direct military intervention appeared to have met its limits as a viable strategy against Third World revolutionary nationalism. A new period began in which various attempts were made both to accommodate the changing strategic and economic position of the United States *vis-à-vis* its allies and the Soviet Union, and to reconsolidate US hegemony in the Third World.

Corresponding to the US defeat in Vietnam, the economic power of the United States declined relative to that of its major allies further limiting its military power. By the early 1970s, Washington had lost its strategic monopoly, an historic reality that no future administration could ignore.[18] The decline of America's capacity to intervene everywhere in the Third World to protect its interests thus rendered containment simply too costly in economic terms, regardless of other concerns.

The Vietnam defeat, moreover, fuelled the growth of the Vietnam Syndrome within American society. As a significant and growing constraint on American foreign policy, the War Powers Act was passed by Congress over the President's veto in November 1973, as well as other restrictions on the President's powers to wage war in an attempt to increase Congressional control over the activities of the US armed forces.[19] Restrictions were also imposed on the covert operations of the CIA and other intelligence agencies.

Responding to this growing loss of support for interventionist policy, as early as 1969 the Nixon Administration attempted to rebuild public support for an alternative national security doctrine. Nixon sought to safeguard American interests however broadly defined while taking account of the constraints on the projection of US power. The result was the articulation of the Nixon Doctrine, regarded by some as the 'doctrine of surrogate gendarmes'. As a variation of military containment, the US would rely on the heavily bolstered military power of strategically placed local elites, such as the Shah of Iran and President Somoza of Nicaragua, to combat revolutionary nationalism still defined as communism. Arms control and trade, meanwhile, would be used to bargain with the Soviet Union and China as a way of managing these powers. Nixon was intent on maintaining appearances of omnipotence even though US power was declining.[20]

In the late-1970s post-Vietnam era of uncertainty, national humiliation and self-criticism, Washington maintained this 'concert of powers' approach while it adjusted to the reality of its diminishing capacity to defeat Marxist insurgencies directly. The defence of strategic and economic interests, as always, remained central to US foreign policy calculations, and revolutionary nationalism was still considered a major threat to national security. Also US business and multinational corporations needed American power to safeguard their interests in the Third World. The desirability of a multiple alliance system to maintain US hegemony was thus ensured. Moreover, the *détente* Nixon forged with the Soviet Union and the Chinese provided the incentive for the Soviets to not undertake or back Third World revolutions.

Both the Nixon Doctrine and *détente* were expressions in part of the growing perception in the 1970s that the real threat to US hegemony came not from 'communist' powers as such but from indigenous Marxist revolutionary nationalism against which direct military force had proven less than effective. As the liberal persuasion gained strength in Washington, the United States sought a new approach to Third World revolution. Policy makers redefined the nature of the international regime and how it should be ordered. With this assessment the 'trilateral' or 'managerial' approach to world order became dominant. Successive administrations pursued a more liberal approach using world trade and economics to maintain America's global hegemony, while seeking less confrontation with Moscow and Peking.[21]

President Ford, regarded by some as heading the first trilateralist administration, nevertheless inherited and continued the policy of regional surrogates or 'Vietnamising' US foreign policy. Militarised allied regimes in the Third World reduced the need for, and therefore the domestic repercussions of, direct American intervention against revolutionary forces. For some time this strategy seemed successful, particularly in the 'southern cone countries'. However as the 1970s progressed, this strategy of surrogate containment was faltering. Basically inflexible, it relied too heavily on military solutions, which thereby imposed new limits on the maintenance of US interests.

Early in the Carter years, the militarists reached their nadir and the trilateralists their point of maximum influence. Carter's general foreign policy focus was on restructuring relations between capitalist states rather than on anti-Soviet politics. The Third World also became more central to American foreign policy calculations as US national interests and threats to these interests were redefined to promote human rights, displacing the US–Soviet rivalry as the central theme of Washington's foreign policy. Carter purged many militarists from influential positions within the national security apparatus; the armed services and the CIA were cut back, and the latter forced to undergo public scrutiny of its secret operations.

President Carter however had to come to terms with a political culture teetering between isolationism engendered by the Vietnam experience and demands for renewed military interventionism by the emerging neo-conservatives of the 'New Right'.[22] For the most part, Carter attempted to pursue a middle course. As a result the US eschewed overt involvement in Angola and later in Nicaragua but nevertheless sanctioned intervention if needed to protect vital US interests such as Middle Eastern oil. But by the end of 1979, Carter was overtaken by crucial international and domestic developments which discredited managerialism and fuelled the arguments of those advocating military interventionism. More of LIC's origins lay within these developments.

Resurgent Militarism

Though the militarists had lost influence by the early Carter years, by the end of his presidency a full ideological turn-around had occurred. The militarists re-established their influence in Washington and initiated what some argue was the 'Second Cold War' by returning the US–Soviet rivalry and interventionism to the central focus of American foreign policy. Neo-conservatism regained such favour domestically that President Carter was swept from power in 1980.

Ultimately the militarist resurgence was aided by international developments that forged consensus within the foreign policy elite for the readoption of military containment. Just as Vietnam signalled the collapse of military interventionism, together the fall of the Shah of Iran and President Somoza in Nicaragua and the continuing Iran hostage crisis, among other events, largely discredited managerialism. What Halliday referred to as the 'third wave of revolution' was thus an important factor generating militarism's resurgence.[23] Between 1974 and 1980, no less than 14 states were taken over by revolutionary forces. In spite of US attempts to bolster its allied regimes these revolutions suffered few reverses. By 1979, Nixon's 'world order' strategy had failed. Consecutive 'losses' to the West in Angola, Iran and Nicaragua brought the perceived threat of Third World revolution geographically much closer to America, causing considerable alarm in Washington and fuelling the growth of neo-conservatism. The emerging New Right considered *détente* a 'sellout' and the managerial approach as only accommodating Soviet expansionism. President Carter's failure to combat what was considered to be Soviet expansionism by proxy meant that the 'dominoes' were falling. However, from the Administration's perspective, it was pressured from both sides as the lingering memories of Vietnam still constrained the adoption of direct intervention.

Frustrated by perceptions of paralysis in US foreign policy, Carter's 'weak-kneed liberalism', and the relative loss of US power to deal with these threats, neo-conservatives and those of the broad militarist persuasion quickly rallied. The Vietnam Syndrome was to be overcome: it had sapped domestic confidence in US power with disastrous consequences for American foreign policy for far too long. As early as 1975, retired intelligence officers, military contractors, right-wing business figures and ideologues organised to lobby against *détente* and to agitate for the restoration of US power. The newly re-formed Committee on the Present Danger, which re-emerged in 1976 as a spearhead for the New Right, dominated the loose groupings and coalitions that formed.[24] Many members of this influential group, and others which coalesced around it, were also members of America's national security state[25] – even Ronald Reagan was a member of the CPD.[26]

The CPD agitated for the reassertion of aggressive military containment. By the end of 1976, it believed that the American public's mood was shifting from pacifism to patriotism, with growing support for a US military build-up. As in the days of NSC-68, the CPD perceived military force to be the supreme calculus of political power. The group's purpose was straight-forward: 'to alert American policy makers and opinion leaders and the public at large to the ominous Soviet military build up and its implications, and to the unfavourable trends in the US–Soviet military balance'.[27] In short, it strongly lobbied for the reinstatement of military containment as the cornerstone of American foreign policy. Through the mass media, seminars and other channels, the CPD persistently alerted public opinion to an alleged US 'vulnerability' to the Soviets, arguing that the Soviet Union was prepared to fight and win a nuclear war and that arms control and *détente* were not a credible foreign policy alternative to a build-up of US military power. By lobbying in this manner the CPD was a major domestic factor in the demise of SALT II.

In the late 1970s, the Coalition for a Democratic Majority and the Committee for a Free World as well as other 'think-tanks' supporting the Committee on the Present Danger,[28] emerged as the frontline of the New Right. This coalition embraced a number of basic ideological interest-group perspectives including neo-conservatives, groups from the 'old right' and representatives from the military-industrial complex.[29] The alliance of these groups broadly came into being through the Coalition for Peace Through Strength (CPS), an *ad hoc* lobby group modelled after the 'Emergency Coalition Against Unilateral Disarmament'. Like the latter, the CPS originated in the American Security Council (ASC), referred to by some as 'the heart if not the soul of the military-industrial complex'.[30]

This coalition was spearheaded via a marriage of political expedience to combat the institutional authority of the executive in foreign policy formulation. The CPD needed the organisational skills and network offered by the CPS, while the latter needed the CPD's influence and expertise. A potent alliance was thereby formed of hard-line, anti-Soviet, anti-communist groups that reshaped Washington's foreign policy agenda in accordance with the Committee's bipolar perception of the world, eventually getting one of the CPD's own members elected as President of the United States.

The Militarist Offensive

The militarists charged that while the managerialist 'world order' approach appeared to be an active foreign policy, in reality it was more isolationist. They argued that Moscow was expanding its influence in the Third World by proxy to minimise the risk of direct confrontation with the United States. Moreover, they regarded Kissinger's 'stability with peace' approach of the mid-1970s as immoral because it failed to combat this expansionism.

From 1976 on the CPD led an intensive press and propaganda campaign against Carter's foreign policy. The militarists sought to convince the

American people of the need to 'rearm' and 'roll back' Third World revolutions, and to forge no more 'deals' with the Soviet Union.[31]

As it emerged, the anti-Carter campaign was quite significant because of its diverse participants. Many right-wing evangelicals joined, linking their strong conservative stance on social issues with the need for strong national defence. Bureaucrats, academics and others critical of the Administration's emphasis on human rights and *détente* also joined them. In particular response to Carter's purge of the Central Intelligence Agency, a number of former CIA officers became active in the campaign,[32] forming a group known as the Association of Former Intelligence Officers which sponsored speakers to tour the country calling for an end to 'national security' leaks and for a 'crackdown on traitors'.[33]

During this campaign, the CPD virtually functioned as Reagan's 'shadow cabinet', accusing the Carter Administration of losing its nerve when faced with Soviet aggression. Some even thought Carter was indirectly responsible for the 'loss' of Iran.[34] Essential to this attack was the perception that Soviet aggression was shifting focus in the Third World, a perception inflamed by the continuing wave of revolution in the late 1970s. Focusing on Angola and then the Ethiopia–Somalia conflict in 1977, the Soviets appeared to be on the move along a so-called 'arc of crisis' extending from Western Africa to Asia.[35]

As a result of this campaign US foreign policy increasingly focused on the Third World which had grown in importance to both the US and the international capitalist system as an increasing supplier of raw materials. Whether perceived to be Soviet-inspired or a function of strictly anti-Western indigenous nationalism, revolutionary activity was considered a most serious threat to US interests.[36] There was thus a growing consensus among America's foreign policy elite for the resurrection of military containment, even before the fall of Somoza and the Shah.

Under increasing pressure, Carter finally accepted that revolutionary nationalism challenging US interests was Soviet inspired. The 'third wave of revolution' had been integral to this change of perception, and by the late 1970s, the managerialist position thus appeared severely flawed. *Détente* had not produced Soviet cooperation in curbing Third World revolutions nor had it constrained the expansion of Soviet military power. With the fall of the Shah and Somoza, and therefore the apparent failure of the strategy of regional surrogates, the managerialist position became indefensible.[37] As a result, fuelled by the Iran hostage crisis, the Soviet invasion of Afghanistan and the loss of Nicaragua, in 1979 the Carter Administration embraced an interventionist foreign policy. The Carter Doctrine was formulated, which committed the United States to protecting the Middle East and its oil from Soviet aggression. By embracing the theme and essence of NSC-68,[38] the Carter Doctrine signalled not just the end of the world order approach, but also a return to military interventionism.[39] By defining both Nicaragua and

Iran as vital to 'US national security', in one fell swoop it also extended America's national security perimeters to the Persian Gulf.[40]

Carter's adoption of an interventionist approach, however, did not appease his critics. Fuelled by the Iran hostage crisis, the momentum of growing neo-conservatism led to the election of Ronald Reagan, who pledged to make America 'great again' by restoring US military dominance. Nevertheless, while Reagan's victory may have confirmed a resumption of Cold War politics, the theme of this 'Second Cold War' proved more anti-Soviet than anti-communist.

Militarism Reasserted

US foreign policy had thus turned full circle. In 1980 the Reagan Administration set about further reasserting an interventionist posture as many neo-conservatives and other militarists, newly appointed to the Administration, began to acquit their responsibilities with a zeal and ideology reminiscent of the 1950s. Reagan's foreign policy was both direct and simple: it targeted the Soviet Union as the source of all 'evil'. Gone was the sophistication of Nixon and Kissinger's *détente* and Carter's earlier emphasis on human rights and the problems of the 'South'. Instead, Reagan intensified Carter's newly found 1979–80 belligerence and anti-communist policies. However, the full extent of the new Administration's redefinition of US national interests was not clearly evident in 1980. Only much later, with the development of LIC and the Reagan Doctrine, did the extent of the re-definition become clear.

In 1980 the Committee on the Present Danger virtually became the Reagan Administration, with many of its members gaining the highest positions of control in the key institutions that determined foreign policy, including the National Security Council (NSC), the Department of Defense and the CIA. Many CPD members became Reagan's top national security advisers including Arms Control Negotiator Eugene Rostow, Paul Nitze, Fred Ikle and William Van Cleave.[41] By 1981, more than 50 CPD members had been appointed to key posts and the Reagan Administration's *de facto* foreign policy was determined by the CPD.[42] Attempting to reassert 'roll-back', the Administration repudiated *détente* and, while increasing its bellicose anti-Soviet language, began a rapid build-up of conventional and nuclear arms.

Continuity in Foreign Policy

Seen in context, Reagan's interventionist approach established broad continuity in US foreign policy. Anti-communism was restored as the central focus of US diplomacy as the Administration, espousing the rhetoric of 'roll-back', reasserted the strategy of military containment of the Soviet Union.

Initially, the broad thrust of Reagan's foreign policy was to combat the Soviets on all fronts simultaneously, as outlined in the findings of the Committee of Santa Fe, a foreign policy group of right-wing intellectuals attributed with defining the nature of Reagan's approach towards Central America.[43] Specifically, this meant restoring 'roll-back' as the foundation of US security policy in the Third World. According to this doctrine, appropriate US military action depended on the dimension of the perceived Soviet threat. America's global dominance in political, economic and military terms had to be re-established, thereby demanding the Administration pursue a major build-up of nuclear and conventional weapons. However, to diminish Soviet influence globally also meant the US should increase its focus on the Third World, the emerging arena for the intensifying superpower rivalry in the 1980s. A major consequence of this focus was the emergence of low intensity conflict.

LIC as Continuity

The development of the strategy of low intensity conflict also represented continuity in Washington's Cold War 'coercive diplomacy'. It highlighted a number of factors consistent in the evolution of US foreign policy since the Second World War. Covert action, intelligence activity, economic pressure, displays of military strength for political purposes and other diplomatic action, all dimensions of LIC, have always been a part of Washington's foreign policy arsenal. Each has played a prominent role in the foreign policy of the United States since 1945 as the goals of Washington's foreign policy became 'militarised'. All derive from long-held realist assumptions by many US foreign policy elites that military and other interventionist policies and strategies are a continuous and necessary requirement to ensure that US security needs are met. LIC reaffirmed the pattern in US foreign policy of competing isolationist and interventionist influences. In this case, it represented a further manifestation of interventionism.

The emergence of LIC also established continuity with earlier US national security doctrine. As a strategy to combat what was seen to be Soviet-backed revolutionary nationalism, LIC represented another interpretation of containment. However it was not carefully planned, designed nor orchestrated. Instead, the convergence of a number of diverse factors actually spawned this strategy. Factors such as the militarist persuasion achieving dominance within Washington, and a number of historical, cultural and political determinants together gave this foreign policy approach its distinctive character by 1987.

As seen in the nature of its selective applications, LIC also revealed the competing tendencies of moralism and realism within the Reagan Administration itself.[44] Other elements of foreign policy continuity include the involvement of US business elements and private agencies as both instruments and determinates of foreign policy strategy. Just as they had in the 1950s, the involvement of US business and private interests is clearly evident in the CPD's influential role in formulating US foreign policy. US business interests have a long history of influencing American foreign policy, often quite overtly as was the case in the 1970s when a close working relationship developed between the US government and giant American multinational corporations such as the International Telephone and Telegraph Company (ITT): with their interests threatened by President Allende's nationalisation programme, ITT, among others, collaborated with the Nixon Administration to overthrow the Chilean government in September 1973.[45]

LIC's emergence also further demonstrated how US presidents often restrict or at least carefully manage foreign policy information available to Congress. The American Congress and the Legislature have a complex relationship which often forces US presidents to try to circumvent Congress in a variety of ways if they wish to avoid congressional restraints, such as the War Powers Act, or adverse public opinion in order to achieve their foreign policy goals.[46] As I examine more fully in Chapter 6, President Reagan openly flouted Congress by waging LIC in Central America. However, he was not setting an entirely new precedent for further presidential action: in the early 1960s, for example, President Johnson effectively duped Congress in the Gulf of Tonkin incident,[47] and later the Ford and Carter Administrations openly flouted the War Powers Act or at least only paid it lip service.[48] Therefore by deluding Congress over his administration's role in attempting to subvert the Nicaraguan government, Reagan was only establishing further continuity.

A Reactive Strategy

Like earlier US national security doctrine, LIC emerged as a reactive strategy in response to a foreign policy question the Administration long sought to address. In general, postwar US foreign policy has conspicuously lacked true positive purpose and instead has been more reactive than active. US policy making has thus been described as a series of reactions to major crises, a characteristic trait of a nation that possesses a global outreach but lacks the power to police everywhere at once. In the case of LIC, it emerged as a reaction to the threat posed by resurgent revolutionary nationalism, which was seen to be driven by Soviet expansionism.

The major expression of a militarist foreign policy is direct military intervention. As such, the Reagan Administration often appeared very militarist. For example, its invasion of Grenada followed very much the pattern of US interventionist action in the 1950s and 1960s. However, in many crisis areas created by revolutionary nationalism in the 1980s, direct military intervention was not an option, particularly in the case of the Philippines and Nicaragua. Since the Second World War, a number of inhibiting factors have prevented the US from pursuing direct military intervention in many target states. During the Cold War these included: a perceived need to use nuclear weapons, the prior presence of Soviet troops, some other component of the US decision-making structure apart from the President such as Congress, vetoing an intervention decision, an absence of armed conflict, or the absence of a specific request for intervention. With these factors in mind, some argue that the United States has pursued direct military intervention only if these factors were not present and there was an overt threat of a communist takeover.[49] However, in the case of the Reagan Administration, other factors prevented direct military intervention in many parts of the Third World, and forged the necessity for the development of an alternative strategy such as low intensity conflict.

LIC's Specific Applications

Though many observers perceived low intensity conflict to be global in application during the Reagan era, in practice its full profile emerged in only a few specific target environments. As an important national security strategy to pursue US objectives in the Third World, LIC's applicability was limited by a particular combination of domestic, regional and international factors. These factors included circumstance, opportunity and the feasibility of the goal to be achieved. Moreover, Washington's objectives often differed from case to case (as will be seen in later chapters) which also determined the extent of the strategy's development.

In addition to those determinates of LIC's application as described above, the factors determining the full development of LIC in target states were both objective and subjective. They related to perceptions within the Reagan Administration of threats to 'national security' interests within a particular region, the likelihood of US involvement in a protracted war if more conventional military solutions were pursued, and the extent of US domestic and international opposition likely to be provoked by such involvement.

Most determinants of US foreign policy formulation relate to questions as to what constitutes America's national security interests, and the perceived threats to those interests. To adequately define what constitutes US national security interests is a complex task. It must incorporate questions such as what, and who, do these interests serve: the state, the business sector, the welfare of the population, and so on? Are these interests ideological, strategic, or economic and how much does the target environment define the interest at stake? National security interests can include the maintenance of subjective images such as global prestige and reputation, or the objective interest of maintaining US forces in some strategic Third World country. Perceived threats to US defence interests and perceived needs to combat ideological, military and strategic challenges can all be included under the national security interest umbrella, as can access to critical Third World markets and resources.

In 1988, the Reagan Administration related its foreign policy directly to national security. The Administration stated that its 'National Security Strategy' reflected US interests and that it had a broad plan for achieving the 'national objectives that support those interests'. The Administration listed these 'key' interests as including: the survival of the United States as a free and independent nation with its fundamental values intact, a healthy and growing US economy, a stable and secure world free of major threats to US interests, the growth of human freedom, democratic institutions, and free market economies throughout the world underpinned by healthy alliance relationships.[50]

However, in low intensity warfare environments, the Reagan Administration consistently perceived these interests as synonymous with nothing more than opposition to communism, the Soviet Union and its perceived proxies. The Administration's worldview embraced the notion that successful opposition to communism was one of the United States' most important interests. As a manifestation of a global challenge to US supremacy, Moscow's proxies were considered a threat to America's national security, and Marxist revolutionary nationalist forces were also similarly identified.[51] Richard Pipes, a foreign policy adviser to Reagan, identified Soviet proxies and hence Soviet expansionism by proxy as assuming three forms: expansion by means of the armed forces of other communist countries, or countries in common cause with the Soviet Union; Soviet-supported guerrilla movements in the Third World, and terrorist groups similarly supported and directed by the Soviet Union.[52] In contrast to Carter's initial managerial approach, the Reagan Administration, seeking to maintain 'the security of our nation and our allies',[53] targeted those nationalist forces engaged in Marxist revolution or those already in established revolutionary regimes. More specifically, it claimed that US national security objectives included maintaining access to 'critical resources, markets, the oceans, and space' and wherever possible reducing Soviet influence and its use of subversive forces.[54] The Reagan Administration's national security interests therefore refocused on Third World revolutionary movements, as opposed to the heavy emphasis both Ford and Carter placed on the threat posed by Soviet troop concentrations in Eastern Europe.

With Marxist revolutionary nationalist forces thus posing such a perceived threat in the 1980s, the increased potential for Reagan to recommit US military forces into another round of costly, protracted wars in the Third World determined the development of LIC. With regard to Central America, for example, a US intervention in El Salvador would have easily provoked a region-wide guerrilla war just as debilitating and futile as Vietnam. Moreover, given the high cost of fuel and other military 'consumables', a prolonged US military involvement in the Third World was likely to cost far more than the economic interests it was supposedly designed to protect and also produce a new round of crippling inflation in the United States.[55]

Apart from economic costs, the Reagan Administration also had to consider the electoral costs of such involvement. Short-duration conflicts in which US conventional forces could achieve their objectives and extricate themselves quickly if necessary, as in Libya and Grenada, were situations in which the Reagan Administration could risk direct military intervention without fearing significant domestic opposition. However, involvement in protracted Third World conflicts ran the risk of rekindling memories of defeat in Vietnam and of incurring political costs that would easily outweigh the worth of the objective sought. Further, this risk would be compounded if the immediate objective of such intervention could only be vaguely or abstractly defined. Evidence of a potential groundswell of domestic and international opposition to any prospect of direct intervention was therefore a major determinant in the development of LIC in the 1980s. As I demonstrate later, there was significant public opposition to prospects of direct US intervention in Central America; while there can be no conclusive proof, it is reasonable to suggest that had there been clear public support for such a stance, Reagan's Central American policies would have been considerably more belligerent. In this respect, public opinion was a significant factor in the development of LIC in specific target states, just as it has been on US foreign policy making in general. Recognising this, the Administration engaged in campaigns to win public support for interventionism by appealing to anti-communism, religious sentiments and the fear of terrorism. In this respect the development of the Reagan Doctrine, which was a major manifestation of this campaign and an integral part of the LIC strategy, was in itself an indication of the strength and power of US public opinion as a factor in foreign policy making.

LIC as Discontinuity

LIC, while representing further continuity in US foreign policy in terms of its objectives, in its nature actually represented an element of discontinuity. While the basic tenets of US foreign policy have not changed since the Second World War, particularly regarding its guiding principles and ultimate goals, there has been an element nevertheless of discontinuity, what some might wish to call 'adaptation' in such policy. This discontinuity can largely be confined to the means or tactics used to achieve US goals. In this respect, LIC was an adaptation in US foreign policy to changing circumstances, and was a strategy developed as an alternative to direct military intervention. But LIC was, and is, more than just an alternative. While multidimensional, it is primarily a political strategy which not only emphasises the civilianisation of the pursuit of foreign policy objectives but also its privatisation. In this respect the emergence of LIC forged a relatively new era in foreign policy where US foreign policy strategy was actually carried out, in part, by civilians and civilian agencies often in a private capacity and often illegally.

OLD AND NEW

Considerable debate has taken place in academic and military circles over the status of LIC and the degree of foreign policy innovation it represents. Some argue that LIC was new and innovative, developed in think-tanks in the United States in the 1980s, and tested in El Salvador and Nicaragua in Central America before being applied elsewhere, while others argue that it was battle tested in the proving ground that was the Philippines.[56] Still others contend that it was and is simply counterinsurgency and no more charac-teristic of Reagan's foreign policy than earlier administrations, particularly

President Kennedy's attempts to combat revolution in Latin America and the early stages of the Vietnam War in 1960–61.[57] Some even argue that low intensity conflict is merely a synthesis of counterinsurgency and unconventional warfare tactics already pursued in the Third World for decades.[58]

The latter argument has much to commend it. Activities comprising LIC are not in fact new. To some extent all were present in varying degrees in different forms of US intervention in the Third World after the Second World War, and even as far back as the turn of the century. Some were even derived from the experiences of European colonial powers, particularly the British and French colonial regimes which established many important precedents for LIC activities in their counterinsurgency campaigns in Malaya, Algeria, Northern Africa and Vietnam in the 1950s and early 1960s. Possibly the most important case study was provided by the British experience in Malaya in the early 1950s. In combating the communist-inspired 'Emergency' (as it was called), the British built up an efficient intelligence network and adopted a strategy of aggressive small-unit patrols to harass and pursue the opposing guerrilla forces. Their counterinsurgency policy consisted actually of limited military action. At no time during the Emergency did the British actually use artillery, aerial bombardment, tanks or more than 25 infantry and police battalions, which meant no mass destruction and minimal 'civilian' deaths. More important, however, was the political campaign that was conducted in concert with the limited military approach. The British pursued a 'hearts and minds' strategy by broadening autonomy and then granting independence to cut local support for the insurgency.[59] This primarily political approach proved extremely successful: in the early days of the Kennedy Administration, the Malayan experience was regarded as a model of how to deal with an Asian communist insurgency.[60]

The French experience in Algeria in the 1950s also provided valuable lessons for the later proponents of LIC. One was the necessity in counterinsurgency activity to avoid unnecessary brutality which would undercut attempts to win over the support of the target population.[61] Another related lesson, again, was the importance of the 'political war' in either supporting or defeating revolution.[62]

In the Philippine war of independence and the later anti-Huk campaign of the 1950s, the United States devised and perfected many activities which were also later identified as elements of low intensity conflict.[63] The campaign against the Huks, for example, directed by Colonel Edward Lansdale and Ramon Magsaysay,[64] made use of many psyops operations as well as related civic action and pacification operations.[65] This campaign, which was responsible for defeating the Huks politically and psychologically, was considered so successful that Lansdale was later given the responsibility of overseeing the same psyops and military operations in Vietnam. In both these conflicts, Lansdale worked closely with the CIA carrying out paramilitary actions that relied heavily on locally gathered intelligence.[66]

In the early 1960s, in response to the apparent success of Maoist people's war in the Third World, the Kennedy Administration embraced the doctrine of counterinsurgency, considered by many to be low intensity conflict under a different name. Traditional military activities were combined with political and economic action in an attempt to win the support of the contested population. As part of this strategy, the Administration upgraded the Special Forces (Green Berets) and other units specifically for use in these conflicts, particularly in Vietnam where many elements of LIC can be identified.[67] Moreover, in Latin America the United States used the 'Alliance for Progress' as its political front to actively promote the third way, with rhetoric that heavily emphasised the benefits of democracy and Western economic modernisation. This strategy also heavily relied on the Latin American Peace Corps Program as one vehicle for pursuing American objectives.[68] Other elements of LIC are also identifiable in the economic blockade of Cuba in the early 1960s.

In Eastern Europe in the late 1940s and 1950s, the CIA and its forerunner, the Office of Strategic Services, also undertook clandestine operations that could be considered elements of low intensity conflict.[69] Moreover in 1950, NSC-68 enshrined several LIC elements as tools for US foreign policy, for example: 'We should take dynamic steps to reduce the power and influence of the Kremlin inside the Soviet Union and other areas under its control' including the use of 'covert psychological warfare' and 'operations by covert means in the fields of economic warfare and political and psychological warfare'.[70]

A more recent pursuit of LIC-like activities (in its counter-revolutionary form) however was in Vietnam, albeit for a relatively short while as these activities were eventually discredited. The unconventional warfare tactics waged by US Special Operations Forces were displaced by more 'conventional' warfare tactics when it was perceived that 'pacification' as a counterinsurgency strategy was failing to stem the guerrilla war. Reflecting the dominance of conventional military thinking within US policy-making circles during this period, these LIC tactics still remained discredited in the late 1970s, even after the disastrous conventional campaign involving nearly half a million troops was defeated.

In the 1970s, following the Vietnam debacle, the US concentrated on the more familiar European theatre, avoiding direct military involvement in Third World conflicts. This new cautious mood was symbolised by the passing in Congress of the War Powers Act and the Clarke Amendment which prevented US military involvement in Angola. Nevertheless, the Vietnam defeat still remained pivotal in the emergence of low intensity conflict as a national security strategy in the 1980s, when the advantage of hindsight allowed for a more realistic analysis of the US failure in Southeast Asia.

The strategy of low intensity conflict should be considered a mixture of both old and new. While many LIC activities are old (disputed by those who argue that LIC was new and innovative, as argued in the case of Nicaragua), the extent of the organisation and coordination of its diverse activities was new (as indicated by the extensive campaign Reagan waged to mobilise public support for the Contras). So too was the ideological and operational coherence this strategy achieved (particularly when presented as 'ambiguous warfare' at the time by Secretary of State George Shultz).[71] This feature is overlooked by those who argue that LIC is merely old counter-insurgency and unconventional warfare tactics under a new name.[72] In previous contexts, and particularly in Vietnam, LIC activities as part of counterinsurgency appeared *ad hoc* and unrelated to each other because they were pursued alongside major military campaigns. But under the Reagan Administration the coordination of these activities formed a distinct conflict profile with the objective of political/psychological victory. Moreover, the waging of low intensity conflict also became a foreign policy end in itself, due to a recasting of US foreign policy activities to avoid future 'Vietnams'.

A Political Approach

The fact that LIC is more a political than a military doctrine is what most distinguishes it from earlier counterinsurgency and unconventional warfare strategies and techniques pursued by previous administrations. In this sense, its emergence during the Reagan era does establish a degree of discontinuity in US foreign policy. While an expression of adaptation to changing political, economic and other circumstances (itself a continuous feature in the pattern of US coercive diplomacy), LIC is primarily political in nature. Low intensity conflict as it emerged not only incorporated significant attempts to politically mobilise US public support for foreign policy objectives, but it also subordinated military action to serve political ends. LIC tailors military activities, as it does other dimensions of action, to serve the political objective of attacking the credibility and legitimacy, hence the support base, of the target regime or revolutionary movement. In this sense, LIC broke the postwar pattern of heavy reliance on 'militarised diplomacy' which had become the dominant theme of US foreign policy.

Moreover, LIC relies heavily on psyops. Revolutionary conflicts during the Reagan era were portrayed as popular struggles against 'communist terrorism' waged by 'democratic forces' supported by private US agencies involved in an anti-Marxist crusade. While such psyops campaigns disguised the extent of US government involvement, the fact remained that they were designed to enlist civilian and private, as well as foreign, 'interest' or support group involvement in these conflicts, either as agencies of the Administration, or allied groups pursuing their own similar agendas. Unlike earlier administrations enlisting the assistance of similar interests, the Reagan Administration actively appealed to varied Christian fundamentalist groups to gain support for activities that could circumvent Congressional restraints and thereby enable it achieve its foreign policy objectives, albeit 'illegally'. In this sense, the significant degree to which this emergent strategy was 'civilianised' and 'privatised' demonstrated that LIC was not only quantitatively different but also qualitatively different from earlier strategies, including Kennedy's 'flexible response' and Nixon's 'Vietnamisation' approaches. This policy established further discontinuity by effectively 'contracting out' the pursuit of US foreign policy in select parts of the Third World.

LIC also differed with respect to its organisational and command structures that developed within the Reagan Administration. While I examine this later, it is worth noting here that by 1987 the strategy had coalesced into an innovative thrust in US foreign policy. Forced to respond to the political, economic and military realities of the 1980s, the Reagan Administration through the National Security Council devised a distinct LIC command structure reaching from the NSC downwards. This structure distinguished LIC from earlier loose or partial forms of this strategy, not only because of the extent of the NSC's involvement but also because of its coherence compared with earlier strategies often implemented haphazardly, with little cross-communication.[73]

THE STATUS OF LIC

To many observers, LIC appeared a new and comprehensive strategy the United States could use to project its power, within what it tacitly regarded as its limits, to overcome Marxist revolutionary nationalism and reassert US dominance in the Third World, if not globally. LIC was neither simple nor short term, nor did its proponents consider it to be a 'second-best' strategy to replace direct military intervention.[74] Instead it was regarded as the most appropriate means of dealing with the kinds of political and social challenges facing US interests at that time in Third World. However, analysis of LIC's applications in practice proves that this overstates the Reagan Administration's translation of this strategy from conceptual model to specific LIW environments.

A Selective Strategy

During the Reagan era, LIC above all else was purely a selective strategy. A decisive factor contributing to its emergence in particular Third World states was the existence of favourable local conditions for the pursuit of LIC activities.[75] These 'windows of opportunity' depended on such factors as the local people's culture, lifestyle and sensibilities, the terrain and local history. They also depended on the extent these could be covertly (and even overtly) manipulated and exploited (particularly using psyops) to destroy or at least weaken the target government or movement. Other factors included the availability of local individuals or groups who could lead or already were leaders of the revolutionary movement or the 'democratic alternative'; the existence of social cleavages such as religious and ethnic differences that could be exploited;[76] or better, the pre-existence of revolutionary groups or movements, such as the Mujahideen in Afghanistan. However, in countries without a democratic tradition, or in cultures in which democratic traditions were alien such as in Afghanistan or Kampuchea, it was difficult to promote a democratic revolution. LIC in these cases could only be partially developed and usually with an emphasis on its military and economic dimensions.

Finally, the development of the full LIC conflict profile depended on the nature of the US objectives in the target state and the feasibility of achieving them. This partly depended, in turn, on perceptions of potential US public opposition to both the means and ends of such policy. US objectives varied from attempting to combat direct Soviet aggression as in Afghanistan, to destabilising and overthrowing Marxist revolutionary nationalist regimes such as in Central America. Policy goals also varied over time. In Nicaragua, for example, while a Contra military victory appeared out of the question, one acceptable primary objective was to demonstrate to other movements in the region the extent of US resolve in opposing revolutionary nationalism. Another was engineering the acceptance of the Contras as legitimate participants in peace negotiations, thereby achieving a political victory which enabled the US to achieve further objectives.

Apart from members within the National Security Council and associated agencies deciding that a particular movement or government was to be opposed, it should not be readily assumed, therefore, that in the first instance there existed a formal decision-making procedure within the Administration wherein the relevant factors were weighed and then a decision was made to implement LIC in a particular target state. As already noted, low intensity conflict was and is more a 'reactive' strategy. LIC activities emerged in a target state over time pursued by agencies that would exploit and take advantage of opportunities (often unforeseen) as they arose.

THE DEVELOPMENT OF THE FULL PROFILE

Low intensity conflict was theoretically applicable throughout the Third World, and elements of the strategy were developed by agencies of the Reagan Administration in many target states including Afghanistan, Cambodia and Ethiopia,[77] but up until the end of 1987 the strategy was fully developed only in Angola, El Salvador, Nicaragua and the Philippines.[78] This suggests that LIC at that time was much more easily developed in states where pro-US authoritarian regimes existed and were being challenged or, as in the case of Nicaragua, had been overthrown by revolutionary nationalist forces. In such cases the latter had exploited the discrediting of 'democracy' by these regimes, which particularly in Nicaragua and the Philippines had ruthlessly pursued the anti-communist charter outlined for them by the Nixon Doctrine. In these environments it was relatively easier and more convincing to proclaim that, though suppressed or endangered, a democratic tradition existed which provided the basis for a viable 'third way' and, covertly, a vehicle for the maintenance or reassertion of US power and influence. Also in these environments, the existence of oppressive authoritarian regimes could especially facilitate the conditions for pursuing LIC. Under such regimes there usually existed an educated middle class (often alienated from the political process) within which support for the democratic alternative could be moulded. On the other hand, where such a regime had been overthrown, there would exist among the disaffected socioeconomic elements that had comprised its support base a source of resources and recruitment for the formation of a 'democratic' revolutionary movement.

Low intensity conflict thus emerged with a coherent image based on a characteristic response to revolutionary nationalism over time by agencies of the Reagan Administration. As operational policy in this era it appears, nevertheless, to have had definite parameters and limited applicability defined by a specific set of criteria. However within the US's own sphere of influence, LIC had particular relevance and hence utility as a replacement for the discredited Nixon Doctrine as those staunch advocates of this doctrine, such as Jeane Kirkpatrick, steadily lost favour within the Administration to those championing 'democratic revolution'.[79]

AN EXPECTED FOREIGN POLICY INITIATIVE?

Reagan's election represented an interventionist influence again achieving dominance within Washington and perhaps the US political culture at large. Moreover, the President's foreign policy statements embraced the essence of *realpolitik*, including for example, his belief that 'the lesson of history is that among the great nations only those with the strength to protect their interests survive'.[80] However, although Reagan's assumption of power indicated the public's desire for a return to 'strong leadership', its lingering reluctance to again countenance direct military interventionism renders the emergence of LIC somewhat of an expected foreign policy initiative. In accordance with the assumption that 'the promotion of American interests above all else is the only acceptable moral obligation the US must consider',[81] the Administration not only asserted US military power abroad conventionally, but in the face of potential domestic opposition also pursued its interests by alternative means in the Third World. The following chapter traces the emergence of LIC as an 'alternative' interventionist strategy within the military and policy-making circles of the Reagan Administration.

3   FROM APPROACH TO STRATEGY

As a *de facto* US national security strategy, in terms of theory and practice low intensity conflict was developed quite separately before these two levels converged into a coherent foreign policy tactic articulated by the Reagan Doctrine. Theoretically, the strategy was conceptualised within US policy-making circles and academic think-tanks, which attempted to understand and evaluate how appropriate was the further pursuit of LIC-like activities already practised in Third World states by both 'official' and 'private' US agencies. In this chapter I look at this theoretical level of LIC's development, tracing LIC's conceptual evolution within the United States and its eventual acceptance by the Reagan Administration and the US military as a coherent strategy with which to combat revolutionary nationalism.

Initially, low intensity conflict did not receive full support within the Reagan Administration or the military. Some more conventionally minded military personnel argued that LIC should not have the status of a strategy. They regarded it instead as nothing more than a rehash of Kennedy-era *ad hoc*, unrelated counterinsurgency and unconventional warfare techniques already discredited in Vietnam and lacking ideological credibility. Only later when the Reagan Doctrine was enunciated did LIC appear to find majority acceptance. This was because the Doctrine articulated a publicly acceptable ideological rationale for LIC and, by defining its objectives and parameters of application, gave it operational coherence.

By the end of 1987, the Reagan Administration had accepted LIC as a legitimate national security strategy: its operation, or 'footprint' (so termed due to its reliance on many covert activities) was identifiable in a significant number of Third World states. Also, the command apparatus of both the US Administration and the military had been restructured to facilitate the coor-dination of LIC, at least by government agencies. Moreover, by this time the strategy had also achieved sufficient operational coherence in the Third World to enable the Reagan Administration to address effectively what Colonel Harry Summers regarded as the basic fundamentals of war, namely questions like 'what are we trying to do? ... how are we going to do it?' and 'who is going to command and control it?'[1]

SELF-ANALYSIS AND DEBATE: THE INFLUENCE OF VIETNAM

While elements of LIC are certainly not new and had been discredited prior to the 1980s, central to its conceptual emergence as a strategy during the

Reagan years was a long period of theoretical debate within academic think-tanks, the armed services and the Administration itself over the problem of how to deal with low intensity warfare. There was much critical analysis of the lessons to be derived from US experiences in Central America, the Philippines and elsewhere, and also from the experiences of other colonial powers in earlier attempts to combat revolutionary nationalism. Meanwhile, the credibility of this approach was enhanced increasingly by the apparent successes of LIC activities already being pursued in target states. The major influence in this process of strategy formulation, nevertheless, remained the reassessment of the US experience in Vietnam.

America's defeat in Vietnam had shocked successive administrations and the military into rethinking not only the rationale for US intervention into such Third World conflicts, but even its global role as the 'defender' of democracy. During the 1970s, the United States retreated into a long period of self-criticism: academics and theorists within the US armed services and intelligence branches paid considerable attention to the lessons that could be learnt from Vietnam.[2] Meanwhile, the US military, eschewing counter-insurgency as a failed strategy, instead turned to its erstwhile preoccupation with orthodoxy, conventional containment and preparations for battle in the European theatre.

Two Schools of Thought

Keen to reassert US hegemony in the Third World, theorists such as Sarkesian, Colonel Harry Summers and Edward Lansdale could be broadly divided into two opposing schools of thought based on their diverging analyses of the nature of Third World revolutions, their different conclusions as to why the US failed in Vietnam, and their conflicting interpretations of the lessons to be learnt from that failure. As participants in the broader debate, the two groups effectively competed for doctrinal hegemony and acceptance within the Administration and US military. The first school advocated a return to Clausewitzian notions of conventional war 'with its center of gravity on the destruction of the enemy armed forces',[3] and within which military power was the ultimate determinant of victory. The second school, in which Lansdale was very influential, consisted of those who could be considered LIC proponents. They were convinced that the counterinsurgency method of 'pacification' used in Vietnam was the most appropriate means of countering revolutionary nationalism, and argued that a predominantly political/psychological approach would assure America achieved not just a narrow military victory in the short term, but 'total' victory in the long term.

The first or 'conventional' school of which Summers was an influential proponent, proved dominant within the US military during the 1970s. It argued that the 'pacification' school ignored the international dimensions of the Vietnam conflict and that conventional strategies of massive firepower should have been used from the outset. At the core of this analysis was the 'umbilical theory' of revolution which provided the basis for Reagan's initial strategy toward revolutionary movements in Central America.[4] This theory posited that Marxist revolutionary movements such as those in El Salvador and Nicaragua in the Third World were essentially dependent on military supplies and other support from sympathetic 'outside' powers such as Cuba and the Soviet Union. The support provided by these outside powers was thought to resemble an umbilical-like process.[5] Hence for America to defeat such insurgencies, either the outside powers or the 'umbilical supply cord' linking them to the insurgencies had to be eliminated, assumedly by using conventional military force. Summers' essential conclusion was that from the outset the United States should have waged all-out conventional war against North Vietnam (the outside power) and left the waging of counter-insurgency within South Vietnam (against the internal enemy) to the South Vietnamese Government Forces (ARVN). He argued, subsequently, that the US military should not be primarily engaged in civic action or other pacification operations in target states as this was a misdirection of crucial resources. In the Vietnam conflict, counterinsurgency was therefore only part of the answer because South Vietnam faced not only internal insurgency but also outside aggression. Summers thus claimed that the United States lost in Vietnam because doctrinal confusion over the role of the US military meant it was 'shackled' early in the conflict. US forces were prevented from fighting a war, which should have emphasised the 'classic' strategic offensive, which, Summers claimed, carried the war to the enemy, and by destroying 'his' armed forces and will to fight, would achieve victory.[6]

Because of the ascendancy of this view during the 1970s, mainstream US military thinking on tactical doctrine underwent significant changes resulting in the creation of the US Army Training and Doctrine Command (TRADOC). Counterinsurgency doctrine was virtually abandoned and conventional war tactics were re-emphasised. Symbolising this shift was the stress placed by the revised new Army Manual FM 100–1 on the fundamental role, principles and precepts governing the employment of US armed forces in conventional warfare.

Nevertheless, what could be later considered as the 'LIC school' endured. Its proponents, who constituted a minority within the military, intelligence bodies and academia, were still convinced of the suitability of their approach.[7] They argued that the main source of revolution in Third World states lay within internal economic, political and other conditions from which discontent and desperation germinated, and upon which alternative ideologies such as Marxism and violent nationalist revolution flourished.

By 1980 the LIC school was rapidly gaining influence. Many former advocates of the pacification or psyops approach had acquired positions of influence within the newly elected Reagan Administration. These included appointments within the Pentagon, State Department and diplomatic missions abroad, as well as in many New Right think-tanks that guided the development of Reagan policy.[8] Perhaps more importantly, the LIC school's interpretation of the US defeat in Vietnam appeared much more compelling and relevant to the predominant threat contemporary revolutionary nationalism posed to US interests in the Third World at that time. Moreover, the need to revise America's approach to this threat became more urgent as the Sandinista victory in 1979 and the Iranian hostage crisis in 1980 indicated that the 'third revolutionary wave' appeared to be gaining momentum. With the spectre of new Vietnams looming, the US military and the Reagan Administration were forced to reconsider the most appropriate means for combating such forces despite the still lingering memories of defeat in Vietnam. Moreover, the political 'right', though demanding that conventional and nuclear forces should be increased to combat the Soviet threat if necessary, was also calling for the development of a new strategy that could effectively combat revolutionary forces in the Third World. As a consequence, the LIC school increased its influence to such an extent that even Edward Lansdale commented: 'I think they're going to listen to us this time.'[9] This listening process essentially meant absorbing the LIC school's analysis of the lessons to be learnt from Vietnam.

The LIC Lessons/Conclusions from Vietnam

In Vietnam many LIC tactics were virtually abandoned as the conflict's dynamics drew the US increasingly into conventional warfare and then defeat. In the years that followed, these tactics remained discredited, even though evidence showed that the pacification approach, as opposed to conventional warfare, was successful where applied. Ultimately, only when attempting to respond to revolutionary nationalism did the Reagan Administration accept the LIC proponents' analysis of what was to be learnt from defeat. The following conclusions thus formed the basis of the LIC strategy eventually conceptualised and pursued by the Reagan Administration.

First, of the two strategies used in Vietnam, the pacification or 'hearts and minds' approach was relatively more successful in achieving set objectives than the strategy of 'attrition', or the conventional military approach. Attrition, though complemented by counterinsurgency techniques borrowed from earlier conflicts (such as strategic hamletting, zoning, and search-and-destroy operations) relied heavily on the concentrated application of firepower. While this strategy emphasised troop mobility, capturing territory and inflicting heavy casualties, LIC proponents argued that this actually worked against the war effort because it alienated the local population, as many of them became casualties of such actions.[10] Also, the more the US increased its firepower, paradoxically, the more local sympathies for the revolutionary forces grew, thus stiffening their resistance. This was partially summed up in the oft-quoted analogy at the time: 'You cannot crush a shadow with a steam roller.'[11] Similarly, they argued that the high profile of US personnel in the conflict fed the growth of local nationalist sentiment which in turn fed the strength of the insurgency. The more Washington escalated the conventional conflict, the more America was losing. Conventional military escalation in counterinsurgency or counter-revolutionary conflicts was counterproductive, and the role outside forces could play in Third World conflicts was inherently limited. In this sense, US military superiority was not sufficient nor perhaps even relevant for combating revolutionary nationalism.

Alternatively, the pacification approach avoided alienating local populations as it combined civic action and psychological operations with only selective repression. Its principal objective was to destroy the grassroots support base of the revolution by winning over the loyalty of the local people, a goal deemed more important than victory on the battlefield. Though short-term success was possible using overwhelming military power against a popularly supported guerrilla force, in the long term, victory could be achieved only with support of the local population and control over the government.[12]

This alternative approach was only sparingly used early in the Vietnam War by US Special Forces (SOFs). Associated with pacification were aid and development programmes and propaganda as well as other psychological operations such as infiltration and assassination operations and other means of selective terrorism. Possibly the most famous pacification operation was 'Operation Phoenix'. This covert assassination programme accumulated all known data and information on the Viet Cong in select provincial record centres, enabling the CIA-created Provincial Reconnaissance Units and their Special Forces advisers to more easily identify and target Viet Cong suspects for 'elimination'. According to former CIA Director William Colby, the programme was successful, resulting in the assassination of over 20,000 Viet Cong.[13] Success, as such, in the pacification approach was perceived differently to the way it is normally understood in conventional war. The latter meant military victory, the former meant victory not only militarily, but also economically, politically and psychologically.

Second, it was concluded that the language, culture and sensibilities of the people, their worldview and historic particularities had to be taken into account.[14] The counter-revolution needed to be fully immersed in the local human environment. Only in this way could locally acceptable and relevant alternatives to the revolution be validated. Moreover, a convincing government, free from corruption and able to offer a secure and appealing way of life, had to be created. In other words, a process of nation building had to be undertaken. This meant a far greater emphasis on gathering and analysing local intelligence.

Third, both US forces and their local allies had to believe in the objective for which they were fighting. Otherwise victory would be difficult to achieve. As Zindar noted, in Vietnam:

The North Viets and the VC had a cause. They believed and the South Viets never did! That was clearly the ultimate mistake. We always assumed what they wanted was what we wanted for them. When we left, the South Viets had something like the fifth largest army in the world ... But it didn't mean a damn thing if these guys didn't want to fight for it. That's really the big thing! ... The grunts have to believe.[15]

Implicit in these comments was the asymmetrical nature of the Vietnam War. While the United States and its South Vietnamese allies were fighting a 'limited war', their opponents were absorbed in a 'total' conflict. Therefore to engage effectively in low intensity warfare, America had to adopt a total war approach both in the target state and within the US itself.

Fourth, the major impediment to pacification in Vietnam was opposition from within the US military establishment itself. Many of its tactics broke with orthodox military doctrine, which emphasised large formations and high-technology concepts of war. Consequently, there was a distinct lack of cooperation and coordination between sectors of the US military, as there also had been between the military and US civilian authorities. Though effective and cheap, pacification was only given one-tenth of the total resources dedicated to the war.[16] LIC proponents thus argued that the US military had to develop new attitudes to innovation and reorganise its services to accommodate low intensity conflict. Opposition to pacification and other elements of unconventional warfare had to be broken down and a cohesive and united approach adopted by the military and the Administration. A unity of command had to be established, as Summers even acknowledged, to coordinate the efforts of the Department of State, the US Agency for International Development (USAID), the US Information Agency (USIA), the Department of Defense, the Department of Commerce and the CIA, as well as other agencies and their LIC activities.[17] To do this a supranational command short of the President needed to be established within the Administration to control operations on a day-to-day basis.

Finally, it was concluded that large-scale intervention in foreign military conflicts tended to generate US domestic opposition over time, which was a significant factor in America's defeat in Vietnam (which Summers argued could have been avoided had America declared war).[18] US Secretary of Defense Caspar Weinberger observed: 'In Korea, and then Vietnam, America went to war without a strong consensus or support for our basic purposes and, as it turned out, without the firm commitment to win ... never again should the imperative of public support be ignored.'[19] Full public support for the overt aspects of a long-haul, low-cost strategy such as LIC was therefore an essential requirement, even though domestic opposition would be lower as US casualties would be lower.

In the wake of Vietnam, US public support was unlikely to approve of American troops being involved in protracted wars in the Third World for vaguely defined objectives. The American public would support only quick operations such as the US invasion of Grenada. Caspar Weinberger observed: 'Before the United States commits combat forces abroad, the US government should have some reasonable assurance of the support of the American people and their elected representatives in the Congress ...'[20]

The US could not combat an insurgency through direct military intervention without popular support both in the target state and at home, unless the conflict was of limited duration. However, the nature of revolutionary warfare in the Third World tended to be protracted. New approaches were thus needed that reflected the understanding that either the US had to get in and out very quickly, or intervene in an entirely different fashion. It could not afford to engage its forces for any considerable length of time without clearly defined strategic goals and a guarantee that it would enjoy domestic support for continuing the conflict. This meant that the local 'democratic' forces had to take the major role in the struggle against revolutionary nationalism. US troops and government agencies could not be perceived as the major actors in the conflict.

LIC proponents thus concluded that conflicts waged by revolutionary nationalist forces were primarily political in nature as they were essentially promoting competing political systems. Support of the local people was thus the primary strategic target in these conflicts, a fact perhaps unwittingly acknowledged by Summers in his reported exchange with a North Vietnamese officer in Hanoi in 1975: 'You know you never defeated us on the battlefield', said the US colonel. The North Vietnamese colonel pondered this remark for a moment. 'That may be so,' he replied, 'but it is also irrelevant.'[21] Military power was ultimately irrelevant in these conflicts if the target population could not embrace the political system imposed upon it. This, it was noted, was borne out by the need of many Third World regimes combating popular revolutionary nationalism to seek external, and primarily US assistance. Therefore, counterinsurgency without popular local support was a formula for ever-deepening US involvement in a protracted war. Warfare waged by revolutionary nationalism needed to be combated by total warfare, hence the need to consider the revolutionary tactics of people's war, and a form of intervention that stressed a political–psychological approach.[22]

LIC proponents thus argued that US policy makers and the military needed to grasp the peculiar, predominantly political, nature of the Vietnam War and similar wars in the Third World, and not attempt to interpret them in conventional military terms. Also, the US needed to redesign the way local governments and local militaries might relate to their own populations, not just militarily, but in political, social, economic and psychological terms so that these local forces could play the key role in dealing with insurgent or revolutionary war. By embracing this approach, LIC proponents argued, insurgent movements or revolutionary governments could be forced to collapse through a 'flexible combination of economic sabotage, political attacks, psychological warfare and military pressure'.[23]

The Forums for Strategy Reappraisal

The reappraisal of US strategy during the Reagan period was spearheaded by think-tanks and service seminars devoted entirely to low intensity warfare, many of them funded by the Pentagon for the express purpose of developing strategy and tactics for low intensity warfare (LIW). Several Congressional committees also considered the most suitable approach to Third World conflicts. In January 1987, General Gorman acknowledged before the Senate Committee on Armed Services the difficulty of ascertaining the desired objectives for the US in LIW and the appropriate strategy over the long run to achieve them.[24]

As part of this strategy reappraisal process, an important LIC conference was conducted at Fort McNair on 14 January 1986. It was attended by Secretary of State George Shultz, Secretary of Defense Caspar Weinberger, White House Communications Director Patrick Buchanan, and other senior Administration officials, the military, the press, academics and others. The conference agenda included an analysis of the various components of low intensity warfare, notably the military options, civic action and the role of public opinion. Noting that low intensity warfare comprised a 'permanent' war being waged against the United States in the Third World, conference speakers reflected on LIC's growing coherence and theoretical conceptualisation within the Administration and the US military by arguing that it was a much needed strategy with which to respond.

By January 1985, the US military had acquired a considerable appreciation of the nature and threat of low intensity warfare through the various Pentagon-funded think-tanks and studies.[25] Admiral William Crowe, for example, noted that a purely military solution would not work in a low intensity environment in Central America. Instead a national strategy supported by more focused organisational arrangements was needed as well as a fully integrated security assistance programme. The military therefore acknowledged it needed to improve its capabilities to engage in such warfare.[26] This was especially indicated by the revival of interest in Special Operations Forces (SOFs) and unconventional warfare as it had developed during the Kennedy years.

The increasing acceptance of LIC, however, generated considerable debate within both the Administration and the military on the true nature and applicability of this emerging strategy. This debate was somewhat inconclusive for it involved studying *ad hoc*, piecemeal, if not fluid, measures already being implemented on the ground, particularly in Central America. Moreover, US agencies in the field were to some extent already refining and coordinating these measures into a more cohesive conflict profile, thereby filling the vacuum left by failed attempts at containing Third World revolutionary nationalism militarily.

THE DEBATE WITHIN THE REAGAN ADMINISTRATION AND THE MILITARY

Within the Reagan Administration, the debate over appropriate responses to revolutionary nationalism often took place between the Departments of State and Defense, with the former generally appearing to favour the LIC approach more than the latter.[27] This difference was evident in the diverging positions of Gaston Sigur, Assistant Secretary of State for East Asia and the Pacific, and Richard Armitage, Assistant Secretary for Defense with respect to the Philippines.[28] The CIA also appeared to favour the LIC approach. Its director, William Casey, became an active participant in this informal national security debate. He realised the importance of 'native' insurgents waging 'irregular, partisan guerrilla warfare' in successful revolutions in history and the necessity of supporting them.[29]

Indicative of their positions within this foreign policy debate, the State Department's Office of Public Diplomacy and the Office of the President lobbied for the integration of all elements of low intensity conflict, including security assistance, economic support, development aid and military pressure into a comprehensive programme for the pursuit of US interests, particularly in Central America (where this debate was primarily focused). Moreover, LIC proponents played down military solutions to conflicts in this region. In 1981, Secretary of State Alexander Haig (not an advocate of LIC), in opposition to those supporting the use of covert action in Central America, lobbied for a military blockade of Cuba to stop the flow of arms to El Salvador. Haig argued that covert action, which involved funding and directing the conflict, was a 'contradiction in terms' as secrecy was impossible. He believed the Nicaraguan problem was fed by Soviet and Cuban intervention and thus needed a broader response. He also argued that support for the Contras would only escalate the conflict and draw the United States into more complex problems in Latin America. Pastor noted that Haig felt strongly that the US ought to address Nicaragua's external behaviour rather than, as Haig noted, 'tell others what form of government they must have'. In this sense he correctly judged that the Contra strategy would tempt the Administration to slide toward the objective of overthrowing the Nicaraguan government, which Haig saw as 'unlikely and as a source of problems for the United States in Latin America'.[30] Haig in this instance was 'overruled'.

Opposition within the US military to the LIC approach was both doctrinal and organisational. It was doctrinal in that an emphasis on political/psychological actions compromised the orthodox US military belief that military issues should be kept separate from political questions. Philosophically, those who espoused this position strongly favoured relying on conventional military means and strength of firepower in Third World conflicts. As Sarkesian argued, this was because of the strong psychological and philosophical linkage between the US military and US society, and the American perception that the most immediate threat was from the Soviet Union. This fostered a 'Pearl Harbor' mentality within the US domestic mind and rendered the US military far more able to posture and prepare itself philosophically, morally and practically for a major war against the Soviets than to engage in low intensity warfare. Moreover, such a 'mindset' was less willing and able to grapple with the serious ethical and operational dilemmas inherent in LIW environments.[31] Accordingly, opposition to LIC was also organisational: at the end of the 1970s the US military capability was primarily conventional and high technology in nature.

During this controversy Senator Edward Kennedy, in an address to the Congressional Committee on the Armed Services, effectively summarised the LIC advocates' criticism of such opposition within the military. He also indicated Washington's increasing acceptance of the need to engage more in 'political warfare' in the Third World. The senator argued that guerrilla warfare was essentially an appendage of a 'far vaster political contest that no matter how well it was combated militarily ... cannot possibly make up for the absence of a political rationale'. Kennedy argued that Third World conflicts centred far more on political, social and economic concerns than military action. Thus in training its military, the United States needed to concentrate more on 'the importance of political infrastructures, civic action and psychological operations to meeting human needs and to accommodate radically different cultures and traditions'. Further reflecting the opposition to LIC within the services, Kennedy also argued that the military had not encouraged the most able personnel to pursue special operations, which 'have actually hampered the development of expertise in low intensity operations'.[32] This was supported by General Gorman in his address to the Senate Committee on the Armed Forces when he claimed that sectors of the military establishment were reluctant to come to grips with LIC. In 1986 a DOD report essentially came to the same conclusion. Moreover, the Senate Committee concluded that many high-ranking policy makers, including Shultz, Kissinger and Kirkpatrick, had come to believe that LIW was the type of conflict that the United States was the most likely as well as the most ill-prepared to deal with.[33]

Within the US military, many of those who actually advocated the pursuit and refinement of LIC came from Southern Command (SOUTHCOM) based in Panama. Referring to Central America, they argued that simply 'going in' or invading militarily was 'an event, not a strategy', that would only lead to a Vietnam-like quagmire. Instead, a more comprehensive strategy was needed to deal with the political nature of the war waged by revolutionary nationalist movements (such as the Farabundo Marti National Liberation Front (FMLN) in El Salvador). Moreover, they argued that US domestic support had to be mobilised behind attempts to assist the 'democratic' forces in these protracted conflicts, and that piecemeal foreign policy initiatives had to be abandoned and replaced by a coordinated and farsighted strategy. SOUTHCOM military planner Lt Colonel David Caldon advocated a 'security development' approach within which the Army's mission would be extended beyond its traditional role to include small unit training, civic action initiatives, psychological warfare and other 'non-traditional' operations to be implemented in 'conjunction with civilian agencies' responsible for development assistance.[34] Caldon also argued that the US could not separate the internal defence of target states from internal development, a position echoed by Gorman who argued that the US needed a 'broader range of instruments' in LIW rather than just relying on SOFs.[35] In terms of policy development, however, the ensuing debate focused not merely on the pattern of activity or conflict profile already emerging in Central America and the Philippines, but on the need for a more coherent and universal Third World strategy.[36] The United States had the option of either continuing its *ad hoc* approach and further moulding it into a primarily political/psychological strategy, or of relying more on military means including direct US intervention. Neither course of action was considered mutually exclusive. Direct military involvement by conventional means was still regarded as an option should the LIC approach fail. Indeed for some, LIC constituted a preliminary stage leading to direct intervention.

The recognition by many in 1987 that the United States was ill-prepared for LIW was both a further indication of the seriousness of this debate and of the military's growing acceptance of the perception that low intensity warfare posed a substantial threat to America's national security. Senator William Cohen of the Senate Committee on the Armed Services, for example, agreed with others (including General Wallace Nutting),[37] that the US needed to confront the challenges posed by terrorism and guerrilla insurgencies. He also argued, however, that the current US defence posture reflected an inability to understand 'the form and substance of this direct challenge to our interests'. This, Cohen suggested, was manifest in the Services' lack of 'unity of effort', a lack of training, organisation and materials, and a support system to combat 'political violence'.[38] In acknowledging that the United States lacked a coherent strategy to deal with LIW, Cohen was stressing the need for the development of such a strategy.

EVIDENCE OF LIC GAINING COHERENCE

By 1987, the operation of LIC in many areas of US influence in the Third World was one indication that within the Reagan Administration LIC had gained acceptance as a valid national security strategy. Another indication was the development over time of a greater US capacity to pursue this strategy, particularly with respect to America's ability to conduct covert action and, more specifically, unconventional warfare, intelligence operations and psyops in target states.

From the outset, the Reagan Administration sought to facilitate the operation of covert action in US foreign policy over and above the emphasis placed on these activities by President Carter in his last year in office. While Carter reinstated the importance of pursuing covert action against the Soviets and their allies after the invasion of Afghanistan, between 1980 and 1984 Reagan increased the use of covert action by 500 per cent and a command structure within the Administration was created for overseeing it.[39] In 1981, President Reagan created a restricted subcommittee known as the National Security Planning Group (NSPG) within the NSC to make decisions about the use of US covert action in Central America. The NSPG included the Vice-

President, the Secretaries of State and Defense, the Director of Central Intelligence (DCI), the NSC adviser and various important aides. The practice of regulating intelligence activities by executive order, namely Executive Order 12333 issued on 4 December 1981, was also continued. Describing covert action as 'special activities', the order specified that the NSC was the 'highest Executive Branch entity that provides review of, guidance for and direction to, "special activities"'.[40] Using National Security Decision Directives (NSDDs), President Reagan thus approved the use of covert action internationally by the Administration's various foreign policy agencies.

Reagan's increasing reliance on covert instruments of statecraft was also reflected in the rapid build-up of the relevant US military and intelligence organisations' capabilities. The training of the military and the development of its expertise in guerrilla warfare was stepped up significantly and reoriented to develop its capability to engage in LIW. The greatest emphasis in this reorientation was placed on the development of the Special Operations Forces, which played an extensive role in LIC in the form of Military/Mobile Training Teams (MTTs) used to train government or insurgent forces. By 1985 the use of MTTs had increased five-fold. In September 1984, MTTs were reported present in 17 countries including Grenada, Honduras, El Salvador, Costa Rica, Colombia, Lebanon, Saudi Arabia, Somalia, Tunisia, Morocco, Liberia, Zaire, the Philippines and Thailand.[41] In 1988, SOFs made up 25–35 per cent of all US MTTs abroad; they were training armies in Latin America, Africa, the Middle East, Asia and Europe.[42] As Caspar Weinberger noted in 1984, the high priority given to the revitalisation of the SOFs reflected the Administration's recognition that low intensity warfare, for which the SOFs were uniquely suited, was the most likely threat the US would encounter through to the end of the century.[43] Unlike the CIA's covert operations, details of SOF activities did not have to be reported to Congress, and were therefore particularly suitable for use in covert activities which might otherwise be restricted by Congressional oversight.

The build-up or 'revitalisation' of US Special Forces, deemed by the Reagan Administration to be one of its highest priorities, was considerably enhanced by Secretary Weinberger's Defense Guidance Directive instructing each of the armed services to develop a special operations capability. According to Weinberger in a 1984 report, SOFs 'meet threats at the lower end of the conflict spectrum – where the use of conventional forces may be premature, inappropriate or politically infeasible'.[44] After 1981, funding for the SOFs more than tripled, its staff numbers increased by 30 per cent and its weapons stockpile similarly increased.[45] Of particular note in this reorganisation was the establishment of the First Special Operations Command (SOCOM) at Fort Bragg, North Carolina in 1982 to enable the Army to develop the necessary leadership capability to respond effectively to warfare in 'less-developed' areas. The Command was to focus specifically on unconventional conflicts. The forces it included under its operations umbrella consisted of SOFs, Ranger Units, psychological warfare and civic action units, and special units from other services designated to cooperate in joint ventures.[46] In linking SOF operations with small-unit commando activities and limited conventional war capabilities under one organisational structure, this policy suggested a similar posture for special contingencies. The Army also later formed the 'General Officer Steering Committee' to provide direction over SOF expansion.[47] The multi-service Joint Special Operations Agency (JSOA), an interservice planning agency for Special Operations that reported directly to the Joint Chiefs of Staff, was established in 1983 (and activated on 1 January 1984).[48] A Special Operations Policy Advisory Group made up of retired officers was also established within the Department of Defense. Similarly, the US Air Force amalgamated all its SOFs into a newly created 23rd Air Force, which became its Special Operations Wing.

During the early 1980s the US military also emphasised the formation of 'Light Divisions', which were much smaller and more rapidly deployable than their conventional counterparts. Hailed by some as most effective in low intensity warfare, and a valuable means of generating greater Pentagon support for involvement in this type of conflict,[49] these formations, however, were incompatible with the nature of LIW. Nevertheless, the differences of opinion over the appropriateness of Light Divisions reflected the greater debate within the Administration and US military on how the US could best engage in low intensity warfare. Though this debate appeared by 1987 to have reached a consensus in lieu of a formal strategy of reinforcing *ad hoc* measures already conducted in practice, the expansion of the Light Divisions indicated the US was prepared for direct intervention in low intensity wars should this be needed as a last resort.

The intelligence capability of the Administration's military and civilian agencies, a fundamental component for waging LIC, had also been significantly expanded by the end of 1987. One of Reagan's key programmes upon coming to office was rebuilding and revitalising the national intelligence system, particularly the CIA which was much criticised and weakened under President Carter. In this task, Reagan enlisted the cooperation of Vice-President George Bush (a former CIA director), and CIA director and close friend William Casey, a veteran of Office of Strategic Services (OSS) clandestine operations. Former Captain John Zindar claimed:

LIC originated a lot from the Reagan Administration ... Reagan came to power and then found out that Carter had suspended all the instruction of military intelligence in Central America and Latin America in general ... Reagan was just appalled ... and a Presidential Directive came out of the White House ... saying ... 'We will organise and teach intelligence by the end of the year' and this was in 1982. By the end of 1982 we had already taught one full-year course in intelligence in Panama and had gone to a lot of other places and set up little schools in support ... such as El Salvador and Honduras.[50]

Hundreds of covert action experts lost to the CIA during the Carter years were thus rehired. The CIA's paramilitary capability also expanded as it developed its own unconventional army of soldiers and guerrilla warfare specialists. Zindar further claimed:

Under Reagan we were ordered to get guys down there [Central America] and teach them intelligence. But what kind? First it was US vs Soviet stuff and then we started pulling the Vietnam stuff off the shelves. That's how it started ... We saw what we initially were teaching was ludicrous and went back and learnt from Vietnam and the Brits who were the past masters of it.[51]

The intelligence operations on which the US agencies now concentrated were essential to waging Maoist-style people's war. Intelligence focused on creating low intensity warfare environments, not high intensity warfare as in the European theatre. More than fifty covert operations including para-military action and espionage were reportedly in progress by 1984 (representing the 500 per cent increase in operations in Carter's last year). Half of these operations were in Latin America.[52]

In addition, the Reagan Administration expanded the mechanisms for waging psyops within the US itself by creating a domestic propaganda arm in the form of executive branch organs such as the White House's Central America Policy Outreach Group and the State Department's Office of Public Diplomacy. These groups actively promoted aspects of Reagan's policies in Central America to win US public, Congressional and international support. Reagan also established the Kissinger Commission, chaired by the former CIA official and retiring Deputy Secretary of Defense Frank Carlucci, which also campaigned for bipartisan consensus for US actions in Central America.

Other indications of LIC's increasing coherence and acceptance included the Administration's efforts to coordinate and supervise agencies already implementing elements of the LIC approach. This was manifest in the creation of a command structure in 1987 responsible for administering LIC activities. For example the position of Assistant Secretary of Defense for Special Operations and Low Intensity Conflict (ASD[SO/LIC]) was established within the National Security Council to 'overwatch interagency actions on Low Intensity Conflict'.[53] Congress had legislated for both this position and the creation of a Board for Low Intensity Conflict within the NSC in late 1986, in spite of DOD reluctance due to the lingering 'conventional' opposition to LIC and SOFs within the US military. As noted by Assistant Secretary of Defense Richard Armitage, this new position would be 'responsible for overall supervision (including oversight of policy and resources) of Special Operations ... and Low Intensity Conflict ... activities within the Department of Defense'.[54] The US Congress also mandated the creation of a unified command, the Joint Special Operations Command (JSOC), and the assignment of all SOFs within the US to this command. It sought to eliminate 'organisational problems responsible for deficiencies in planning and preparing Special Operations Forces'.[55] Congress was concerned that the SOFs were fractured along service lines, impeding unified action, effective planning and integration of strategy, and also that they were receiving insufficient resources from a reluctant conventionally orientated military leadership.

The establishment of such a command structure accommodated the desires of LIC proponents both in and out of government. They were virtually unanimous in calling for the concentration of a LIC policy- and decision-making authority within the NSC, as well as for a reorganisation of existing bodies (and the creation of new ones) throughout the Administration into a hierarchy that would stretch from the NSC down. The 'Mandate for Leadership 11', the source from which it is claimed the second Reagan Administration gleaned its foreign policy direction, also recommended the creation of a special group for LIC within the NSC, asserting that 'changes in the role of the National Security Council should boost the chances of the Reagan [Doctrine] succeeding'.[56]

In 1985 the interagency body known as the '208 Committee' was created to coordinate the support of 'anti-communist insurgencies' in the Third World.[57] Reminiscent of the '40 Committee' which administered covert wars during the Johnson and Nixon Administrations, this committee was responsible for conceptualising operations, goals and timetables, and for the budgeting and paramilitary logistics of US covert operations. It was a key agency coordinating the private dimension of LIC. The Committee's decisions were ratified by the National Security Planning Group, included in which were the President and his key national security advisers.

Other bodies, some transitory, included various interagency groups formed for specific administrative functions, such as the Restricted Interagency Group (RIG). In its early years the Reagan Administration's Nicaragua operations were managed by a RIG headed by the Assistant Secretary of State for Inter-American Affairs, Thomas Enders; it was later taken over by Langhorne Motley. Other members included General Paul Gorman, Head of the US Southern Command, Deputy Secretary of Defense for Inter-American Affairs Nestor Sanchez, the then White House liaison to the National Security Council and paramilitary expert Marine Lt Colonel Oliver North, and the CIA's operations director for the covert war, Duane Clarridge, alias 'Dewey Maroni'.[58] Another group, the semi-governmental 'Special Warfare Advisory Group' (SWAG), drew up a 'Low Intensity Conflict' strategy blueprint and included such influential LIC proponents as former General John Singlaub, Edward Lansdale, Daniel Graham, Andy Messing, Ed Littwak and Fred Ikle.[59]

Among other indicators of the growing coherence of LIC strategy and its command infrastructure, particular mention must be made of the US Army's increasing attention to its role in low intensity warfare. The Army issued field manuals specifically addressing this type of conflict and published many research articles and studies which included, for example, 'Low Intensity Conflict Issues and Recommendations', Volume 2 of the *Joint Low Intensity Conflict Project Final Report*.[60] Moreover, General Galvin, Commander-in-Chief of US SOUTHCOM, in describing the strategy of his command in Latin

America to the Senate Committee on Armed Services on 23 February 1987 offered what amounted to a description of LIC conduct. He claimed that his 'tools' for carrying out overall US military strategy in the region included 'security assistance, forward deploying forces, training opportunities, intelligence sharing, humanitarian and civic action, peacetime psyops, combined training exercises', all of which were fundamental elements of LIC. Further, in claiming that his command was 'supporting counterinsurgency operations' in El Salvador and helping other Latin American countries with national development and collective security initiatives to combat 'terrorism' and insurgency, Galvin actually outlined the operation of counterrevolutionary LIC. He also highlighted one key aspect of revolutionary LIC which the US military used in 'psyops' actions directed against the Sandinista government. He stated that Sandinista 'aggression and intimidation' was deterred through the presence of American forces in 'comprehensive exercise' programmes (in other words demonstrations of military strength designed to intimidate the Sandinistas) (see Chapter 8).

Also relevant were a number of National Security Study Directives that elevated formerly piecemeal counterinsurgency tactics to the status of doctrine. These included the NSSD adopted as policy in January 1985 in response to developments in the Philippines (see Chapter 9). This directive was essentially a compromise between the State Department and the Pentagon. State Department pragmatists led by Michael Armacost sought a Lansdale-like approach that advocated a power-sharing agreement in the Philippines before easing Marcos out of power and establishing the 'democratic alternative'. In contrast, the Pentagon sought to retain Marcos in power. In this case, in supporting the former line of action, the directive virtually enshrined LIC strategy as policy.[61]

THE STRATEGY EMERGES

Sarkesian's criterion for measuring a strategy's coherence was how well it achieved stated national objectives by ideologically legitimate means that closely linked foreign policy with operational doctrine.[62] If one is to use this measure, LIC achieved considerable strategic coherence over time. By 1987, a conceptual operational doctrine was finally developed within the United States, one which could accommodate a foreign policy orientation that attached priority to the political objective of winning support for the 'democratic alternative' in the Third World. However the directives, initiatives, actions and service reorganisations described above (which largely corresponded to the structural requirements and policy changes advocated by LIC proponents) were relevant to an approach already operational and even effectively replacing military containment in several Third World states. While some infer that LIC was intentionally developed both conceptually and practically in 'laboratories' in Central America,[63] this is not the case at all. In reality, the theory of LIC largely developed separately from its practice. Only with the conjunction of the two did this approach assume the status of a coherent and ideologically legitimate strategy. The articulation of the Reagan Doctrine in fact provided the nexus between these two levels when the Administration was forced to justify those LIC actions pursued by its agencies in its 'secret war' against the Sandinistas, which by 1984 were being exposed to the world. In this sense, LIC's emergence was inevitable. It was the only means by which the Reagan Administration could justify illegal foreign policy activities already undertaken and legitimise those it sought to continue.

4 THE REAGAN DOCTRINE: SELLING LIC TO AMERICA

In this chapter I examine the development of the Reagan Doctrine and its relationship to LIC, revealing that the essential target of LIC was not just the support base of revolutionary forces the US opposed but the American public itself. Moreover, LIC as strategy was not an expression of the Reagan Doctrine. In fact the Reagan Doctrine itself was an expression of low intensity conflict in action. By providing formerly *ad hoc* LIC activities with operational coherence and ideological justification and therefore legitimacy, the Reagan Doctrine elevated LIC to the level of a national security strategy. In so doing, however, the Doctrine itself became part of the psyops dimension of this emerging strategy.

The Reagan Doctrine as outlined in a number of US foreign policy statements, had largely emerged by 1985. At that time, the political mood both within Congress and the US public was receptive to a doctrine which while ruling out direct foreign intervention still stressed an interventionist role for America in the Third World. The Reagan Administration had conceded that the causes of revolutionary nationalism were both internal (due to social and economic inequalities among other factors) and external. It also considered the Soviet Union or its proxies to be willing to exploit revolutionary nationalist movements or regimes with military and other support. This was no different from the Kennedy Administration's analysis and earlier US attempts to address similar revolutionary nationalist challenges (primarily in Latin America). However, under Kennedy the US response to such challenges in Latin America lacked ideological and operational coherence. Kennedy had developed 'The Alliance for Progress' to address economic and political problems while pursuing aggressive military measures to combat 'communism' in the region. This two-pronged uncoordinated approach eventually proved contradictory as it defended oppressive regimes and power structures that were often part of the problem because they fed revolution in the first place.[1] The Reagan Doctrine possessed no such ambiguity: it clearly provided a coherent ideological framework for an active interventionist policy to combat Third World revolutionary nationalism, usually portrayed as Marxist aggression.

The Reagan Doctrine provided ideological legitimacy for an approach that was in part a synthesis of earlier analyses of the causes of revolution. By promoting the 'third way', LIC promised to address both external and internal causes of Third World revolution and it therefore possessed the potential theoretically for universal application. Thus while there was not complete bipartisan support for the Reagan Doctrine, throughout 1985 the US domestic political climate grew steadily more supportive of it.

WHAT WAS THE REAGAN DOCTRINE?

Adequately defining the Reagan Doctrine is problematic because of the lack of clearly enunciated statements by President Reagan himself (nor did Reagan actually claim the Doctrine as his own). One of its most notable features was its vagueness, a factor which made Administration officials reluctant to define it as an actual doctrine.[2] This foreign policy 'thrust' eventually achieved doctrinal status because enough statements were made by Secretary of State George Shultz, other prominent Administration figures, and by the President himself in his 1985 and 1986 State of the Union addresses. Together these statements and utterances defined a distinct US foreign policy direction with relatively coherent goals and a strategy to achieve them.

Unlike other national security doctrines, the Reagan Doctrine therefore does not really have a specific 'birthdate'. It emerged more as a tendency or calculated emphasis in foreign policy direction, which assumed doctrinal status over time. As Charles Krauthammer argued, before 1985 the term 'Reagan Doctrine' was used indiscriminately, but after Reagan's State of the Union Address in that year the Doctrine meant specifically US support for 'anti-Communist revolution as the centrepiece of a revised and revived policy of containment',[3] thereby reasserting active interventionism as a major theme in US foreign policy. In this regard, February 1985 is the generally accepted date of the Doctrine's emergence.

While vague in some aspects, Reagan's foreign policy direction compared more than favourably with the foreign policy doctrines enunciated by either Nixon or Carter, both of which sought to 'contain' Soviet expansionism by directly supporting the counterinsurgency actions of regional powers or by threatening unilateral US intervention. The Reagan Doctrine, however, proposed a 'new' official approach – one that supported indigenous local insurgencies in their struggles against 'vulnerable' newly acquired Soviet client states. As such it was heralded as a direct challenge to the Brezhnev Doctrine which proclaimed that socialist revolution was irreversible.

The Reagan Doctrine has also been alternatively labelled the 'Shultz Doctrine' because of the US Secretary of State's major role in its articulation and later interpretations in a number of speeches. Of these, Shultz's address to the Commonwealth Club of San Francisco on 22 February 1985 is generally regarded as the most important and possibly the clearest enunciation of the Doctrine.[4] Shultz argued that Americans should accept the 'moral responsibility' for leadership of the 'free world' and for supporting 'people who have made their own decision to stand and fight rather than see their cultures and freedoms quietly erased'. The United States should support these struggles not 'only out of our historical sympathy for democracy and

freedom but also, in many cases, in the interests of national security',
because, Shultz argued, promoting insurgencies against non-communist
governments in important strategic areas had become an expensive way for
the Soviet Union to extend the reach of its power and to weaken its
adversaries, 'the pretext for subverting any non-communist country in the
name of so-called "socialist internationalism", while the Brezhnev Doctrine
holds that once you're in the so-called socialist camp, you're not allowed to
leave'.[5] Shultz therefore advocated first, that the overt revolutionary
dimension of US foreign policy had to be supported and material aid should
be supplied to those struggling against 'communist tyranny'; and second,
that 'pressures and sanctions' be imposed on communist states.[6]

Reagan himself actually did make some important statements that helped
shape the nature of the emerging Doctrine. By the beginning of his second
term, Reagan was already advocating that the US should support 'freedom
fighters' around the world who were struggling against Marxism, such as
the Mujahideen in Afghanistan and the Contras in Nicaragua. The clearest
articulation of this theme came in his State of the Union Address in 1985,
which he reiterated in the context of the same speech in February 1986: 'To
those imprisoned in regimes held captive, to those beaten for daring to fight
for freedom and democracy – for their right to worship, to speak, to live and
prosper in the family of free nations – we say to you tonight: you are not
alone Freedom Fighters.'[7]

Reagan, however, made it clear that the United States would support the
right of these forces fighting for 'freedom' in Afghanistan, Angola, Cambodia,
Nicaragua and elsewhere, *only* 'with moral and material assistance'.[8] By
explicitly avoiding making any pledges of direct US military commitment to
these conflicts, Reagan thus implicitly further defined the Doctrine as being
non-interventionist, at least in terms of direct military involvement.

In January 1988, President Reagan gave further content to the Doctrine
in the White House publication *National Security Strategy of the United States*,
in which he claimed that the US supported 'liberalisation' (hence support for
the 'third way'), and sometimes 'liberation' in regional conflicts, the latter
being in accord with the US policy of 'helping anti-Communist insurgents in
their battle to bring self-determination, independence, and human rights to
their own countries'.[9] In other words, the Reagan Doctrine could be
construed as 'sometimes' committing the US to supporting revolution
because it proclaimed support for 'democratic' insurgent movements.
However, the Doctrine could also be considered to commit the United States
to 'sometimes' assist counter-revolution in the Third World because to
support the liberalisation of states could mean supporting 'democratic' forces,
including governments, under challenge by 'undemocratic' forces –
including revolutionary nationalist movements.[10]

Intention and Goals

The Reagan Doctrine proclaimed the Administration's intention to supply
moral and material assistance, where 'opportunities exist', to 'democratic'

resistance forces resisting Marxist aggression sponsored and supported by the Soviet Union.[11] Implicitly this also meant opposing those anti-US revolutionary nationalist forces, thought to be Soviet backed, which were agitating for self-determination.

The Administration's tactical objectives as outlined by the Doctrine were to isolate the battlefield and then assist, where opportunities arose, the local democratic resistance forces achieve victory. The Reagan Administration also sought to demonstrate to communist and non-communist nations alike that communism was not the inevitable, irreversible future. President Reagan argued that: '... freedom fighters in Afghanistan, Ethiopia, Cambodia and Angola ... are fighting to undo the infamous Brezhnev Doctrine, which says that once a nation falls into the darkness of communist tyranny, it can never again see the light of freedom'.[12]

However, though the Administration was issuing a direct challenge to the Brezhnev Doctrine, implicit in the Reagan Doctrine was the message that Marxist revolutions and regimes could be defeated and overthrown without direct US military intervention, avoiding costly and protracted wars, as had been the case in Vietnam.

Strategically, the Doctrine proclaimed the Reagan administration's intention to protect the 'free world' from what it considered to be Soviet expansionism. The foremost proponents of the Reagan Doctrine, including Richard Pipes and David Horowitz, argued that the Soviet Union was pursuing a 'grand strategy' of outflanking the West by expanding into the Third World.[13] Hence, any US 'defensive action' should not be undertaken by static containment, which the Administration found morally untenable; instead, the US should first support the 'roll-back' of Soviet influence by 'democratic forces' at the 'empire's' periphery, and then support either the destruction of this influence at its centre, or alternatively the democratisation of the Soviet Union by force.

Aware of the obstacles to be overcome to achieve such goals, the Doctrine's supporters claimed that in reality the Administration initially sought less ambitious objectives: to reverse the gains Moscow made in the 1970s which had greatly extended the Soviet 'periphery', and to increase the cost to the Soviet Union of maintaining its influence in the Third World, thus ultimately straining the Soviet system itself. Like other decadent and oppressive empires, the Soviet Union, they argued, suffered from internal decay and was beset with many other problems including grave economic difficulties, the war in Afghanistan, unrest in Poland and the general unpopularity of the Soviet regime itself. It was therefore deemed appropriate that the United States should use all the leverage at its disposal to indirectly force the retraction and ultimate collapse of the Soviet system.[14]

The Reagan Doctrine's exponents justified the pursuit of a low intensity conflict (LIC) approach by arguing that the best way to sap Soviet strength at the periphery of its 'empire' was to engage it in costly struggles against local 'democratic forces' and thereby absorb it in a plethora of its own 'Vietnams'. Nicaragua was thus represented only as a minor but necessary target of a doctrine that prescribed global action. As Henry Kissinger, Chairman of the Bipartisan Commission on Central America, stated: 'If we cannot manage in Central America, it will be impossible to convince threatened nations in the Persian Gulf and in other places that we know how to manage the global equilibrium.'[15] Though ostensibly global in reach, in practice however the Doctrine was limited to a number of Third World states such as Nicaragua, the Philippines, Afghanistan and Angola wherein LIC was being developed. Nevertheless, to its supporters outside the Administration, the Doctrine heralded a newly assertive phase in US foreign policy in which the US, in serious competition with the Soviet Union for hegemony in the Third World, would confront and gain the upper hand over its adversaries in an area where Moscow had previously enjoyed a virtual monopoly.

The reality of the Doctrine's application, however, soon revealed that within the Reagan Administration there existed differing rationales for its emergence. It is important to distinguish between the rationale held by the Doctrine's neo-conservative supporters both within and without the Administration, and that of its actual 'architects', those 'realist' members in the National Security Council (NSC) primarily responsible for the Doctrine's articulation. As the reality of the Doctrine's application suggest, Reagan's foreign policy architects, while publicly articulating neo-conservative goals as well as ostensible reasons for the Doctrine's emergence, were actually pursuing other objectives.

The Reality of the Doctrine's Rationale

From the perspective of its neo-conservative supporters, the Reagan Doctrine emerged as an aggressive and timely response to the Soviet Union's intentions, strengths and weaknesses. The Doctrine's inspiration and rationale appeared to be derived from the worldview that advocated destroying the 'Soviet Empire'. This worldview assumed Moscow was vulnerable because its expansion into the Third World in the 1970s and 1980s left it seriously overextended and facing a spontaneous worldwide eruption of democratic resistance to that expansionism. These 'wars of national liberation' were similar to those the Western colonial powers had once confronted. Importantly, however, Moscow lacked the necessary economic and administrative skills and resources to deal with such challenges. The growth of such organised resistance was considered the result of a serious misreading of popular attitudes in the target countries.[16] The Soviet Union was considered to be under-prepared for the scale of this popular resistance and compelled to rely on permanent repression to stifle unrest. Theorists supporting the Doctrine argued that Marxism was incompatible with popular expectations and aspirations in contested countries and thus incompatible with freedom. As a consequence, Marxism had unleashed yearnings for liberation that had transformed into powerful forces opposing Soviet-imposed client regimes.[17] The 'empire's' overextension had thereby facilitated the growth of resistance within its periphery. The Soviet Union was also considered to be economically highly vulnerable. The Doctrine's supporters argued that Moscow's expansionist strategy had proven extremely costly and that its clients had to pay for the large military outlays necessary to combat the 'freedom fighters' opposing them. These economies were thus deprived of funds and resources, which in turn forced a reduction in basic public services and provoked greater dissatisfaction and unrest, thereby strengthening the resistance of the internal democratic forces. In addition, Soviet-sponsored development projects were considered incompetent and insufficient to offset such growing economic hardship in the periphery of its 'empire' and, consequently, the appeal of the democratic alternative.[18]

Such a neo-conservative analysis concluded that the 'empire's' weaknesses and vulnerabilities left the Soviet Union the option of either shouldering increasingly heavy economic burdens to assist its client states, or countenancing their economic and military collapse. While US actions in the Third World were unlikely to provoke violent confrontation with the Soviet Union, it was thought that by forcing Moscow to divert scarce resources for the defence of its overseas clients, thereby obliging it to overextend itself still further, these actions could play a considerable part in bringing about the eventual collapse of the Soviet regime. Ultimately, Moscow's difficulty in supporting its proxies was interpreted as a military vulnerability that could be exploited by 'democratic' resistance forces, which by virtue of their popular support would be able to function with little assistance. Local resistance forces offered the potential for creating a spontaneous revolt of democratic forces throughout the periphery of the empire and even within the Soviet Union itself. However, it was also argued that such spontaneity demanded that the resistance forces be supplied and assisted from outside the 'conflict arena', since such spontaneity 'typically entails penalties of weakness in the organisation, training, discipline and armaments of democratic resistance forces'.[19] Therefore these forces needed to be, and could be, supplied quickly before the Marxist states were able to consolidate their grip on power.[20]

From its supporters' point of view, the legitimacy of this interventionist Doctrine rested on the Administration's argument that it had a moral responsibility beyond defending America's own national security interests to champion and defend the cause of democracy and freedom and to support peoples everywhere resisting Marxist aggression. By implication, the Administration argued that it had an unlimited right to intervene in the Third World to further the interests of the 'global democratic revolution, self determination, and support for "freedom fighters"'.[21] A central tenet of the Doctrine was that Washington's support for anti-Soviet forces should not be perceived as mere attempts to gain strategic, economic and military advantages, but that these forces also championed moral principles such as the universality of human rights and freedom of human choice, values perceived by the Doctrine's supporters as integral to the American way of life. The Reagan Administration argued that it was morally justified to export democracy to the Third World and to pursue the destruction of Marxism,[22] not by providing merely moral support for 'democratic forces' but by military and other forms of aid. As Shultz noted, 'The forces of freedom cannot place their trust in declarations alone.'[23]

Supporters of the Doctrine believed that it also sanctioned foreign intervention on grounds of preserving peace. President Reagan, for example, warned Congress in March 1986 of 'the dangerous and destabilising international impact that even unpopular Leninist regimes can have'.[24] The Doctrine's supporters argued that since the domestic nature of Soviet client regimes posed a threat to world peace, they had to be pressured to reform, or failing that be overthrown. The proper task of the United States was to use all pressure and force at its disposal to bring about 'reform, self determination – hence freedom, and world peace'.[25]

Though presented as a response to a global outbreak of democratic resistance to Marxist oppression, the reality of the Reagan Doctrine's emergence, however, was quite different. Closer scrutiny indicates that the Doctrine was articulated in the first instance not to herald a global anticommunist crusade, but rather as a response to the public exposure of many LIC operations pursued by Reagan's foreign policy agencies in Nicaragua. As these operations were in fact 'illegal' because of Congressional opposition expressed through the Boland Amendments (as outlined in detail in Chapter 5), the Doctrine's emergence was more an attempt by its architects to justify and legitimate these actions and gain public support for their continuance.[26]

In this sense the Reagan Doctrine established precept after foreign policy practice, legitimising LIC activities waged by Washington's various agencies by promoting such activities to the level of national foreign policy, which it claimed served US national security and the defence of democracy and freedom in the Third World. In this manner, the Reagan Doctrine provided the nexus between theory and practice, and LIC assumed the status of a *de facto* strategy which the Administration could pursue to achieve interventionist foreign policy objectives.

The most telling evidence in support of this argument is the timing of the Doctrine's emergence. The statements forming the main thrust of the Doctrine were enunciated between 1984 and 1986. During this time, numerous operations of the CIA and other US agencies in Central America that directly contradicted the stated policy of the US government were exposed by freelance journalists and others working for media organisations such as the *Washington Post* and the *New York Times*. As Jeane Kirkpatrick claimed, these statements were designed to sanction 'covert activity' not 'normally defended by Administration spokespeople'.[27] Furthermore, almost all of these statements referred to the conflict in Nicaragua, or at least emerged in the context of support for so-called 'freedom fighters', the most popularised symbol of which were the Contras.[28]

Among other evidence is the fact that the Doctrine's architects were either proponents of LIC themselves or essentially linked to them. Many had been involved in the Vietnam War and the reappraisal and critique of America's defeat and had assumed positions of influence within the Reagan Administration and the New Right generally. As noted earlier, many also belonged to the Committee on the Present Danger, which virtually became President Reagan's first Administration. From such positions, these individuals directed the executive apparatus' pursuit of the LIC strategy and, it can be assumed, the articulation of the Reagan Doctrine.[29]

The Legitimisation of Low Intensity Conflict

The Reagan Doctrine legitimised the pursuit of LIC activities in the field because it publicly articulated the basic premises, parameters and 'overt' conflict profile of this approach, proclaiming that the US was pursuing a policy of assisting indigenous forces in the Third World to resist Marxist aggression. The Doctrine's neo-conservative supporters argued that conventional military containment was both an impossible and unacceptable option: impossible because Marxist aggression in all its dimensions (military, political and psychological) could not be held 'static' by conventional containment, and unacceptable because attempting to contain such aggression by conventional means was merely to 'react to Soviet behaviour' and thereby seek only a stalemate. Instead, real 'containment' of Marxist aggression was considered synonymous with its roll-back because in reality to contain it meant defeating it. However, such a military offensive was not an option because of the obvious risk of war with the Soviet Union. Therefore, the Reagan Doctrine's commitment to export democracy and support freedom fighters was termed neither 'containment' nor 'roll-back', but 'containment plus' or 'maximum feasible containment' because it advocated the more feasible option of combating and destroying Marxist aggression and influence using a combination of proxies and covert action.[30]

The Reagan Doctrine also implicitly outlined LIC's revolutionary and counter-revolutionary forms. With regard to revolutionary LIC, the Doctrine stressed the US would aid and support 'democratic freedom fighters' resisting (primarily by way of insurgency) the oppression of Marxist governments in the Third World. In his message to Congress on 14 March 1986 entitled 'Freedom, Regional Security and Global Peace', Reagan argued that there is:

> ... no historical basis for thinking that Leninist regimes are the only ones that can indefinitely ignore armed insurgencies and the disintegration of their own political base. The conditions that a growing insurgency can create – high military desertion rates, general strikes, economic shortages, infrastructural breakdowns, to name just a few – can in turn create political fissures even within a leadership that has had no change of heart.[31]

Reagan's statement was timed to influence Congressional votes on the Administration's request for $(US)100 million in aid for the Contras, which further suggests that the Doctrine's emergence was prompted more by a need to support US operations in Nicaragua aimed at overthrowing the

Sandinistas, than to outline the logic of an ideological position. In calling upon Congress to support revolutionary actions against Nicaragua and other leftist states, Reagan further defined the objectives of LIC indirectly by articulating an ambitious programme for repulsing Soviet advances achieved in the 1970s and for extending democratic revolution into states that had recently endured socialist revolutions. Further, by taking a leaf out of traditional communist revolutionary doctrine, the Administration, using LIC language, proclaimed that the US should support democratic revolution worldwide. Shultz argued, 'A revolution is sweeping the world today – a democratic revolution ... this hemispheric trend ... is something to be applauded and supported',[32] thereby legitimising US support for insurgent movements in Nicaragua (hence LIC operations in support of the Contras), Afghanistan and Angola. As regards LIC's counter-revolutionary form, familiar US aid and support was reiterated for friendly democratic governments combating Marxist-inspired insurgent movements supported by the Soviet Union.

LIC's selectivity in operation was also inherently justified and rationalised by the Reagan Doctrine's proclaimed targeting of the periphery of the Soviet empire in order to minimise the possibility of 'direct' superpower conflict. However, it was first necessary to demonstrate the existence of local 'democratic' forces which could provide the rationale, hence window of opportunity, for US assistance. This furnished the Administration with the public justification for a qualified application of the Reagan Doctrine and for the pursuit of LIC in states such as Nicaragua, but not, for example, in states like North Korea. The Administration could rationalise and justify the actions of LIC agencies already operating in target states without committing itself to combating Marxism everywhere in the Third World; hence the contention that the Doctrine was not so much a prescription for future action but a justification for past and present covert foreign policy.

The Doctrine Defines the Nature of Low Intensity Conflict

Also implicit in the Reagan Doctrine is its description of the predominantly political/psychological nature of LIC and its objective of creating 'total war'. By proclaiming Washington's intention to wage a total effort against the spread of Marxism in the Third World – to wage 'total war' against communism in economic, political, ideological, psychological and military terms – the Doctrine effectively revealed LIC's multidimensional character.

The notion of combating terrorism was as central to the Reagan Doctrine as it was to the psyops operations of low intensity conflict. Not only Soviet-sponsored communism, but Islamic revivalism and revolution, criminal acts and many other international activities were all labelled as terrorism by Administration spokespeople.[33] Secretary of State George Shultz argued that there existed a worldwide terrorist conspiracy pitted against the United States, which involved Iran, Nicaragua, Libya, Cuba and the Soviet Union. In this manner the Reagan Doctrine circumvented ideology and domestic arguments opposed to Cold War configurations manifest in the post-Vietnam Syndrome and invoked instead a universal rationale that championed the defence of democracy and freedom against the ravages of Soviet-inspired terrorism.[34] The labelling of revolutionary nationalist movements and states opposed to the United States as international terrorists linked to Moscow thus replicated LIC's dominant psyops message. By urging that terrorist groups threatening US national security be combated, the Reagan Doctrine not only reflected LIC psyops but sanctioned them in the process. Also, it further served the objective of personalising distant conflicts by tying the threat of 'terrorism' posed by nationalist revolutionary struggles to the current pre-occupations of US domestic politics. The American public could identify and fear irrational terrorism far more readily than abstract ideologies and foreign wars. The use of the 'terrorist' label thus provided an effective and persuasive rationale for US intervention.

Emotive images of terrorists transcended old crusades against communism, which previously rationalised US involvement in questionable and costly conflicts in the Third World. The Reagan Doctrine consequently allowed the Administration to challenge directly the Vietnam Syndrome. By attacking 'terrorism', the Doctrine established the legitimacy of a possible military intervention into, or an 'active military response' against, states perceived as supporting this form of activity. For example, Secretary of State Shultz argued that the Reagan Administration recognised that 'terrorism is being used by our adversaries as a modern tool of warfare' against US strategic interests around the world. 'Given the nature of the threat', therefore, Shultz claimed that the United States was fully justified in using military power to overcome it.[35]

The Reagan Doctrine also reflected the use of religion as a psyops tool in LIC, proclaiming that American support for freedom fighters and democratic governments in the Third World was necessary to defend the 'unalienable rights of all God's children', including their 'right to worship'.[36] Implicit in the Doctrine was the argument that the US was involved in a worldwide conflict to protect Christianity, which was everywhere threatened by godless communism, often considered synonymous with international terrorism. This use of religion distinguished the Reagan Doctrine quite sharply from its predecessors, which were primarily concerned with military and political threats to US interests. The Reagan Administration considered that a politicised popular church, such as that embracing liberation theology in Latin America, posed a considerable threat to American values. This was indicated in the Committee of Santa Fe document (considered to be influential in guiding the Republican Administration's policy) which stated that US policy in Latin America must counter liberation theology: 'The role of the church in Latin America is vital to the concept of political freedom [founded in] private property and productive capitalism.' Liberation theology was therefore to be combated because it was considered 'less Christian than Communist'.[37]

Civilianising Conflicts by Covert Action

The Reagan Doctrine similarly legitimised the LIC emphasis on civilianising conflicts by publicly stating US support for freedom fighters as a matter of national doctrine. Unlike previous foreign policy doctrines, the Reagan Doctrine openly proclaimed the intention to 'export democratic revolution'. By claiming US support for 'freedom fighters', either in the form of 'democratic' insurgent forces such as the Contras in Nicaragua, or alternatively 'democratic' forces combating insurgencies (hence vigilante groups such as those in the Philippines), the Doctrine sanctioned the LIC objective of supporting and even creating paramilitary groups in target countries as a relatively inexpensive and less dangerous means of achieving US goals. In supporting this civilianising process the Reagan Doctrine thus diverged quite sharply from the theme of Kennedy's 'flexible response' which in placing a primary emphasis on the use of US Special Forces still emphasised a military approach by US personnel. It also went further than the Nixon Doctrine because it sought to mobilise target populations not just militarily but politically, rather than relying on bolstering local armies of 'regional surrogates'. The Reagan Doctrine also differed from Carter's reliance on Rapid Deployment Forces to 'extinguish' trouble in the Third World where US interests were threatened, because it explicitly avoided committing US combat troops for foreign intervention.

By supporting the civilianising of conflicts the Reagan Doctrine gave LIC further operational coherence and political legitimacy. First, it reinforced the notion that Washington sought to wage total war by incorporating civilians into its revolutionary and counter-revolutionary projects to defend democracy. Second, it provided an ideological explanation for the military, political and other activities of the many private organisations and individuals that were already directly or indirectly serving as LIC agencies. In so doing the Reagan Doctrine legitimised many of these agencies' illegal covert operations in Central America by locating them within the context of pursuing the laudable US foreign policy objective of supporting democratic revolution in the Third World. However, these operations were pursued both covertly and illegally because the Reagan Administration in its determination to crush Marxism in Central America sought to circumvent Congressional opposition to its attempts to overthrow the Sandinista government. Third, by proclaiming support for local 'democratic' forces and avoiding, at least explicitly, directly committing US combat troops into these conflicts, the Reagan Doctrine rationalised LIC's low-risk approach which promised a 'high political pay off'.[38] In so doing, it legitimised the objective of roll-back by less high-intensity means than conventional warfare; means which included exploiting opportunities for political initiatives and covert action which were central to LIC. Low intensity conflict was thus given coherence by a Doctrine that first outlined the primarily political nature of the strategy and its many dimensions, and then articulated the foreign policy objective of supporting 'democratic revolution' (essentially involving local civilian groups and para-military forces) that this strategy was 'designed' to achieve.

The Reagan Doctrine also further established LIC's legitimacy by arguing the strategy's ideological acceptability. It was presented not as a strategy for military intervention but rather a strategy that assisted the 'worldwide revolution' of democracy championed by indigenous 'freedom fighters' who were equatable with America's own 'founding fathers'. In this manner the Reagan Administration was able to answer its domestic opponents and take the moral high ground in justifying its activities in Central America.

THE REAGAN DOCTRINE AS AN EXPRESSION OF LOW INTENSITY CONFLICT

From the perspective of its neo-conservative supporters outside the Administration, the Doctrine offered first a blueprint for combating communism and Soviet influence in the Third World and also a means of reasserting US power and influence. Second, it implied that ultimately the US had a right to intervene unilaterally in other countries as an act of 'self-defence' and to maintain and promote democracy, liberty and freedom. The Doctrine also signalled that America had shaken off the paralysing Vietnam Syndrome proclaiming that the United States sought to reverse its failures in the Third World in the post-Vietnam era (by assisting local forces) in for example, Angola, Nicaragua and Afghanistan, and to restore democracy and freedom globally. US action taken against the Sandinistas therefore appeared for public consumption as only one facet of a strategy for global action. According to neo-conservative analysis, the Reagan Doctrine offered a turn-around from the succession of defeats and humiliations the US had suffered ever since the Bay of Pigs debacle in Cuba in the early 1960s.[39]

To its neo-conservative supporters, the Reagan Doctrine also appeared to be 'revolutionary' in nature, not because it was new but because it was concerned with waging indigenous 'democratic revolution' against nationalist and socialist revolutions, both those in their infancy and those already successful in forcing regime change in the Third World. However, as noted, the reality of the Reagan Doctrine's professed applications did not fit the neo-conservative analysis of its supporters. This incongruity between theory and practice revealed a degree of tension within the Administration itself (between neo-internationalists or moralists, and realists). More specifically, it revealed tension between those of its supporters who, motivated by their moral and ideological opposition to communism, were advocating that the Doctrine should be applied universally, and those of its architects who favoured a selective or pragmatic approach determined more by questions of national security. The selectivity of the Doctrine's professed targets indicated that its architects were more interested in confronting revolutionary nationalist forces (perceived threatening to US interests) rather than proxies of the Soviet Union (though both were portrayed as synonymous by neo-conservatives) throughout the Third World.[40] This led to severe criticism of the Reagan Administration by many of the Doctrine's staunchest supporters,[41] sparking a debate within the wider political culture between neo-conservatives and what Charles Krauthammer argued was a growing wave of realists. This mirrored the growing theoretical debate within the Administration concerning when and how the Reagan Doctrine should be implemented.[42] It also ignored the practical reality that the Doctrine was more a justification after the event, rather than a blueprint for future action.

Further reflecting the practical reality which the Doctrine evolved to serve, much of this debate was concerned with the question of supplying aid to the right-wing forces in Angola which Shultz (ironically it appeared) opposed, arguing that such backing would jeopardise possible negotiations that would see the Cubans withdraw from Angola, and which might also produce 'a stalemate at higher levels of violence'.[43] The criticism that Reagan's foreign policy lacked consistency evolved to such an extent that some suggested the departure of the Doctrine's most ardent supporters from the Administration, including such figures as William Clarke, William Casey, Jeane Kirkpatrick and Constantine Menges, had actually weakened the Administration's resolve to fully implement the Doctrine appropriately.[44] However, this argument appeared ignorant of the reality of the Doctrine's evolution, which in actuality did indicate a degree of consistency in the Administration's accounting for the primarily covert foreign policy it was conducting in Central America in defiance of Congress.

Ultimately, the Reagan Doctrine appeared to have been applied only in the Philippines, Afghanistan, Nicaragua, El Salvador and to a limited extent in Kampuchea and Angola. In response, the Doctrine's erstwhile supporters argued that insufficient action was undertaken not only in these countries but also in the other countries that had already 'succumbed' to Marxist rule in the 1970s. These countries included Vietnam, Ethiopia, Mozambique and South Yemen; all of which, except for Vietnam and South Yemen, were claimed to have active anti-communist insurgent movements challenging Soviet-backed governments. These movements, the neo-conservatives argued, needed outside aid and assistance to ultimately triumph and thereby render the popular vision of the invincibility of Third World communist revolutionary movements to be a myth.[45] However, the selectivity of the Doctrine's focus remained consistent with those target states within which LIC operations were already being waged. This further suggests that the Reagan Doctrine, rather than stating a new foreign policy direction, was instead a justification for LIC activities already occurring and, in the case of Nicaragua, actually illegal.

In sum, the Reagan Doctrine did not herald or guide the implementation of a new US national security strategy, but instead sought to justify the emergence of low intensity conflict to the American public, or at least the features of it that had been rendered overt. The Reagan Doctrine, therefore, was itself an expression of the psyops dimension of this all-embracing strategy. With particular regard to Nicaragua, by promoting the righteousness of supporting local democratic forces, the Doctrine sought to sanction LIC operations already in progress and to create domestic support for LIC's objectives, which included direct intervention should the need finally arise.

LIC emerged as a national security strategy because the Doctrine only sought to sanction the initiatives of the Administration's 'official' agencies and not the 'privatised' activities that evolved independently but were nevertheless an interrelated expression of the strategy. In this sense, the Doctrine did not provide the strategy with greater administrative effectiveness or geographical reach, but it did provide the nexus between theory and practice and facilitated greater resources being committed to the waging of LIC, as the lifting of the Clarke Amendment indicated. The private dimension of low intensity conflict thus remained covert. For the Doctrine to expose or bring unwarranted attention to the many illegal activities being conducted in this dimension and infer that the Administration supported or assisted, or was at least associated, with these private operations would only jeopardise the continued pursuit of LIC, as the exposure of the Iran-Contra operation and the related scandals and consequent public outrage threatened to do in 1987.[46] Therefore, the Reagan Doctrine never completely outlined LIC's full conflict profile. Only if we examine the operations of this multidimensional strategy in practice in the 1980s can the emergence and nature of this strategy, as well as its implications for US foreign policy in later years, be thus fully understood.

In later chapters I examine the forms and success of the domestic psyops aspect of the Reagan Doctrine. What is important to highlight at this point however is precisely the Doctrine's domestic focus as compared to earlier National Security doctrines. While all previous doctrines served as a guide and rationale for US foreign policy action and sought to generate US public support, the Reagan Doctrine was aimed primarily at legitimising actions (some illegal) already undertaken. It was also used as a psyops tool for combating the Vietnam Syndrome. In this respect the US public were as much a target of LIC as the revolutionary movements and governments Reagan sought to destroy. And as a result, for America itself, truth, responsible democratic government and a moral US foreign policy were perhaps the greatest casualties.

5 CENTRAL AMERICA: THE STRATEGY'S PROVING GROUND?

In the early 1980s, the Reagan Administration sought to combat revolutionary nationalism in Central America with a range of *ad hoc* measures according to opportunity, circumstance and necessity. These measures represented the operation of low intensity conflict in practice, and particularly in Central America largely formed the basis for the germination of this strategy in LIC literature and policy-making circles. In this region, the preconditions existed in El Salvador for the emergence of the full conflict profile of LIC's counter-revolutionary form.[1] They also existed for the revolutionary form of LIC in Nicaragua where Reagan was determined to overthrow the Sandinista government, which had come to power in 1979 via a popular revolution.

In this chapter I overview these preconditions or more precisely the determinants of what became the operational profile of this strategy in Central America, and particularly LIC's revolutionary strand in Nicaragua. In so doing, I demonstrate that Central America was perhaps less the 'laboratory' or proving ground of LIC and more a troubled region spawning many unrelated counter-revolutionary and revolutionary measures waged by the US and the governments and paramilitary groups it supported. In other words, LIC emerged in practice in an *ad hoc* form in Central America prior to, and quite separately from, its theoretical formulation in US academic and military circles and its rationalisation and legitimisation via the Reagan Doctrine.

The importance of demonstrating that LIC emerged in an *ad hoc* form in Central America is that it indicates Reagan lacked a coherent foreign policy strategy to combat revolutionary nationalism in the first instance. While intent on reversing Marxist influence and perceived Soviet gains in the Third World, the Administration was in fact unwilling to bear the cost of the full range of measures necessary to do so, which in Nicaragua's case included direct military intervention. As a result, the Reagan Administration was left groping for some in-between response and thereby pursued a mixture of overt and covert activities including sponsoring the Contra insurgency to remove the Sandinistas from power.

CENTRAL AMERICA AS THE FOCUS OF US FOREIGN POLICY

Buoyed by the groundswell of patriotic sentiment during and in the wake of the Iranian hostage crisis, the Reagan Administration believed it possessed a mandate for an assertive foreign policy and so it came to power intent on combating revolutionary nationalism within the US's sphere of influence. Early in Reagan's first term, the Administration indicated that it would renew America's former emphasis on playing the global 'policeman' and using aid and direct military intervention if necessary to assist 'friendly nations' combating revolutionary nationalism (largely assumed to be Soviet-sponsored). Intent on rearming but constrained by Carter's budget for Fiscal Year 1982, Washington ordered the US military to prepare itself to protect American interests in the Third World as far as US resources would 'permit'. As already outlined, it also invigorated, expanded and improved the military's capacity for pursuing covert action and intelligence operations in the Third World. However, while America's conventional military build-up was undertaken to outstrip the Soviet Union's military capability, it was also perceived as an essential way of controlling Third World revolutions that threatened US interests.

Situated on the US southern border and within its most immediate sphere of influence (as defined by the Monroe Doctrine), the new Administration perceived Central America to be 'infested' by Cuban-backed (and thus Soviet-sponsored) insurgent movements, and dominated by the Marxist Nicaraguan 'Government of National Reconstruction'.[2] Fearing the creation of more 'Cubas', Reagan thus paid close attention to the region, focusing first on El Salvador and then on Nicaragua.

This of course was not an entirely new foreign policy orientation. In his last year in office, President Carter had also adopted a militarist approach to the region, particularly these two countries. During this time the Pentagon, CIA and State Department initiated and upgraded covert operations,[3] and in January 1981 President Carter ordered a total of $5 million in military aid and US advisers to be sent to El Salvador.[4] As early as 1979, after the invasion of Afghanistan, Carter also considered direct military intervention into Nicaragua as a means of staging a US show of force for the Soviet Union's benefit.

Reagan thus initially appeared to be continuing, and in fact strengthening, Carter's late emphasis on an interventionist foreign policy in the region. In its first week in office, the new Administration virtually equated both Marxist governments and movements alike with terrorist organisations and declared that 'international terrorism' waged by these Soviet and Cuban proxies would be met with 'swift and effective retribution'.[5] However, in surprising contrast to the militarist rhetoric, Reagan's response to the consolidation of the Sandinista regime in Nicaragua actually proved less directly interventionist than might have been expected. This was due in large part to the strong US domestic opposition continuing to constrain any notions of direct military intervention. Though the Reagan Administration was also restricted by the relative financial constraints of the early 1980s and international opinion, the lingering Vietnam Syndrome still remained the major stumbling block for achieving its goal of ridding Central America of 'communism'.

THE DETERMINANTS OF LIC

Similar to the Carter Administration, the United States under Reagan sought to 'draw the line' against communism in both Central America and the Caribbean and to send a clear message indicating this resolve to Moscow. The Reagan Administration's broad approach to combating what it perceived to be Marxist-inspired revolutionary nationalism in Central America initially consisted of three elements. First, it sought to defeat (or at least manage) the insurgency in El Salvador; second, to develop short-term US interventionist forces for Grenada-type operations; and third, to isolate the Sandinista government in Nicaragua, both politically and militarily, and then remove it from power by means that accommodated the constraints that existed on such interventionist actions.[6]

Reagan's election victory inspired a flurry of activity in Central America and particularly in El Salvador. In that country the Farabundo Marti National Liberation Front (FMLN) stepped up its revolutionary activities which included launching a final offensive in January 1981. The United States responded by claiming the Sandinistas were clandestinely shipping arms to the FMLN.[7] And, in a move that was reminiscent of the increasing involvement of the United States in Vietnam, it increased its aid to the Salvadoran government and dispatched more advisers to assist the government's counterinsurgency campaign.[8]

The increased activity of the FMLN early in 1981 prompted several senior members of the new Reagan Administration, including Secretary of State Alexander Haig and UN Ambassador Jeane Kirkpatrick, to advocate firmer measures to combat revolutionary nationalism in the region. These included military force to crush 'communism' in Nicaragua and a strengthened blockade of Cuba, which was considered the major supplier of arms to Marxist forces in Central America.[9] However, apart from Haig and his supporters, the predominant view within the Administration was that the direct introduction of US forces into Central America and elsewhere in the Third World was premature. Secretary of Defense Weinberger and the Joint Chiefs of Staff, for example, are known to have opposed the dispatch of US Marine Forces to Lebanon in 1982–84 and continued to oppose direct US military intervention in Central America. Nevertheless, Haig and his supporters were successful in lobbying for at least the consideration of direct intervention in the region, in particular in El Salvador, and the Administration refused to rule out this possibility.[10] However, domestic consensus in the United States for such intervention still had to be secured, though there was hope nevertheless that, in the absence of such consensus, Reagan's foreign policy objectives might be achieved alternatively through covert operations and third parties. Thus while the Reagan Administration did not publicly rule out direct intervention, and notwithstanding its later 'clinical' strike against Grenada, it did not pursue such action above the level of dispatching advisers. Moreover, though Washington increased its economic and military aid assistance to El Salvador above the levels of the previous administration, in Central America it moved initially with considerable caution.[11]

The Discrediting of the Umbilical Theory

Though divided over how to actually intervene, the Reagan Administration was nevertheless united on the urgency of ridding Central America of perceived communist influence (in practical terms opposing the FMLN in El Salvador and the Sandinistas in Nicaragua).

One view within the Administration initially accepted the assumptions of the 'umbilical theory' of Third World revolution, which argued that 'Marxist' revolutions were directly supported by the communist powers. According to this theory, in order to defeat revolutionary movements in Central America the flow of aid and support from Cuba, and through Cuba the Soviet Union, had to be severed.[12] In El Salvador's case, the FMLN could be cut off and isolated by a combination of covert action, diplomacy and support for the counterinsurgency actions of the pro-US regime.

With many adherents in the Pentagon, the umbilical theory was a unifying factor behind the Administration's initial Central American strategy, providing the public rationale for attempts in 1981 to cut off the alleged flow of arms and other aid from Nicaragua to the insurgent movement in El Salvador. In pursuing this 'limited objective', it also provided an initial public justification for the Administration's support of the Contras. However, when the aid flow to the FMLN had been cut and the movement still fought on, the Reagan Administration found that it had to formulate other forms of intervention that could achieve its objectives and yet still accommodate America's domestic opposition.[13]

The Vietnam Syndrome and Public Opinion

Even after Reagan's election, the Vietnam Syndrome (or the 'Nicaragua Syndrome' as it came to be known in the Central American context) remained a major obstacle to achieving US goals in the region. Prospects of direct intervention were ruled out in the first instance and the Administration's pursuit of covert action as an alternative for achieving the same foreign policy objectives were hampered.

Though a militant public backlash helped sweep Reagan into power, his foreign policy still faced significant opposition from the American people, the international peace movement and from within the European community. As well as opposing Washington's build-up of conventional military forces and nuclear arms, in 1981 a large portion of the American public remained opposed to any notion of direct US military intervention in the Third World.[14] Opposition existed to such an extent that any prospect of direct military intervention into Central America potentially provided the spark for the formation of a massive anti-war movement right across the United States involving people from all sectors of American society, in particular, many church organisations and Hispanic and black communities.

It was soon apparent to the Reagan Administration that the American people were not sufficiently committed to its objectives in Central America, even though the public still generally favoured support for the junta in El Salvador and the Contras, at least with economic and non-lethal aid. This aggravated the difficulty of explaining or justifying US involvement in the region, particularly any projected escalation.[15] Washington under Reagan had committed itself to reversing communist gains in Central America, but found it extremely difficult to argue cogently that either alone or together the Sandinistas or the leftist guerrillas in El Salvador constituted a serious military threat to US interests in the region, let alone to the United States itself.

In the face of such significant opposition to its foreign policy, which was also reflected within Congress, the Reagan Administration realised the necessity of toning down its rhetoric and proceeding more cautiously. It linked its military aid packages with political reforms and began to publicise – and expect more attention to be paid to – human rights from the forces it supported in the region. From within the Administration, nevertheless, Haig and his supporters continued to work diligently to achieve public support for a direct military interventionist policy. In contrast to the publicity that internal disputes over the 'means' of foreign policy attracted, the Reagan Administration thus remained very much united on policy direction. Meanwhile covert intervention by the US was continued in both Nicaragua and El Salvador as primary policy.[16] However, by the end of 1981, paradoxically, Reagan's covert operations had become virtually a 'public secret' due to their constant exposure by American investigative journalists and others.[17] Nevertheless, public acceptance of direct intervention was still promoted should such covert activities fail to achieve their objectives.

To counter the Vietnam Syndrome and thereby eliminate a significant foreign policy constraint, the Reagan Administration entered into an enduring domestic propaganda campaign to portray the struggle against the FMLN's offensive as a strategic and decisive battle for Central America. This was done to legitimise US covert activities and support for allied forces in the region.[18] As a result, a two-track foreign policy emerged in which the United States pursued both political and land reform, as well as covert action.[19] Aid to the Salvadoran regime, including training of Salvadoran troops in the United States, was also stepped up. Though Congress acquiesced in support of such an indirect escalation of US involvement, as did public opinion, it remained opposed to direct intervention, an option that was gaining increasing attention within the Administration itself.

By the end of 1981, however, a deadly combination of the Salvadoran Army, military aid and US advisers managed to contain the FMLN insurgency. Other factors also contributed to this achievement, including a heavy reliance on psychological operations by the counter-revolutionary forces, America's support of land reform, the promotion of President Duarte as the 'middle way', and the death squads of the Salvadoran 'right'.[20] As a result both the necessity and likelihood of direct intervention into El Salvador diminished and Reagan's attention shifted to Nicaragua. With the exception of Grenada, in the 1980s Nicaragua thus became the primary focus of US foreign policy in the region and potentially a major target for direct military intervention.

Was Grenada a Practice Run for Nicaragua?

America's military intervention into Grenada in 1983 appears, at least superficially, to contradict the argument that Reagan was severely constrained from pursuing direct military intervention in Central America or elsewhere. Admittedly, the Grenada episode provides clear evidence of Washington's willingness to use large-scale direct military intervention to achieve its objectives should prevailing circumstances permit. However, the invasion of Grenada was not a rehearsal for the direct invasion of Nicaragua, as expected and indeed feared by many at the time.[21] Instead it pointed precisely to America's inability to pursue this course of action in Nicaragua. Grenada was a small island with a small population, easily isolated, invaded and overwhelmed. In contrast to Nicaragua, Grenada was well suited to direct intervention by US forces. Moreover, it provided an easily attainable *fait accompli* to present to the Administration's foreign policy opponents.

Since entering office, Reagan had indicated that he would not rule out military force if it were needed to protect US interests and Grenada certainly did not present as another possible 'Vietnam' with all its commensurate military and political costs, as either El Salvador or Nicaragua did.[22] There also was a significant opportunity for US military intervention to crush Marxism in Grenada in October 1983. Internal feuding had split the ruling 'New Jewel Movement' apart, and the murder of Prime Minister Maurice Bishop and his supporters within the leadership provided an opening for just such a US 'liberation'. With the leadership embroiled in internal conflict and Reagan able to argue that US citizens within Grenada were threatened, it was thus relatively easy to justify and rationalise military intervention to protect US 'interests'.

Nicaragua, however, could not be another Grenada. Although certainly not as big as Vietnam in terms of size and population, it was still far bigger than Grenada with over 400 times the territory and over 20 times the population. With respect to these factors alone it would be much more difficult to invade. Moreover, Nicaragua at that time had a battle-hardened army of over 30,000 soldiers and a people's militia considered to be as many as 200,000.[23] Direct military intervention in Nicaragua, as Washington recognised, therefore would have produced very different results. Victory would not have been achieved quickly: the invading force would have had to combat not only the experienced Sandinista regular forces, but also engage a guerrilla army built on a support structure and broad popular base carefully developed during the anti-Somoza revolution. In terms of material and human costs, an invasion of Nicaragua was clearly prohibitive. According to one estimate, such an invasion would have cost at least $16 billion.[24] According to Lt Colonel John Buchanan, a total of at least 125,000 US troops would have been necessary to defeat the Sandinistas.[25]

It is reasonable to assume nevertheless that the United States might have achieved initial military success in Nicaragua, but then what? Here again the situation was far from comparable with Grenada, either in terms of achieving an end to the military conflict or ensuring the consolidation of a pro-US 'democratic' government. As widely recognised, Grenada and Nicaragua had experienced fundamentally different revolutions. In Grenada the Marxist regime of Maurice Bishop had attempted to impose revolution from the top downwards. Rather than achieve success through an insurgency that required a deep commitment from the population to defend its hard-won gains, as was the case in Nicaragua, Bishop came to power through a palace coup in 1979 (ousting the government of Sir Eric Gairy). While Bishop was personally popular, he lacked an organised and armed power base among the population and thus Bishop was himself similarly deposed like Gairy (though Bishop was later executed) by a hard-left faction of Grenada's military on 13 October 1983. The new regime led by General Hudson Austin, however, was particularly brutal in its suppression of civilian demonstrations and imposition of martial law. When US forces invaded Grenada on 25 October, they therefore encountered very little resistance from a divided and unpopular military junta and a largely indifferent and unarmed civilian population. In Nicaragua on the other hand, US forces would have encountered a committed opposition (hardened by the anti-Somoza revolution) among both the armed forces and the general public. For example, Eden Pastora, the leader of the Contra group known as the Democratic Revolutionary Alliance (ARDE),[26] claimed that a US invasion would only provoke 'a national war, a patriotic war',[27] and would have almost certainly ensnared the United States in a protracted conflict against indigenous guerrilla forces waging people's war (as the US would also have confronted in El Salvador), confronting Washington with the prospect of incurring heavy casualties over time for questionable goals.[28] Moreover, to achieve political stability in Nicaragua a sustained application of US power would have been required, which the US public was not likely to have supported.

As for a US military victory in Nicaragua by proxy, as early as 1983 the Pentagon and the CIA acknowledged that the Contras had no chance of defeating the Sandinistas. Even if they could, an estimated 80 per cent of the population would still support the Sandinistas.[29] To pursue a Contra victory as its major strategy, the Reagan Administration thus risked facing the consequence of a humiliating defeat. This therefore meant involving US forces in the first instance if Washington wished to avoid such a foreign policy disaster. The desired alternative, therefore, was for the Contras to maintain constant military pressure on the Sandinista government while the United States applied political, psychological and economic pressures simultaneously to force its collapse.

Its limitations aside, in the Caribbean the Grenada operation proved relatively successful. It considerably assisted the Administration's pursuit of interventionist activities elsewhere as it played a valuable role in eroding the Vietnam Syndrome. As a successful foreign adventure, the Grenada operation actually attracted considerable domestic support, albeit much after the event, when it was presented as a major step in Reagan's plan for rolling back communism in Central America.

An Alternative Strategy for Nicaragua

The Grenada success could not be repeated in Central America. Particularly in Nicaragua, the pursuit of US objectives demanded an alternative strategy that combined diplomatic, political, economic and covert military activities. Direct US military intervention in Nicaragua required committed and sustained US domestic support. The Reagan Administration not only lacked that support but also faced formidable opposition both at home and internationally to an interventionist policy.

A series of US opinion polls indicated the strength of public sentiment against direct military intervention in Nicaragua.[30] A *New York Times*/CBS News Poll, for example, published on 15 April 1986, showed public opposition running at virtually two to one against aiding the Nicaraguan Contras. When asked directly, 62 per cent said they feared the US would get involved in Nicaragua the same way it did in Vietnam.[31] Other polls conveyed the same weight of opinion.[32] Such opposition was even more intense earlier in 1983 through to January 1984 wherein public support for overthrowing the Sandinistas was generally only in the low 20 per cent range.[33] By the mid-1980s over 20,000 national organisations and 1,000 local groups had formed in the United States to pursue 'anti-interventionist public education in Central America'; in the process these groups became somewhat of an embryonic anti-war movement.[34] The considerable strength of this domestic opposition was also reflected in the periodic reluctance of the US Congress to grant even covert aid and support to the Contras.[35]

Such was the intensity of this domestic opposition that the Reagan Administration was obliged to legitimise its policy towards Managua as much as possible. In so doing Washington argued that Nicaragua, as a proxy for Soviet expansionism within the US sphere of influence, threatened vital US military and strategic interests, trade routes and access to markets and resources. In particular, it argued that Nicaragua threatened US control over the Panama Canal, which was essential to US security. In his presidential campaign Reagan had strongly opposed President Carter's Panama Canal treaties (signed on 7 September 1977) arguing that they (the treaties) were a 'surrender of vital interests, [and] they were a dangerous invitation to the enemies of the United States'.[36] Subsequently, Reagan broadly defined his

objectives in Central America as rolling back communism and, more specifically from a military and strategic viewpoint, keeping Nicaragua free of
Soviet and Cuban influence. This, it was argued, would prevent Nicaragua
from being used by these two countries as a military, naval or intelligence
base from which other Marxist insurgencies could be initiated in the
region.[37] Secretary of State Shultz argued that the United States had to
oppose the Sandinistas 'not simply because they are Communist', but
because 'they are Communists who serve the interests of the Soviet Union
and its Cuban client, and who threaten peace in this hemisphere'.[38] The
Administration claimed that the future of democracy in the region was at
stake, as was US prestige if Washington was subsequently perceived as
unable to control regions within its sphere of influence.[39]

The implications of this US perception were not lost on the Sandinista
government. Nicaraguan Foreign Minister Miguel D'Escoto noted that 'in
the US there is an underlying fear ... that we will become a base for the Soviets
that will threaten the national security of the US'. He argued that the
Sandinistas attempted to 'oppose the propaganda of those who oppose us in
the United States with peace proposals ... We have bent over backwards to
demonstrate we insist on the right of the Nicaraguan people to determine
their own destiny without foreign intervention.'[40] Regardless of Sandinista
attempts to allay US fears, however, the strategic importance of Nicaragua
within Central America ensured that any noncompliant or recalcitrant
Nicaraguan government, be it communist or not, would be considered a
security threat to the United States. The Reagan Administration perceived
Nicaragua's military build-up in the early 1980s as particularly menacing
and it eventually acknowledged publicly that it aimed to overthrow the
Sandinista government and was increasing its covert action and military
support for what it termed the 'Nicaraguan freedom fighters'.[41]

Military action against the Sandinista government began with the Contras
destroying two bridges in northern Nicaragua on 14 March 1982; for the
next three years the United States, aside from diplomatic and economic
activities, pursued covert action and assisted the Contras as its primary
strategy for overthrowing the Sandinistas. During this time, with the
continuing failure of the Contras to achieve their objective, a US military
invasion did at times appear imminent however.[42] Certainly with the failure
of the umbilical strategy, it appeared a desirable option to many neo-conservatives. But for those reasons already cited, direct intervention was out
of the question. Moreover, the persistence of US domestic and international
opposition hindered not only the dispatching of military advisers and
increased military aid to El Salvador, but also even the Administration's
policy of supporting the Contras.

Interventionist Debate

The considerable opposition at home to Reagan's foreign policy was
highlighted in the prolonged debate between 1982 and 1985 over the whole

issue of intervention in Nicaragua. Reaching right into Congress, the controversy reflected the conflicting ideological positions evident in the US after the Sandinistas were victorious in 1979.[43] Opponents of US intervention viewed most revolutionary nationalist movements in the Third World as not necessarily threatening US strategic interests. Instead, they advocated a policy of coexistence and cooperation, and welcomed the easing from power of such former Third World client dictators as Anastasio Somoza Debayle. Though interventionism had emerged as the Reagan Administration's preferred strategy, its desirability in the eyes of both Congress and the public at large thus continued to be the subject of intense debate and indecision. While no clear motive for supporting counter-revolutionaries was articulated in the debate, the neo-conservatives argued that in the case of Nicaragua assistance to the Contras added leverage to the diplomatic pressure Washington could exert on the revolutionary government in Managua to negotiate for a settlement of US–Nicaraguan differences on US terms.

The Reagan Administration's failure to articulate clearly its objectives and its strategy for achieving them in Nicaragua, or even provide a convincing rationale for such actions, served ultimately to increase public opposition to its policy of opposing the Sandinistas. At times, its regional objectives appeared confused and contradictory, an impression confirmed by the comments of former Assistant for National Security Affairs to President Carter, Zbigniew Brzezinski, in January 1987. Brzezinski claimed that his:

... willingness to support the Contra effort, which I do support, is conditioned on the notion that it ought to have a defined political objective. In my view, right now, that objective is unclear, undefined, and perhaps not clearly limited. Are we trying to overthrow the Sandinista regime? Are there no circumstances under which we would be prepared to accept it? Can we live with it under any set of arrangements? Those are the areas of ambiguity in our current policy in my judgement.[44]

Such confusion as there was over US objectives stemmed in the first instance from the Administration's initial claims that it sought to use the Contras only to interdict arms supplies to the FMLN in El Salvador, when in contrast the Contras themselves had claimed from the outset that they sought to overthrow the Sandinistas.[45] Moreover, the sabotage activities pursued by US agencies in Nicaragua indicated not only Washington's complicity in this objective, but also that its arms interdiction exercise was intended merely to deflect actual and potential domestic opposition to US policy.[46] Reagan's objective of overthrowing the Nicaraguan government was not easily justifiable to the American public. There was little if any evidence to prove that the Sandinista government constituted a military threat (particularly in view of its military strength and capabilities) to the United States and its interests in the region, or that Nicaragua even harboured anti-US designs.

Indicating the Administration's somewhat contradictory pursuit of a 'two-track policy' *vis-à-vis* Nicaragua virtually from the outset, the strength of this domestic opposition ultimately forced Washington to tone down its hard-line position and soften its image. It argued that Carter had also taken a 'militarist' approach to Central America. Publicly, Reagan also appeared to promote the hope of a political solution to conflict in the region. Meanwhile, the Reagan Administration continued covert operations aimed at destroying the Sandinistas, even though these operations were continually being exposed, leading to further public confusion over Reagan's objectives. It was not until 21 February 1985 that Reagan, perhaps in response to these revelations, publicly admitted his Administration's objective was the removal of the Sandinista government, adding that his aim was to force the Sandinistas to cry 'uncle'.[47]

During the course of this debate, the Administration was determined to maintain the Contra forces and to pursue the objective of removing the Sandinistas from power. However in so doing Reagan was thus faced with a dilemma. To avoid public opposition to intervention in Nicaragua, Washington was forced to covertly support an insurgent movement that, paradoxically, just to survive needed a significant amount of backing from the US public.

By 1983, the constant media revelations of covert activities waged by US agencies in Nicaragua had provoked enormous opposition both within the United States and internationally, in particular, in response to the CIA mining of Nicaraguan harbours, bombing an airfield and issuing a covert operations manual that included within it instructions as to how best to carry out assassinations.[48] By 1984, regardless of periodic outbursts of optimism from those advocating direct intervention in Central America, the American public remained clearly, if not increasingly, opposed. Even the most stalwart neo-conservatives such as Jeane Kirkpatrick soon recognised this fact and the political sensitivity of this issue. In March 1984, Kirkpatrick vetoed a plan by SOUTHCOM Commander General Paul Gorman in which he proposed that CIA-operated, AC-130 surveillance planes be used to strafe guerrilla strongholds in El Salvador.[49]

The Boland Amendments and the US Private Dimension

The most hostile manifestation of congressional opposition to the Reagan Administration's Central American policy came in the form of the Boland Amendments of 1983 and 1984. These prohibited US support for the Contras, thereby severely constraining the pursuit of the Administration's objectives in Nicaragua. The 1983 Boland Amendment directed that US military aid to the Contras be stopped. However, reflecting the growing outrage at continued US actions in Nicaragua, the October 1984 re-enactment of the amendment went further: it directed that all aid to the Contras be terminated including CIA assistance in any form. This effectively made all assistance to the Contras illegal and deprived Reagan of the 'legal' means to wage covert war against the Sandinistas.[50]

As a result, the private dimension of Reagan's foreign policy in Central America expanded rapidly and the National Security Council assumed primary responsibility for directing the conflict. Within the NSC, Admiral John Poindexter, Lt Colonel Oliver North, Robert McFarlane and William Casey collectively managed the project. Oliver North was the primary director of activities and virtually the President's representative in the complex machinations of the vast operation.[51] The operation was overseen by the '208 Committee' which included representatives of the CIA, the NSC and the Departments of Defense and State. Its decisions were ratified by the National Security Planning Group (NSPG), which included President Reagan and his key national security advisers.[52]

As part of this project, NSC agents solicited funds and other assistance through the Iran-Contra dealings to maintain the Contra insurgency. President Reagan himself also directed part of this operation in his private capacity. It is known that Reagan personally lobbied the private sector for funds for the Contras, and through the NSPG he was reportedly involved in all facets of the operation's planning and coordination. In April 1984, President Reagan and National Security Adviser Robert McFarlane decided to encourage and coordinate all private aid to the Contras and secured John Singlaub as chief fund-raiser.[53]

The NSC also assumed primary responsibility for the coordination, liaison, cooperation and direction of the activities of such diverse local and international organisations as the World Anti-Communist League (WACL), which became involved in organising aid and assistance. The Reagan Administration and its supporters worked relentlessly to transform public opinion to enable the CIA to once again 'legally' pursue its covert war against the Sandinistas. The Reagan Doctrine, in stressing America's moral obligation to support 'freedom fighters' everywhere, was central to this enduring domestic propaganda campaign. Also, Reagan implicitly portrayed US covert action in Central America as a form of self-defence sanctioned by international law whereby the US had a right to intervene in any nation in the region if the 'common interest' was threatened.[54]

Neo-conservative lobbyists, public relations specialists, private aid donors and media interests also participated in this campaign to sponsor the growth of interventionist sentiments within the US political culture.[55] Symptomatic of this was the promotion of cult heroes such as 'Rambo', and the media-manufactured belief in US 'invincibility'.[56] These organisations and interests worked in conjunction with the National Endowment for Democracy (NED), the NSC, the CIA and two special propaganda offices: the White House Office of Public Liaison and the State Department Office of Public Diplomacy. By mid-1985 this intensive collective effort appeared to be paying dividends as Congressional and public support finally appeared to be turning around and growing for the US-backed Contra war. While this apparent shift in mood can be partly attributed to the intense propaganda campaign the Administration waged, it must also be considered a result of public frustration and anger following the spate of 'terrorist' attacks on US military personnel and civilians in 1985. These included the hijacking of a TWA plane in Athens, the killing of US soldiers in El Salvador,[57] and the exposure of spy rings in the United States. Further, Nicaraguan President Daniel Ortega's visit to Moscow only days after the House of Representatives voted in April 1985 to continue to withhold aid from the Contras, deeply angered Congress. Ortega's visit actually undermined a chief argument of the Administration's opponents – that US aid to the Contras had driven the Sandinistas to a closer alignment with the Soviet Union. The Sandinista leader's trip to Moscow instead suggested that Managua's ties to the Soviets were due to its own ambitions and were not driven by US actions. Further, Ortega's visit indicated that he seemed almost contemptuous of America.[58] As a consequence, by mid-1985 there finally appeared growing support for Reagan as many Americans became hostile and anxious about the rise of perceived communism in Central America with many desiring a display of US strength in the region.[59]

In Congress, many Democrats also began to find the neo-conservative line convincing. They feared that if US public opinion was destabilised it could trigger further Marxist revolutions in Central America and a chaotic flood of refugees into the United States. Democrat Stephen Solarz was one example of the many Congressional figures who began to support an interventionist policy. For example, he advocated $5 million in aid be supplied to the non-communist resistance in Cambodia.[60] The Reagan Administration also persuaded others to support aid to the Contras by shrewdly manipulating the Vietnam Syndrome. Ironically it argued that US troops might again need to intervene in Nicaragua should the Contras fail. In so doing the Administration was thus able to erode anti-interventionist sentiment both within Congress and the US public at large by turning this sentiment against itself. It has also been claimed that Congress was partly intimidated into supporting Reagan by fears of being accused of being 'soft on communism'.[61] The Administration, for its part, appeared intent on exploiting these fears. White House Communications Director Patrick Buchanan, for example, argued in March 1986: 'With the vote on the Contra, the Democratic party will reveal whether it stands with Ronald Reagan and the resistance – or Daniel Ortega and the Communists.'[62] President Reagan stated on national television on 16 March 1986: 'Clearly the Soviet Union and the Warsaw Pact have grasped the great stakes involved, the strategic importance of Nicaragua. The Soviets have made their decision – to support the Communists ... Now Congress must decide where it stands.'[63]

While majority consensus for intervention was still to be achieved, as early as July 1985 US public and Congressional opinion had moved sufficiently in that direction for the House to support the re-establishment of humanitarian aid, and then later military aid to the Contras. On 10 July, Congress lifted the Clarke Amendment banning aid to the Angolan insurgents and flagged the notion that the US President should again have the flexibility to authorise both covert and overt foreign military intervention, wherever deemed necessary, to repel either direct or indirect communist expansion sponsored by the Soviet Union.

Significant bipartisan support for aiding anti-Marxist insurgencies thus emerged by mid-1985; many subsequently interpreted this development as signalling the rejection of the Vietnam Syndrome. Particularly symptomatic of this new mood was the Congressional decision granting Reagan's request for a $100 million increase in military and other aid for the Contras in February 1986, which allowed for the delivery of weapons to the Contras in October 1986. Such a changing public attitude also made it possible for the emerging Reagan Doctrine to assume a central role in US foreign policy declaring interventionist (though indirect) intentions, not only in Central America but elsewhere in the Third World as well.[64]

THE DETERMINANTS/PRECONDITIONS FOR LIC

By February 1986, Reagan had achieved significant domestic support for waging a form of unconventional warfare against the Sandinistas which I have identified as LIC. By June 1986, Washington was confident enough to ignore the World Court which ruled that continuing US actions in Central America were illegal.[65] However, in Nicaragua the LIC conflict profile had already been developing since 1981 and been 'shaped' by a number of important determinants.

One very obvious factor that determined LIC's emergence was the high level of domestic opposition to US intervention, as previously discussed. In accordance with the LIC school's argument within the US military and elsewhere, such opposition meant that covert activities emphasising a civil-ianisation of the conflict needed to be pursued. The other major determinant driving LIC's development was the existence of a 'window of opportunity' in Nicaragua through which the US could promote local opposition to the Sandinista government.

This window of opportunity was provided by the many stark social and political cleavages existing within Nicaraguan society that could be exploited to assist both the formation of legal opposition groups and to nurture the Contra-armed insurgency.[66] There still existed within Nicaragua the core of the business and landowning classes which formerly constituted Somoza's support base and which generally opposed the Sandinistas. The former elites of Nicaraguan society, who had once opposed Somoza, were also potential allies of the insurgency, if not ready sponsors of anti-Sandinista armed resistance waged by ex-Somoza national guardsmen. Many of these businesspeople as well as, and including, large property owners had been alienated by the leftward tendencies of the Sandinista government and its reforms that directly threatened their interests.

Included within the range of disputes that alienated these people was right-wing opposition to the formation of many pro-Sandinista grassroots workers' and small landowners' organisations and associations that the regime wanted to give a political voice.[67] There was also opposition to the Sandinista mass literacy campaign which its opponents charged was nothing less than 'communist brainwashing'.

These right-wing opponents were represented politically by groups and organisations that included the opposition press (for example, Violeta de Chamorro's *La Prensa* newspaper), and business organisations such as the Nicaraguan Business Association (COSEP) which formed a powerful rallying point for anti-Sandinista opposition.[68] With the fall of Somoza, the Sandinistas and COSEP effectively formed a truce. However, soon afterwards, the pro-US COSEP walked out of the Nicaraguan Council of State, established in May 1980, after disputes over many issues including the minor representation of COSEP within the Council relative to the Sandinistas. Reagan's election in America also heightened political polarisation in the country with the right openly rejoicing in Reagan's victory.[69]

Political cleavages also existed within the Catholic Church in Nicaragua which the Reagan Administration could exploit. These stemmed from various disputes including the controversy over the role the Church should take in a revolutionary situation. However, the major cleavage within the Church existed between the conservative Catholic senior hierarchy, predominantly the Bishops, and the more progressive 'grassroots' lower clergy who tended to embrace liberation theology or the 'popular church' which the bishops regarded as being Marxist-influenced.[70] The Catholic bishops of Nicaragua also harboured resentment and significantly opposed the Catholic priests 'who had long standing connections' with the Sandinistas. Ignoring conservative Church opposition three priests, Miguel D'Escoto and Fernando and Ernesto Cardenal, had actually accepted senior positions in the Government of National Reconstruction. Other priests also provoked opposition from within the Church hierarchy by accepting posts in government and Sandinista organisations such as the Sandinista Defence Committees (CDS) and Rural Workers' Associations (ATC).[71] The traditional Church opposed the Marxism of the Sandinistas and the 'atheism' it believed the regime propagated, in particular, the Sandinista-controlled education system and the endeavours it perceived the Sandinistas were undertaking to 'divide the church' and restrict its influence in Nicaragua.[72] For the popular Church's part, it tended to regard the traditional Church, as did the Sandinistas, as allied with the Nicaraguan upper class, thereby indicating a class-based underpinning to these ideological cleavages.

The powerful conservative hierarchy of the Church, headed by Archbishop Obando y Bravo, thus became a prominent centre of opposition to the Sandinista government.[73] Alone, this institution represented a powerful force for organising grassroots opposition to the regime, particularly among the predominantly Catholic *campesinos* (peasants) who were easily mobilised by arguments that the Sandinistas embodied a threat to Christianity. The Church subsequently waged many campaigns to generate opposition to the FSLN including transferring pro-Sandinista religious leaders out of the country; creating pro-Church groups to spread its influence such as the Centro de Estudios Religiosos (Centre for Religious Studies, CER) and the Comision de Promocion Social Arquidiocesana (Commission of Archdiocesan Social Promotion, COPROSA) which were responsible for organising projects to broaden the Church's social base among the poorer sectors of the population; creating Catholic school-based parent organisations and other groups, and allying itself with opposing political parties. Among other activities, the Church undertook an internal propaganda campaign against the revolutionary government, the FSLN and pro-government mass organisations, waging this campaign through pastoral letters, sermons, pamphlets, radio programmes and the press (particularly *La Prensa*). It also regularly condemned laymen, religious leaders and organisations sympathetic to the Sandinistas.[74] To finance these activities the Church used funding it readily received from the Agency for International Development (USAID) and the Institute for Religion and Democracy (IRD).[75]

Another significant and certainly major social cleavage that was exploited to great effect existed between the 'Spanish' (speaking) Nicaraguans on the Pacific Coast, and the 'Mesquito' (Miskito) Indians and 'Creoles' on the Atlantic coast of Nicaragua, the latter having experienced a predominantly British and North American, as opposed to Spanish, influenced history. The Atlantic Coast population differed not only racially and religiously, but also culturally (and linguistically) from those on the Pacific Coast.[76] Moreover, the Sandinistas had antagonised and alienated the Mesquito Indians (amongst whom the Moravian Church enjoyed great influence) on the Atlantic Coast with ill-informed and poorly timed reform programmes (also opposed by the Church).[77] Much antagonism also stemmed from the Sandinistas forced relocation of the Mesquitos away from their traditional lands. The Sandinistas sought to prevent the Contras from recruiting these minority ethnic groups as well as appropriating Mesquito territory and provoking a mass uprising against Managua.[78] The ensuing unrest fed a long smouldering insurgency waged by groups of both Mesquitos and Creoles who resisted Sandinista control. The Mesquito rebels charged that the Sandinista government threatened traditional Mesquito Indian customs, way of life, values and rights, and would ultimately force their assimilation into an oppressive alien culture that would convert them into 'peasants and mestizos'.[79]

The existence of these multiple cleavages thus ultimately provided the United States with a low intensity environment it could exploit to produce an insurgency and thereby remove the Sandinista government from power and replace it with a compliant pro-US government.

There was, however, yet another factor at work which should be mentioned at this stage as a determinant of LIC's emergence. The US pursuit of covert as opposed to overt activities lessened the risk of a more serious Soviet retaliation beyond mere expressions of outrage vented diplomatically. With

Nicaragua well within the US sphere of influence, there was little likelihood of the kind of Soviet response that had occurred earlier in Korea, Vietnam or even Cuba. Any restrictions placed on US actions by the Soviet Union were likely to be minimal and play a far smaller role in tempering US intervention than the more 'local' factors I have already cited, provided of course that the US avoided a high-profile, large-scale direct military intervention.

THE EMERGENCE OF LOW INTENSITY CONFLICT

Low intensity conflict as it emerged in Nicaragua was the product of two factors: the Reagan Administration's need to devise a strategy which took account of domestic opposition to direct intervention, and the window of opportunity furnished by the political and social cleavages that existed in Nicaragua in the 1980s.

'A Proving Ground'?

When reading LIC literature, the argument that Central America was the proving ground or laboratory for the development of low intensity conflict is commonly encountered, a position which at first appears very compelling given that LIC's profile model is based on literature largely concerned with this region. Most analyses of the emergence of LIC draw on the lessons learnt from the US defeat in Vietnam and then focus on Nicaragua and El Salvador. According to these analyses once the preconditions for the operation of LIC were identified in the region the strategy was then appropriately applied to test its effectiveness. Further, once its successes were gauged it was then applied in appropriate environments elsewhere, for example in the Philippines. However this interpretation, which ignores the internal debates over appropriate US responses, places the 'chicken before the egg'. Certainly, the factors making for low intensity conflict were present in these cases. However, the Reagan Administration's response followed no preconceived blueprint or strategic formula. This mirrored LIC's continuing lack of acceptance within US policy-making circles. LIC, far from being tested in Central America, was more a formulation devised by individuals within the foreign policy-making elite to give coherence to a series of unrelated measures in the field, which were already being applied by official and private US agencies as a matter of necessity in the absence of an official strategy for combating revolutionary nationalism. The combined successes of these measures over time, however, ultimately demonstrated that Washington finally had within its grasp an effective strategy to combat revolutionary nationalist movements struggling for, or already exercising, power. In other words, LIC 'grew' out of the Central American experience with a clarification of US goals rather than being externally applied.

By the end of 1987, Reagan's approach to overthrowing the Sandinistas had assumed a predominantly political/psychological character. Indeed, only from this perspective does this approach appear congruent with an identifiable conflict profile. The exacerbation if not fabrication of an indigenous revolution against the Sandinista government relied heavily on 'initiated' and 'self-initiating' psyops. Sponsored and directed by the Reagan Administration, the key objective of these diverse operations was the destruction of the Sandinistas' support base by creating a negative public perception of the Sandinista government not only within Nicaragua, but also in the US and the international community. The principal message conveyed by the American campaign was that the Nicaraguan 'democratic opposition', with US support, was pursuing the goal of 'nation building' which required the overthrow of the totalitarian Sandinista regime. The Contra struggle was thus presented to the American public as morally equivalent to that of the US 'founding fathers', and therefore unquestionably 'just'. Meanwhile, the various players making up the 'unarmed' opposition were portrayed as popular forces struggling to achieve the democratic third way in Nicaragua, the alternative to both the authoritarian extreme right of Somoza and the totalitarian extreme left of the Soviet and Cuban-sponsored Sandinistas. Subsequently, Washington justified exporting 'democratic revolution' to Nicaragua by invoking the ideological and moral spirit of the Reagan Doctrine and by arguing that it was necessary to ensure the survival and eventual triumph of liberty and democracy in the region. It appeared of little consequence to the Reagan Administration, however, that many of its operations in Nicaragua were secret and illegal in terms of the US Constitution, the US Neutrality Act and the Boland Amendments.

In this chapter I have established that certain determinants existed in Nicaragua which provoked the emergence, development and operation of elements of low intensity conflict. What now needs to be undertaken is an analysis of these LIC activities in operation and how they coalesced, rather than being forged and tested together, to form the strategy's revolutionary strand and the clearest and most distinct example of the conflict profile of LIC in action during the Reagan years.

6 NICARAGUA AND REVOLUTIONARY LIC

By the end of 1987, the US response to the consolidation of the Sandinista government constituted the definitive example of the operation of low intensity conflict in its revolutionary form. It is on this multifaceted response that I based the strategy's conceptual conflict profile outlined earlier. In this chapter I flesh out the major features of LIC's revolutionary strand as it developed in practice in Nicaragua. Apart from facilitating a full appreciation of LIC's operation in its revolutionary form, this overview helps in identifying LIC's 'footprint', even in its counter-revolutionary form, elsewhere in the 1980s (and for my purposes the Philippines) and where it has operated since.

By establishing LIC's full operational parameters and the timing of its emergence in Nicaragua, it is also possible to gauge the extent to which LIC influenced, or conversely was influenced by, the conduct of counter-insurgency and unconventional warfare activities elsewhere in the Third World. As such, for these analytical reasons the conflict scenario in the Nicaraguan case is best measured using the same dimensions outlined in my conceptual model.

THE POLITICAL/PSYCHOLOGICAL DIMENSION

International 'Psyops'

Within the international political/psychological, or psyops, dimension of Reagan's response to the Sandinistas, by the end of 1987 the Administration had succeeded in creating a negative image of the Nicaraguan government so as to discredit its legitimacy and isolate it from the world community.[1] Through diplomatic channels, United States Information Agency (USIA) dispatches and other mechanisms, the Sandinista regime was continually portrayed as a Soviet and Cuban-backed communist totalitarian regime that everywhere supported terrorism and revolution, and thereby was a threat to all democratic nations in the region. Wherever possible in the international community, governments were pressured to sever all ties with Nicaragua. Particular attention was directed to the Latin American states, especially the 'Contadora' group comprising Mexico, Panama, Colombia and Venezuela.[2] A common US tactic was to negotiate with these Central American states ostensibly to find a settlement to the conflict, while questioning the legitimacy of those 'democratic' processes pursued within Nicaragua (such as the elections of 1984) and accusing the Sandinista government of breaking negotiated agreements.[3]

One stark example of US diplomatic manoeuvrings aimed at discrediting the Sandinistas (though in this case it came unstuck), was the reversal of the US position on the 221-point Latin American Peace Initiative arrived at by the Contadora group in 1984. The initiative dealt with the most contentious issues of the conflict and called for the removal of all foreign military personnel, advisers and bases, an end to large-scale arms supplies to the region, a prohibition of all cross-border attacks or support by one country of insurgents in another, and the establishment of procedures to verify these agreements. With much fanfare, the United States, though not a signatory to the treaty, pressed the Sandinista government to sign. However, when the Sandinistas eventually agreed in September 1984, the Reagan Administration abruptly changed its position stating that the treaty was not the end of the 'peace process'. Having unexpectedly achieved its public objective of securing Nicaragua's agreement to abide by the Peace Initiative the US itself was not prepared to accept the consequences of such an agreement. Nicaragua's compliance with the treaty meant that the US was at least morally obliged to withdraw its armed forces from Central America which, as noted, was a major condition of the treaty, and with which Washington never intended to comply.[4]

Such an about-face further indicated Reagan's reluctance to enter into a negotiated settlement with the Sandinistas. An earlier indication of this occurred was in 1981 when US Assistant Secretary of State Thomas Enders travelled to Managua ostensibly wishing to seek common agreement with the Nicaraguan government, while at the same time Washington was busy forming the Nicaraguan Democratic Force (FDN).[5] In addition, the US continually demanded that the Contras be included in any negotiations with the Sandinistas arguing that the Contras were a legitimate opposition force. The Sandinistas vehemently opposed this, claiming that Washington was the real force orchestrating the Contra insurgency, and instead demanded direct negotiations with the US, which Washington continually refused. Thus the US consistently demonstrated little real interest in serious negotiations with Nicaragua because in reality the Sandinistas' removal from power was the only objective Reagan could not achieve through negotiations.[6]

The Contras

Until 1986, the Contras were represented by two major groupings, based on the northern and southern borders of Nicaragua, and two Mesquito groups of lesser importance, one on the Atlantic Coast and the other in Honduras. The FDN, as the largest and most successful Contra group, operated in Nicaragua's northern border areas from bases in Honduras. Predominantly made up of former officers and troops from Somoza's national guard and peasantry that were either recruited or cashiered, the FDN's origins are difficult to trace, although much of its structure stemmed from a group originally made up of ex-national guardsmen known as the 'September 15 Legion' led by Colonel Enrique Bermudez.[7] The FDN leadership underwent many changes, with its political front pressured to include non-Somoza figures in order to distance it from the former dictator and the 'guardia', but former national guardsmen always remained in controlling positions.[8] The second Contra group was the Democratic Revolutionary Alliance (ARDE) led by former Sandinista Commandante 'Zero' (Cero) Eden Pastora.[9] based in Costa Rica on Nicaragua's southern border, ARDE comprised former Sandinista fighters loyal to Pastora and Social Democrats disillusioned with the Nicaraguan Democratic Movement (MDN), a legal Nicaraguan 'opposition' body.[10] The Mesquito Indian Contra groups consisted of two major factions, the MISURA closely allied with the FDN, and the MISURASATA loosely aligned with the ARDE and led by Brooklyn Rivera.[11] The CIA backed all of these Contra groups to varying degrees as part of a complicated and shifting relationship in which it was assisted by US Special Forces and other agencies. However, repeated efforts by the CIA to unite the disparate groups failed. Pastora long opposed making any common cause with the FDN, which he charged was a mere CIA proxy made up of nothing more than ex-national guardsmen whom he abhorred; nevertheless Pastora did receive some CIA aid himself.[12]

Domestic Psyops

The American people were an essential target of Reagan's 'initiated' psyops campaign to get rid of the Sandinistas. Washington pursued an extensive media campaign within the US to diminish and discredit domestic support for the Nicaraguan government. Executive branch offices and agencies were created specifically for this campaign of 'perception management'. In January 1983, President Reagan signed National Security Decision Directive No. 77 (NSDD-77) 'Management of Public Diplomacy Relative to National Security'. Classified as secret, NSDD-77 deemed it necessary to 'strengthen the organisation, planning and coordination of the various aspects of public diplomacy ... designed to generate support for our national security objectives' – in other words, to drum up massive public support. In April, the directive was distributed to the State Department, the CIA, the Department of Defense and the USIA for implementation. Along with the USIA, the Office of Public Diplomacy, functioning as a domestic information agency, was a major vehicle for mobilising public opinion in support of US foreign policy. It dispatched representatives to lecture to interests groups throughout the US and produced position papers and pamphlets spelling out Reagan's foreign policy.[13] Moreover, the White House Outreach Working Group on Central America, directed by the President's Director of Public Liaison, coordinated and solidified conservative group support,[14] while other bodies including the Kissinger Commission had more specific tasks such as pursuing bipartisan support for the Administration's foreign policy among elite business and political circles.[15] Even the Office of the President was involved in generating public support, including, for example, a televised speech by the President to a joint session of Congress on 27 April 1983. These agencies thus provided a major institutional foundation for such a domestic propaganda war.

In the private sphere former General John Singlaub's United States Council for World Freedom (USCWF),[16] paramilitary groups such as the Alabama-based Civilian Military Assistance (CMA) (which also had an off-shoot known as the Civilian Refugee Military Assistance (CRMA))[17] and the Soldier of Fortune through its magazine of the same name, church groups, and many other organisations (including a group known as the Enterprise), were also involved in the ongoing domestic psyops campaign. They appealed continually to the public's patriotic and anti-communist sentiments and portrayed the US-backed forces in Nicaragua as anti-Soviet 'freedom fighters' waging a 'holy war' for liberty and democracy.

Reagan's agencies used media and other imagery extensively to equate the Sandinistas (as well as the FMLN in El Salvador) with international terrorism instigated by the Soviet Union. In July 1985, Washington charged that, just like Libya and Iran, Nicaragua was pursuing mindless terrorist goals and the Sandinista struggle against the Contras was nothing but purposeless violence.[18] President Reagan justified US opposition to the Sandinistas as necessary to protect US national security and the welfare of US citizens in accordance with the right to act in self-defence as sanctioned by international law.[19] Moreover, supported by media releases and writings of conservative private organisations including the Heritage Foundation and the Committee on the Present Danger (CPD) through its journal *Commentary*, the Reagan Administration presented the Contras as struggling against such 'terrorism' in their quest to establish democracy in Nicaragua.[20]

The manipulation of the predominant religious beliefs of not only the American people but also the Nicaraguans was another critical tool of this US mass perception campaign, with the Sandinistas portrayed as 'godless' communists who mocked the Pope. By pursuing this emphasis, Reagan harnessed the support of many conservative evangelical groups and anti-communist sects, both internationally and within the United States. These included fundamentalist Protestant organisations and anti-communist sects such as the Reverend Moon's Unification Church, the Christian Broadcasting Network (and its Operation Blessing) and World Vision.[21] Popular fundamentalist Church figures and right-wing US evangelicals who came to the Administration's support included Jerry Falwell and Pat Robertson.[22] Other powerful Church-oriented lobby groups included the Institute for Religion and Democracy (IRD). They claimed to be responsible for promoting the political 'right's' programme in the religious arena, which included combating liberation theology.[23] The role of these groups in generating public support for Reagan's foreign policy, though impossible to measure in concrete terms, was nevertheless significant. Most of these organisations and identities had a high domestic profile within the US and could rally and indeed demonstrate support for the Administration's goals. In calling for aid for Reagan's freedom fighters, these religious groups presented Central America simplistically as a national security problem where communism was challenging Christianity on America's southern border.

A propaganda campaign was also directed against US church and religious organisations sympathetic to the Sandinistas. One principal target was the 'Sanctuary movement', a progressive Christian initiative extensively involved in providing sanctuary within the US for political activists and others fleeing government oppression in El Salvador and Honduras.[24] The Sanctuary movement was commonly accused of being Marxist and illegally importing subversive elements into the United States as part of a left-wing agenda aimed at generating opposition to Reagan foreign policy.

Advocates and supporters of liberation theology both in the United States and in Central America were also targeted and accused of assisting the infiltration of communism into the Catholic Church. As early as 1981, Washington had determined that liberation theology was to be considered a potentially dangerous force, particularly as a rallying point for anti-US opposition in Latin America.[25] The Reagan Administration was perhaps unwittingly assisted by the Pope when he criticised liberation theologists during his visit to Nicaragua in 1983, thereby reinforcing the role of conservative elements within the Church in Nicaragua as a major focus of political opposition to the Sandinistas.

By waging initiated psyops domestically and engaging the support and assistance of conservative 'private agencies', the Reagan Administration essentially 'contracted out' or privatised many support functions for the Contras while avoiding Congressional constraints. The aid programmes and assistance of groups and organisations in the US private and corporate sector helped foster a positive image for the Administration's foreign policy, thereby influencing further domestic support. It has even been claimed that the exposure of some of the secret activities of US agencies in Central America, via 'leaks' to the press, actually suited the Administration as they might possibly generate further domestic support.[26] Private groups such as the 'Friends of the Democratic Center in Central America' (PRODEMCA), the National Defense Council (NDC), the Human Development Foundation, the Nicaraguan Development Council, the Nicaraguan Refugee Fund, the Miami-based Concerned Citizens for Democracy, the World Anti-Communist League (WACL) and the *Washington Times*, became actively involved in such interrelated activities as lobbying, propaganda campaigns and fund-raising. Within Central America some of these organisations, such as the CMA and Soldier of Fortune, also provided 'humanitarian' assistance, material support and training. Many neo-conservative organisations, however, also operated independently from the Reagan Administration, although they directly assisted US foreign policy by providing relief and other aid programs and further logistical support for the Contras.[27]

It is difficult to assess in precise terms the impact and effectiveness of the activities of these private groups save to argue that their involvement certainly worked to maintain the Contras in the field. But it is important to demonstrate the character of these operations and the evolving nature of Reagan's foreign policy in Central America, so that the trends and consistencies of the LIC profile (its footprint) can be identified and compared with US foreign policy activities elsewhere.

Within Nicaragua

Apart from Washington's second-track policy of supporting the Contras, the Reagan Administration certainly exploited the window of opportunity it had in Nicaragua to mould a 'third way' political force from among former elements of Nicaragua's upper class. This force provided a legitimate political front for the Contras, and a pro-US alternative should elections be held. The US objective was to force the Sandinistas to negotiate with the Contras using the Nicaraguan Bishops' Conference as intermediaries, and thereby establish the Contras' legitimacy as an indigenous Nicaraguan opposition force. The US could then work within the local political system using familiar united front tactics, formerly the preserve of revolutionary nationalist movements elsewhere in the Third World. Meanwhile, the Contras were to 'liberate' territory within which they would establish an alternative government that Washington could immediately recognise.

Church figures and members of the Nicaraguan middle class were thus presented as the peaceful face of the democratic revolution. And as such, US activities and assistance in forging a 'legitimate' but disparate democratic opposition in Managua constituted self-initiating psyops. To the Nicaraguan public the emergence of this opposition, which boasted prominent supporters of the revolution against Somoza such as Archbishop Obando y Bravo and Violeta de Chamorro, strengthened the credibility of US claims that the Sandinistas were totalitarians who, sponsored by the Soviets and Cubans, had 'stolen the revolution' from the true democratic forces in Nicaragua.[28]

The US also provided the dominant Contra group, the FDN, with a more palatable democratic image to dispel the popular perception that it was merely a vehicle for the return to power of Somoza's former National Guard. By January 1983, the CIA had recruited six prominent Nicaraguan exiles all possessing anti-Somoza credentials, and retained a Miami-based public relations firm to supply the FDN with the required 'positive image'.[29] Promoted with the now well-worn 'freedom fighters' tag, in June 1985 the FDN were supplied with a new civilian leadership façade with former Sandinistas Arturo Cruz and Alfonso Robelo joining with FDN leader Adolfo Calero to form the United Nicaraguan Opposition (UNO). The UNO was provided with media and conservative lobby group exposure and promoted as the democratic alternative to the Sandinistas by such groups as the

National Endowment for the Preservation of Liberty (NEPL). Many White House officials including Oliver North collaborated in this project.[30] However, after Arturo Cruz resigned in discouragement and the UNO fell apart in 1987, the Contras were more comprehensively reorganised into a group known as the Nicaraguan Resistance. Within this group, which soon was also stricken by factionalism and personal rivalries, the only effective military unit remained the FDN, led by Colonel Bermudez, the Contras' principal military commander.

To cater for all contingencies, Washington also supported other Nicaraguan opposition political parties and trade unions.[31] Before the 1984 election, the 'Coordinadora', a coalition of conservatives and liberals, constituted the major 'legal' challenge to the Sandinista government.[32] The political parties concerned included the Social Christian Party, the Nicaraguan Conservative Party and the Social Democratic Party. Two opposition trade union federations consisted of the Federation of Trade Union Unity (reportedly involved with the CIA),[33] which was affiliated with the International Confederation of Free Trade Unions (ICFTU) and the American Institute for Free Labor Development (AIFLD),[34] and the Nicaraguan Federation of Workers. Both were Somoza creations. These parties and unions joined together with other parties and COSEP in October 1981 to form the Nicaraguan Democratic Coordinating Committee – a grouping that the Heritage Foundation listed for US assistance in 1980.[35] Of these, COSEP with 35,000 members was the most powerful organisation and one of the most effective representative bodies of the internal Nicaraguan opposition. Not surprisingly Washington made COSEP a prime target for support.

One conduit of US assistance for this broadly based opposition was the National Endowment for Democracy (NED), a surrogate of the CIA, which was founded in 1983 and funded by Congress. Backed by Reagan, NED was an organisation dedicated 'to the promotion of democracy overseas'.[36] It channelled funds to Nicaraguan opposition groups with some being redirected to the Contras. NED also later funded the opposition's election campaign in 1990.[37]

Other major agencies supporting the political opposition inside Nicaragua included PRODEMCA, which claimed to be a 'non-partisan citizens' organisation working to establish conflict resolution processes and the strengthening of democracy in Central America.[38] PRODEMCA was formed in 1981 with backing from right-wing foundations but, importantly, it was sponsored by the Reagan Administration to enlist Cold War liberals to support its Central American objectives. Its members included former United Nations Ambassador Jeane Kirkpatrick, Norman Podhoretz of *Commentary* magazine, Albert Shanker of the American Federation of Teachers, Edmund Robb of the Institute for Religion and Democracy (IRD) and William Doherty of the AIFLD.[39]

What is particularly important here is that the nature of PRODEMCA's membership clearly demonstrated the interlocking web of support the

Reagan Administration had built within the US public and private spheres for the pursuit of its foreign policy. Although PRODEMCA was most visible within the US lobbying Congress and funding Contra advertisements in the media, PRODEMCA also funded *La Prensa*, Violeta de Chamorro's opposition newspaper in Managua.[40] As regards other organisations, USAID also supported COSEP and other Nicaraguan domestic opposition groups. It assisted in these groups' 'nation building' projects, such as those pursued by the conservative Nicaraguan Catholic Church, which could compete with the Sandinistas' development programmes.[41] Again, while the impact of these groups is difficult to assess, their operation in support of the Administration's objectives however clearly demonstrates the significant extent to which Reagan's foreign policy became privatised.

The Reagan Administration realised that the Catholic Church was far more able to attract a mass following than the political parties and trade unions tolerated by the Sandinistas, and was able to challenge the regime quite openly. The Church had sponsored social welfare programmes to undercut similar Sandinista efforts, undermining their popular support.[42] In response, the Nicaraguan government blocked USAID assistance to these programmes in July 1982. The Sandinistas decided to prevent foreign aid entering the country that supported private, educational and church groups opposed to the regime.[43] (This response subsequently enabled the Heritage Foundation and the IRD to further condemn the Sandinista government by arguing that it repressed religious freedoms and was constantly harassing the Church and Archbishop Miguel Obando y Bravo.)

Initiated Psyops – Targeting Nicaragua

In a sense, many of the anti-Sandinista activities pursued by the US agencies can be considered 'self-initiating' psyops because, apart from their immediate objectives, they also had a distinct psychological effect on the target population generating both lay and sectarian opposition to the Government. However, directly 'initiated' psyops were also waged extensively against the Sandinista government and its support base in Nicaragua. A major vehicle for these activities was the Contras.

The Contras and the Manual

Perhaps the main indicator of the US's intentional use of psyops activities was the Contra instruction manual *Psychological Operations in Guerrilla Warfare*, authored and supplied to the Contras by the CIA in 1983.[44] The manual contained extensive instructions on how to wage psychological warfare, including selective political assassinations for maximum political and psychological impact.[45] The Contras were instructed to become far more selective in their choice of those to be terrorised and/or assassinated or, in other words, were urged to adopt a more selective use of violence. In this sense, appropriate targets for assassination included court judges, police and state security officials. Other recommended activities included sabotage, blackmail, coercive violence against civilians, mob violence and kidnapping. While the manual's primary purpose was to instruct the Contras on the finer points of waging people's war, and in this respect was significantly influenced by the writings of Mao Tse Tung and Che Guevara,[46] as such, it represented an attempt by the CIA to modify the Contras' use of more conventional military tactics which, to the Administration's alarm, included a tendency to commit acts of unnecessary brutality and even mindless atrocities. Often attributed to 'grudge-settling' by former guardsmen, the sum affect of these activities only further alienated the Contras from the local population.[47]

Aimed at pursuing a 'hearts and minds' campaign to win the support of the Nicaraguan people, the manual stressed a number of important themes including a 'carrot and stick' approach. One theme promoted the use of demands for 'God, Homeland and Democracy'.[48] The manual's authors suggested that the Contras should appeal to the *campesinos*' nationalist sentiments and religious fears by constantly highlighting the dangers of an increased Cuban and Soviet intrusion into Nicaraguan society, and the threat of possible religious oppression by atheistic communists. Thus, as in the initiated psyops dimension pursued within the US, religious beliefs were also manipulated in Nicaragua. Christianity versus 'godless communism' soon emerged as a major theme of the Contra psyops campaign. As articulated in the manual, Christianity was a tool with which the Contras could damn the Sandinistas while simultaneously attracting recruits from among the strongly Catholic *campesinos*.[49] The manual made many references to 'Christian' guerrillas or commanders, advocating that the 'freedom fighters' should use Christian symbolism and stress their Christianity to gain political support.[50] Further, it suggested that in their propaganda and recruitment operations the Contras should constantly express indignation: 'over the lack of freedom of worship, and persecution, of which priests are victims; and over the participation of priests such as Escoto and Cardenal in the Sandinista government, against the explicit orders of his Holiness, the Pope'.[51]

The CIA also produced and distributed a comic book-style sabotage publication entitled 'The Freedom Fighter's Manual'.[52] This booklet, among other Contra literature, displayed the Pope's picture and other religious symbols to politicise both Contra recruits and *campesinos* with the message that the Catholic Church in Nicaragua was under siege by the godless Sandinistas. One particular publication claimed that the Pope commanded the Nicaraguan people to fight against atheism and communism. Presented in cartoon form using monkeys as characters, the story's '*Animal Farm*-like' message depicted that the animals had won the revolution against the guerrillas but then the new group of 'monkeys' had set up their own guerrillas and now it was necessary for a new revolution. The publication's theme stressed that the real revolution in Nicaragua in 1979 had been betrayed by the Sandinistas and now the people should support the FDN to help overthrow the new dictators.

Other Contra-initiated psyops included several ostensibly minor and innocuous features of their military activities. Sandinista Lieutenant Commander Roger Mayaga, State Security Head, 1st Region, claimed that even the sophisticated equipment the Contras used and their attractive US-designed and made uniforms could be considered as psyops tools.[53] Compared to the old and worn uniforms of the Sandinista People's Army (EPS), the Contras in such attire and with such equipment looked far more an army of authority, legitimacy and power and thereby appeared much more impressive to the *campesinos*.

Threats of Invasion/Shows of Strength

US demonstrations of conventional military strength also constituted initiated psyops operations, including naval exercises off Nicaragua's Atlantic and Pacific coasts, and operations such as the 'Big Pine' exercises in neighbouring Honduras in February and August 1983. The frequency of these exercises appeared to many observers to be aimed not at meeting the internal defence needs of Honduras but at serving two other related functions. First, they would provide military aid to the Contras operating out of Honduras when the US forces abandoned military equipment in that country after the termination of the exercises.[54] Second, they would assist in waging an intimidating and damaging psyops campaign against Nicaragua by increasing Sandinista fears of an impending invasion. By conducting what were simply exercises, Washington gave no clear indications to the American public that it was going to invade Nicaragua, thereby not antagonising its domestic opposition. However, by continually undertaking mass troop manoeuvres in Honduras, the Reagan Administration gave the Nicaraguan government the impression that an invasion was imminent,[55] eroding morale and raising tensions within the country and damaging Nicaragua not only psychologically, but also militarily, economically and socially.[56] The exercises obliged the Sandinistas to structure and mobilise their forces for conventional warfare against regular US forces, leaving them off balance and vulnerable to the Contras' guerrilla warfare. The subsequent national mobilisation into constant preparations for an invasion which these US manoeuvres induced distorted normal social and economic activity to the extent that the Sandinistas were forced to abandon social reforms which, in turn, meant the domestic population had to endure increasing hardship.[57] Such preparations included digging air raid shelters in streets, homes and factories, which in demanding such a diversion of the workforce stunted industrial and agrarian production (including the harvesting of cash crops) and further strained Nicaragua's economy.[58]

Such repeated shows of US force were designed to weaken the Nicaraguan people's will to resist and to induce social conflict within the country which would in turn undercut the legitimacy of the Sandinista government.

Further, such shows of strength forced Nicaragua to appear to violate the spirit of the Contadora negotiations: by rapidly expanding their armed forces in preparation for an invasion, the Sandinistas appeared bent on military expansionism further undermining their international legitimacy and increasing their diplomatic isolation.[59]

Manipulation of Opposition Press and Media

Other US-initiated psyops programs included the manipulation of the opposition press within Nicaragua. According to the American psychologist Fred Landis, the CIA virtually controlled *La Prensa*, which was owned and operated by the Chamorro family.[60] The family head, Violeta de Chamorro, though a conservative, was originally a member of the Provisional Government Junta of National Reconstruction but resigned in April 1980 after disagreements about Sandinista proposals to expand the Council of State (Chamorro later joined the opposition and was elected President of Nicaragua in 1990). Landis documented how the CIA manipulated the front pages of the paper to wage a protracted poster-like campaign. For example, by carefully positioning pictures and headlines of incidents of international terrorism, gruesome accidents and other tragedies, as well as domestic and political disputes alongside photos of Sandinista leaders, the government was continually associated with anti-Church sentiments, as well as images of misery, terrorism and death. *La Prensa* also continually printed fabricated stories to discredit Sandinista officials. These stories were often relayed to *La Prensa* by the USIA after first being laundered in smaller press and media operations elsewhere.[61] Closely linked to the other pressures exerted by the United States, this CIA-sponsored press campaign was intended to maximise the growth of anti-Sandinista attitudes and perceptions among the Nicaraguan population.[62]

Finally, extensive anti-Sandinista propaganda was also transmitted through the electronic media. The USIA, through its vehicle the radio station Voice of America (VOA), played a dominant role by extending the range that propaganda could be transmitted into Nicaragua (assisted by other facilities such as the anti-Cuban station Radio Marti in Florida). The Contras also assisted this campaign using powerful radio facilities capable of penetrating Nicaragua on both AM and FM bands.[63]

THE ECONOMIC DIMENSION

Though the Reagan Administration went to great lengths to deny that it was waging economic warfare against the Sandinista government, even to the extent of publishing denials as late as 1985,[64] harsh economic measures were instituted virtually from the day Reagan was installed.[65] On the other hand, in support of the opposition and to highlight grievances against the Sandinistas, Washington implemented extensive aid programmes to assist the Nicaraguan refugees in Honduras and elsewhere. This prolonged use of economic warfare against the Sandinistas undermined both the Nicaraguan economy and the Sandinistas' ability to wage war, while encouraging the growth of an internal political climate that could produce a popular uprising in support of the opposition. This economic dimension of the overall LIC approach to overthrow the Sandinista government can be loosely classified into aid and trade embargoes, and sabotage activities.

In March 1981, the Reagan Administration halted much of its aid to Nicaragua. This coincided with the President's Finding on Covert Action (NSDD-17) which authorised the use of covert action to stop the alleged flow of arms from Nicaragua to the Salvadoran insurgents. In short order, Washington denied Nicaragua both US Export-Import Bank Trade credits needed by merchants, industrialists and farmers to import US-manufactured goods, and Overseas Private Investment Corporation guarantees necessary to underwrite US corporate investments in the Third World and of course in Nicaragua. In September 1981, all remaining US aid was cancelled after Washington accused the Sandinistas of still sending arms to El Salvador as well as accepting assistance from Cuba. In addition, pressure was routinely placed on the World Bank, the International Monetary Fund (IMF), the Inter-American Development Bank (IDB), and the European Economic Community (EEC) to withhold loans to Nicaragua.[66] In some cases the Reagan Administration simply vetoed loans by the IDB and the World Bank. It also put pressure on multilateral development bank (MDB) loans, often 'persuading' the management of these organisations to not bring these loans forward. As a result, Nicaragua received no more MDB loans after 1983. In June 1983, Washington also closed down all Nicaraguan consulates in the country, increasing Nicaragua's difficulties in conducting commercial transactions with the United States.

The aid embargoes impacted crucially on the Nicaraguan economy. Aside from the US, Nicaragua's chief source of aid funding had been the above multilateral lending agencies. Though Nicaragua continued to receive aid assistance from Scandinavian, Western European and some Latin American countries, particularly Mexico, the Reagan Administration also pressured these nations to curtail economic relations with the Sandinista government, with some success.[67]

In March 1983, independently of Congress, President Reagan reduced Nicaragua's sugar quota (worth in excess of $18.5 million) by 90 per cent.[68] Eventually a full trade embargo was imposed on 7 May 1985 under the International Emergency Powers Act with President Reagan proclaiming that Nicaragua represented an 'unusual and extraordinary threat to ... the United States'.[69] Reagan also used diplomatic pressure on other countries to curtail their trade with Nicaragua.

The US also resorted to sabotage to further hurt the Nicaraguan economy and reduce its capacity to earn foreign exchange. CIA agents regularly carried out covert attacks on Nicaraguan oil, harbour, industrial, communication and other facilities.[70] The Contras, meanwhile, attacked the agricultural sector, damaging crops, warehouses, grain silos and farm machinery, as well as trucks, roads and bridges that carried produce. Plantations were attacked and workers terrorised; similar operations were waged against the Nicaraguan fishing industry.[71] While the State Department's Office of Public Diplomacy denied that the US was behind this sabotage campaign, CIA Director William Casey reportedly argued that such sabotage activities made these 'bastards sweat'.[72]

In combating the US economic campaign the Sandinistas were already seriously disadvantaged: Somoza had left Nicaragua with a foreign debt of more than $2 billion and the national treasury virtually empty.[73] Further, the country had been ravaged by an earlier earthquake and the long civil war. The Nicaraguan private sector, which still controlled more than 60 per cent of the gross national product was, for large part, more conducive to forces opposing the Sandinistas than to the Government.[74] The effects of Washington's 'economic war' on Nicaragua were therefore immediate and dramatic. With foreign investment in the country severely cut back, and with Nicaragua's seasonal rural workers fearful of Contra raids and reprisals, the country's harvesting capacity was reduced still further thus exacerbating capital flight.

In response to this virtual economic strangulation, Nicaragua attempted to diversify its economy but, with the Government forced to devote nearly half of its resources to the war, by 1985 the economy was stunted.[75] With a foreign debt totalling more than $4 billion, Nicaragua became the first developing country to fall more than six months behind in its debt repayments to the World Bank. The impact of the economic war was felt harshly at all levels of Nicaraguan society. For example, Rigos Law Downs, a Mesquito Indian from Punta Gorda on the Atlantic Coast of Nicaragua complained, 'I am 23 years old. I am sea diver but cannot work! Our boat engine is American and we can't get parts ... due to the blockade!'[76] This was a typical state of affairs for many Nicaraguans suffering as a direct consequence of the US-imposed aid, trade and oil embargoes.

THE MILITARY DIMENSION

The major agencies responsible for LIC's military dimension within Nicaragua were obviously the Contras, with US Special Operations Forces (SOFs), the CIA and many private organisations playing key roles including participation in combat missions against the EPS.

The Contras

Initially, the Contras were formed to play only a minor role in support of US objectives, acting primarily as a harassing agent to force the Sandinistas to discredit themselves politically. According to David MacMichael, a CIA national intelligence analyst on Central America from 1981 to 1983, CIA officials expected that the Contra operations would provoke the Nicaraguans to mount cross-border attacks. In so doing they would appear militarily aggressive to neighbouring states which would then invoke the Organization of American States' provisions for collective defence.[77] Moreover, it was hoped that the Contras' harassment campaign would force the Sandinistas to further curtail civil liberties within Nicaragua, and by clamping down on their opposition provoke even more internal dissent. Also, it was hoped that the Sandinista government would react against US citizens and diplomats within the country so that Washington could use such open displays of hostility towards the United States to justify its support of the 'opposition'.

By 1983 Washington, however, had reviewed the role of the Contras (primarily the FDN) and actively began to forge them into a 'specific paramilitary force' to oppose the Sandinistas and become a major strategic element in the conflict.[78] The Contras were rebuilt militarily and through active 'recruitment' campaigns, by 1985, their combined strength had grown to an estimated 20,000 men.[79] Nevertheless, even though the Contras were reformed ostensibly as an insurgent movement to oppose the EPS, they remained primarily engaged in economic sabotage operations.[80] This emphasis on attacking Nicaragua's economic infrastructure proved far more fruitful than attempts to establish a liberated zone in which an alternative government could be recognised by Washington.[81] By attacking 'soft' or unprotected economic targets such as electrical grid, water, transportation and communications systems, the Contras could not only cause severe economic disruption within Nicaragua and risk fewer casualties in the process but they could also manage to achieve maximum psychological benefit by demonstrating their 'power' to the local population. These 'soft' operations began as early as March 1982 with the destruction of bridges in northern Nicaragua and later included bombings, other forms of sabotage and ambushes. In July 1984, this plan of action was given increased emphasis on the direction of US Lt Colonel Oliver North.[82]

However, the Contras' operations were not entirely restricted to economic targets. Washington assumed that a fundamental split existed between the Sandinista regime and the Nicaraguan people. To undercut Sandinista attempts to win popular local support, the Contras were directed to destroy all Sandinista reform organisations and social welfare projects, including peasant cooperatives, Christian-based communities, rural schools and local civil defence groups. However, these operations generally proved counterproductive: in carrying out these actions the Contras tended to commit many atrocities including torturing and murdering doctors, nurses and teachers (see later for details of such actions in the context of the civic action dimension) thereby only further alienating themselves from the people.[83]

The Contra operations also included recruitment activities among the local people (primarily among the *campesinos*), but these operations differed both in nature and historically from the recruitment activities of insurgent movements waging people's war elsewhere. Whereas the latter generally incorporated rudimentary justice and land reform programmes to win local support, the Contras, by contrast, relied heavily (though not exclusively) on the use of coercion and financial inducements. For example, the Mesquito Indian, Rigos Law Downs, described an incident to me wherein the Contras, supported by a helicopter crewed by US personnel, had raided his village in January 1985. Their purpose was to recruit local *campesinos*, first by financial inducement and then by threat:

So when the group [sic] came into our village to make an investigation who no cooperate [sic] or who would not join them – they assassinate. They wanted to wash young boys' brains to join them [sic]. He said: 'Right now we will give you five hundred dollars in hand and you can join with me. Right now we will give you the uniform, the camouflage and the arms ... Or if you die fighting, we will give to your parents.' The majority of young boys joined for the money. But ... they then tried to escape from the groups ... then they killed all the young boys! ... So from my village they earned sixty young boys who joined with them and gone [sic] ... in Punta Gorda ... twelve days ago.[84]

This account indicates how such intimidation could be often counter-productive in recruitment operations. Downs claimed that these tactics lost the Contras any support they might have had in his village. But I also asked Downs whether it was true the Contras had considerable success recruiting from the Mesquito Indians? He replied, 'Yes that is true! Because they offer money to my people ... or kill the old people and rape the young girls ... I fled my village because I would not join the groups and they would kill me.'[85]

Further evidence of the Contras' heavy reliance on kidnapping for recruitment was provided by those who had fled the movement, as well as the testimonies of many captured Contras I interviewed in Esteli in northern Nicaragua in February 1985.[86] In the case of the Mesquito Indians, however, the Contras were also able to exploit some poorly judged if not mistaken Sandinista 'relocation' operations designed to outmanoeuvre the insurgency. In January and February 1982, the Sandinistas evacuated more than 12,000 Mesquitos from their Coco River villages on the Honduran Border to an area 80 km to the south, not only to protect them from Contra attacks but also to prevent further Contra recruitment from among their ranks. This, however, allowed the US and the Contras to charge that the Sandinistas were 'repressing' the Mesquitos and undertaking 'atrocious and genocidal actions' against them, which in turn convinced some Mesquitos to join the insurgency.[87]

Apart from kidnapping and intimidation, the Contras' recruitment activities, however, were also assisted by food shortages (in part created by the US trade embargo) and the poor management and other failures of the Sandinistas' agrarian reform strategies. There are no reliable figures on the amount of disgruntled *campesinos* who joined the Contras as a result of severe food shortages or because they were alienated by the Sandinistas' failure to satisfactorily implement agrarian reform.[88] However, it is certain that this did occur and must not be discounted as a factor in any analysis of the Contra recruitment campaigns' effectiveness. Nevertheless, these shortages were also exacerbated by bad weather, increasing speculation and hoarding, growing demand and the Contra attacks.[89]

The CIA, US Special Forces and UCLAs

The Central Intelligence Agency, US Special Forces and CIA-directed mercenaries were integral to the military dimension of LIC in Nicaragua. The CIA, the major director of US policy in Nicaragua until 1984, and US Special Forces such as the Green Berets were involved in supplying, training, directing and even participating in Contra military actions as well as conducting their own. Reports of US Special Forces and CIA involvement in actual combat within Nicaragua are well documented and recorded, as are the activities of US State National Guard Forces. For example, the First Detachment, A Company, Twentieth Special Forces Group of the Alabama National Guard was one among other State Defence Forces that supplied arms and equipment to the Contras.[90]

Under Director William Casey, the CIA waged a military campaign somewhat independently of the other LIC agencies. The CIA relied heavily on the use of mercenaries and specifically its Latin American contract agents (whom it termed 'Unilaterally Controlled Latino Assets' or UCLAs) to mine Nicaraguan harbours and bomb airfields.[91] Related to the Contras but more purely a CIA and Pentagon creation, the UCLAs were made up of mercenaries from many different Central American countries, and included Panamanians, Hondurans, Salvadorans, Chileans, Cuban exiles and Costa Ricans. A covert group specially created to carry out secret CIA missions that could then be attributed to the Contras, the UCLAs came into being as a result of the CIA's frustration with the Contras' incompetence in the field; increasingly the CIA relied on these specially trained covert forces for select combat missions in Nicaragua.[92] Between September 1983 and April 1984, the UCLAs carried out at least 21 direct attacks on Nicaraguan economic targets aiming to isolate Nicaragua by cutting off its supplies from abroad. The UCLAs' targets included port infrastructures, fuel tanks and grain storage facilities, waterways and shipping. Early in 1984, the Contras actually claimed responsibility for the mining of Nicaragua's harbours. However not one Nicaraguan was involved in the operation. It was instead conducted by UCLAs launched from a CIA 'mother ship'.[93] Evidence exists that UCLAs, parading as Contras, were also involved in recruitment operations in Nicaraguan rural areas.[94] For example, Rigos Law Downs identified the Contra group that had raided Punta Gorda in this way:

The mercenary groups had made [sic] up of different types, the Honduran and Panamanians had their own flags. The Cuban spoke different Spanish. I knew he was Cuban. And in one part – the real chief of the guys – he spoke to nobody ... So like he was American, I don't know exactly, but he was white ... like you ... But he didn't speak to nobody, he just gave orders and he was talking through the big radio phone ... and there were women as well! They were foreigners from Costa Rica ...[95]

The different nationalities of these Contra forces indicates that Downs was identifying UCLA mercenaries led most probably by the CIA. Such direct involvement of the CIA (through its UCLA proxies) in combat and sabotage operations, however, was eventually terminated by a hostile US Congress in 1984.[96]

Third-Country Forces

Assisting the CIA and US Special Forces in supplying and training the Contras were the governments of countries which for most part continued their assistance after the 1984 Boland Amendment. These countries included Argentina, Israel, South Korea, Taiwan, Japan, Saudi Arabia, El Salvador, Honduras and Panama; even the People's Republic of China sold missiles to the Contras.[97] Argentina had been involved from the outset in training the insurgents, but withdrew its services in 1983 in retaliation for US support of Britain in the Falkland Islands conflict. Honduras provided sanctuary and base areas for the FDN to the extent that by 1983 it had become the 'command and control center' for the Contra war.[98] Further, its armed forces and those of El Salvador provided conduits for US arms and training. Honduran troops were even reported to be assisting the Contras in military operations. Taiwan and Guatemala also provided military supplies, and the Japanese were reportedly involved in supporting the Mesquito groups as were the Israelis.[99] Most of the above countries have also been credited with supplying finance to the Contras. While Israel denied such claims, observers claim it worked through private arms dealers, South African and other foreign corporations and third countries such as Honduras to supply the Contras with arms and other aid. At times Israel was even reimbursed by the Reagan Administration.[100]

A key question arising from the involvement of third countries in the conflict is the rationale for their support of US policy in the region. The answer lies to some extent in the lobbying undertaken by the Reagan Administration and the congruence of foreign policy objectives between the US and these countries.[101] However, the possibility also exists that the Reagan Administration may have conducted trade deals and secret negotiations with these countries similar to those involved in the 'Iran-Contra' operation.[102]

Project Democracy – The Private War and the Enterprise

An important expression of the military dimension of LIC in Nicaragua was the Administration's 'Project Democracy', directed by the NSC and directly sanctioned by President Reagan. Project Democracy began after the CIA's activities in Nicaragua were formally terminated by the Boland Amendment in 1984 and the National Security Council assumed the major responsibility for the conduct of the Contra war. Lasting until 1986, this illegal operation included the Iran-Contra machinations in which individuals associated with the NSC directed proceeds from arms sales to Iran to the

Contras.[103] The full agenda of this group was never revealed to Congress. As Secretary of Defense Caspar Weinberger argued, 'People with their own agenda ... were doing everything they could to put this agenda into effect.'[104]

Playing a major role in this operation, and in a category all its own because of its totally clandestine operations, was the group known as the 'Enterprise' or 'Secret Team',[105] a shadowy network of some still active but mostly ex-military and intelligence personnel, businessmen, professional criminals, financiers, politicians and others – and the plethora of related organisations and businesses they formed. The Enterprise pursued an extreme right-wing international agenda aimed at destroying Marxist governments and organisations in the Third World. Since its beginnings among the anti-Castro opposition in the early 1960s, there has been much written about the Enterprise and much attributed to it. It has been associated with the Iran-Contra affair, drug trafficking in Central America and Southeast Asia, arms trafficking, money laundering, destabilising foreign governments, and creating and waging insurgencies. It has also been linked to political assassinations, including those of President Kennedy and Martin Luther King. Whatever the credibility of these charges, the activities of the individuals associated with it and the organisation/network in general, particularly in Central America, are well documented.[106]

Though ostensibly a 'private' organisation, the Enterprise was strongly linked to the Reagan Administration through both professional and personal ties and it assumed the role of a *de facto* foreign policy agency and an auxiliary arm of the executive albeit an illegal and illegitimate one, for the conduct of Reagan's secret war in Central America in violation of the Boland Amendment. As a 'compartmentalised network' of front companies to assist in running the Administration's secret war in Central America,[107] the Enterprise was organised and directed by Lt Colonel Oliver North and CIA Director William Casey.[108] Other NSC identities directly involved in this 'organisation' included National Security Advisers Robert McFarlane and Admiral John Poindexter. In the private 'realm', but with strong ties to the Reagan Administration, other leading figures in the Enterprise included former Major General John Singlaub, Thomas Clines, Albert Hakim, General Richard Secord (retired), Thomas Shackley, General Edward Lansdale and Colonel John Waghelstein among others.[109] For most part, the individuals associated with this network acted illegally and unconstitutionally, with many service and intelligence and even Administration personnel often undertaking Enterprise operations in their spare time through a process known as 'sheepdipping'. Often, CIA and other service personnel including SOFs would resign, or take leave, undertake clandestine operations in a 'private' capacity for the Enterprise, and then resume their services.[110]

From within the NSC, Casey and North, through the operations and channels of the Enterprise, directed and financed the secret activities that constituted 'Project Democracy'. John Singlaub was of major importance in the command chain of this operation. As virtual 'commander in the field' of the Enterprise's clandestine activities in Central America, Singlaub is credited with virtually taking full control of the field operations of Washington's covert war in Nicaragua after the forced withdrawal of the CIA.[111]

For the Reagan Administration, the objective of Project Democracy was to keep the Contras in the field in Central America while avoiding Congressional scrutiny, and therefore Executive accountability of this project. The Iran-Contra arms deal was central to this project within which the Enterprise provided the NSC with contacts to private and international funders, and conduits for the supply of both arms and money to the Contras.[112] The funds obtained from the Iran arms sale and from other sources enabled Oliver North, Casey and others to organise a 'private' navy and air force and hire crews to staff the ships and fly the planes that carried US weapons to Iran and supplies to the Contras.[113] The Enterprise also supplied the means and wherewithal for necessary assassinations, Contra recruitment, and front organisations and companies to disguise the project's activities. Moreover, ex-agents, SOFs personnel and mercenaries provided not only a secret transport and supply structure, but also undertook air and naval operations and gathered intelligence. The Enterprise, in alliance with North and Casey, thus became a major party behind the Contras assisting in the supply, recruitment, training and direction of their operations.[114] Though restricted by Congress, the CIA through the activities of Casey and others was aware of these private activities, and apart from the 'sheepdipping' operations of its members, when possible it provided assistance.

A diverse range of other related civilian and paramilitary organisations also became deeply involved in Project Democracy. Prominent among them was the World Anti-Communist League, well known for its support of US foreign policy in Central America. The WACL's public rationale for its existence was to support and assist 'democratic anti-communist freedom fighters of the world'.[115] It had chapters in many countries including the United States where former US General John Singlaub's United States Council for World Freedom, another neo-conservative anti-communist lobby group, was prominent. The WACL (through John Singlaub), with the encouragement of the Reagan Administration, played an important role in organising funds from both private domestic and international sources to buy arms for the FDN. Singlaub was involved in extensive negotiations for assistance for the Contras with South Korea and Taiwan and thus appeared indispensable to Project Democracy. Followed up by Gaston Sigur, Singlaub's negotiations resulted in two donations of $1 million for the United National Opposition (UNO). Singlaub is also accredited with putting pressure on Pastora to join the UNO and to coordinate actions with the FDN.[116]

President Reagan was also extensively involved in fund-raising activities, giving receptions and private audiences to sponsors and potential donors. Also, the National Endowment for the Preservation of Liberty (NEPL), a conservative lobby and fund-raising group formed by Carl 'Spitz' Channell was similarly involved in this project. It used White House briefings and private meetings with President Reagan to convince potential donors to contribute more than $10 million to the Contras by the end of 1986. The NEPL played a significant role as a domestic conduit for funding and weapons for the Contras during the moratorium on official US aid, as did International Business Communications.

Included among the other private groups involved were CAUSA International – the political arm of Reverend Moon's Unification Church (the 'Moonies') and, as noted, the Civilian Military Assistance (CMA) and the Soldier of Fortune.[117] In October 1984, President Reagan publicly supported the activities of private US groups in Central America claiming they were 'quite in line with what has been a pretty well established tradition in our country'.[118] However, these groups were not necessarily operating independently from the Reagan Administration: the National Security Council also directed and coordinated many of their activities.[119]

Many of these private organisations had more in common with the Reagan Administration than ideological orientations and political objectives. There existed close ties of friendship between many key Administration figures and these groups. A close working relationship, for example, existed between Singlaub, North, members of Soldier of Fortune, and Tom Posey who led the CMA. Mercenaries from the CMA, among other groups, not only took over the CIA's role in directing the conflict,[120] but in 1984 also helped replace CIA and Special Operations Forces in training the Contras. By September 1984, this organisation had over a thousand members in Central America and had sent fifteen into action in Nicaragua. It also claimed to have three thousand other men in combat-ready 'freedom fighter' brigades.[121]

Private groups and individuals were a key instrument in the NSC's secret war against the Sandinista government, and Project Democracy represented the contracting-out of Reagan's foreign policy in Central America. Nevertheless, most of these groups also pursued their own operational agenda in the region, quite separate from the Administration. One example was the CMA's planned assassination of the US Ambassador to Costa Rica, Lewis Tambs, in exchange for a $1 million bounty offered by Colombian drug traffickers. The operation was designed to incriminate the Sandinistas and hopefully spark a US invasion in retaliation.

Project Democracy was never intended to be isolated from the greater project of the Reagan Administration. The NSC, instead, intended it to be a bridging operation to maintain the Contras in the field until a repentant Congress unleashed the CIA to again pursue anti-Sandinista activities, which had occurred by 1986. After extensive lobbying by pressure groups, and coinciding with international events previously described, Congressional opinion eventually turned to the extent that in June 1985, the US Congress authorised $27 million in 'humanitarian assistance' and a year later voted to appropriate $100 million for full-scale CIA operations against the Nicaraguan government.[122]

THE CIVIC ACTION DIMENSION

Civic action was a necessary function of the 'nation-building' process and an integral part of the LIC conflict profile that developed in Nicaragua. US official and unofficial agencies and third-country governments were extensively involved in supplying humanitarian or 'non-lethal' aid, consisting of food and medicine, to the Contras and their families in Honduras and Costa Rica. In this respect, economic aid was considered just as important as military aid.

USAID was the major Administration agency involved in civic action in the region. However, private US organisations also assisted in such activities, including the CMA/CRMA, Refugee Relief International, religious groups such as Operation Blessing (run by the Christian Broadcasting Network (CBN) in Virginia) and World Vision based in California.[123] The CMA/CRMA again played a dominant role. For example, between January and September 1984, the CMA/CRMA claimed to have collected upwards of $85,000 in money, food, clothing and medical supplies for the Contras based in Honduras. In 1985 alone it provided $3 million in non-lethal supplies and 15,000 man-hours of training for the Contra rebels.[124] Also involved in raising funds were wealthy business figures such as Joseph Coors and the entertainer Wayne Newton, not to mention the omnipresent John Singlaub who, on behalf of the Administration, coordinated this network of individual and group activities in which many of these individuals had interlocking memberships and directorates. Also included were Americares in Connecticut and Friends of Americares in Louisiana. World Medical Relief, based in Detroit, specialised in medical equipment and transported most of its supplies via an organisation known as the 'Air Commandos Association'. Third-country governments involved in these activities included Saudi Arabia, Taiwan, Israel and South Korea.

As part of the CIA-initiated emphasis on a 'hearts and minds' approach within Nicaragua in 1984, the Contras also heavily involved themselves in civic action programs in regions where they had a presence. The objective was to demonstrate the viability of the 'democratic alternative' to the local population and the concomitant failure of the Sandinistas to establish an effective economic and political infrastructure. The Contras attempted to weaken the influence of the Sandinista government by destroying its social welfare programs (as previously noted) by eliminating doctors, health workers, teachers, engineers, agricultural technicians and others, and then introducing their own.[125] Rigos Law Downs, for example, claimed that the Contras who regularly visited his village for recruitment, intelligence gathering and other purposes often provided aid to the villagers in the form of tinned food, rudimentary medical treatment and money.[126]

NICARAGUA AND THE STRATEGY OF LIC

As I have demonstrated in this chapter, the profile of the conflict waged in and around Nicaragua by the diverse agencies and allied organisations of the United States was multidimensional and primarily political/psychological in nature. By waging what I have identified as LIC, the Reagan Administration was able to create a low intensity warfare environment, which contributed to the Sandinistas' electoral defeat in 1990 at the hands of the US-backed United Nicaraguan Opposition led by Violeta de Chamorro. Though seemingly unrelated, the diverse array of activities pursued by Washington's many LIC agencies collectively did possess significant strategic coherence: they all served to destroy the viability and legitimacy of the Sandinista revolutionary nationalist regime and to undermine its popular support base.

The precise extent of the NSC's jurisdiction, power and influence over the many agencies involved in this operation is impossible to ascertain given the difficulty in measuring the influence of crucial individuals and the informal networks through which they interacted within and outside of the Reagan Administration. On the other hand, the evidence suggests that the NSC did exercise a degree of influence over private agencies which depended in part on the political constituency of the agency, the relationships of its individual members with key figures in the Administration, and its capacity to provide support for the Contra effort. Generally, those groups or organisations that could provide the most assistance had the closest ties with the Reagan Administration, for example, John Singlaub's United States Council of World Freedom, which reportedly had close ties with President Reagan himself and was involved in virtually every stage of the Contra support operation.[127] Moreover, many agencies involved in the vast private network were entangled in a complex web of interlocking directorates: this interrelationship ensured the integration of these US, and other, private groups into the Administration's strategy.

A distinctive feature of LIC as it developed in Central America, therefore, was the contracting-out or privatisation of Reagan's foreign policy. Much of this strategy was rendered covert and unaccountable to Congress and the US public. Though Project Democracy began to unravel quickly in 1986 with the exposure of the illegal Iran-Contra operations and other associated activities in Central America, the 'private war' remained one of the essential features of the Reagan Administration's response to the Sandinista government. It was this distinctive strategy that so many theorists subsequently termed the strategy of low intensity conflict, and on the basis of its emergence over time they argued that Central America was the testing ground for its application elsewhere.

However, the emergence of LIC was not solely the result of revolutionary and counter-revolutionary measures associated with US foreign policy in

Central America. The Administration's approach to Nicaragua (and for that matter El Salvador) and the subsequent conflict profile that developed there also closely resembled the pattern of activity evolving in the Philippines at that time, and to lesser extents in Angola and Kampuchea.[128]

At a conceptual level LIC was also evolving, quite independently, in the policy-making processes within the US national security elite. At this level its development in 'target states' was determined first by continuing domestic constraints on military intervention in the Third World, and second, by the availability and potential within the target state of opposition groups that could be moulded both overtly and covertly into the 'third way'. However, as with many conceptual models, practice does not always follow precept. What needs to be investigated is the extent to which LIC's development in Nicaragua influenced the emergence of LIC elsewhere. An analysis of the nature of the conflict profile of the US response to revolutionary nationalism in the Philippines during the 1980s is therefore valuable. It allows us to determine whether LIC was transplanted there from Central America or instead actually evolved independently in that country as a 'homegrown' strategy which nevertheless assisted LIC's conceptual formulation back in Washington.

7   LIC IN THE PHILIPPINES?

Over the next two chapters I closely examine the counterinsurgency conflict in the Philippines during the 1980s. The US role in combating the Philippines insurgency represents the Reagan Administration's attempt to wage LIC against a Third World guerrilla movement and a target population half a world away from Central America. Careful analysis of the conflict profile in this Asian archipelago reveals the full operation of LIC's other side of the coin – its counter-revolutionary form. It also demonstrates that LIC emerged elsewhere in the Third World at the same time it developed in Nicaragua and was not initially influenced by its emergence in Central America, further dispelling the notion that the latter was a 'laboratory' for a global strategy.

Whereas a revolutionary nationalist government challenged US interests in Nicaragua, in the Philippines a revolutionary nationalist *insurgent* movement challenged US interests maintained by a pro-US regime. The Communist Party of the Philippines (CPP) and its military arm, the New People's Army (NPA), had engaged the Marcos regime in a low intensity warfare (LIW) environment throughout the 1970s and with increasing ferocity in the early 1980s. In response, the regime relied heavily on conventional military means (similar to the eventual US response to LIW in Vietnam) to combat the insurgency. However, in the Philippines (as in Vietnam), the conventional military approach was incongruent with the nature of low intensity warfare and therefore inappropriate. By 1984, the CPP/NPA was steadily gaining ground by waging people's war and exploiting the Marcos regime's corruption.

In this chapter I argue that the Reagan Administration with considerable interests at stake in the Philippines was forced to respond to the growing threat posed by the CPP/NPA. However, there also existed determinants similar to those that operated in Nicaragua which tempered and shaped the US response into what eventually emerged as the counter-revolutionary form of LIC in the Philippines. These determinants ensured many LIC agencies already identified as active in Central America also played a role in implementing Washington's reaction to the CPP/NPA insurgency, which as a result also became significantly civilianised and privatised, two prime characteristics of LIC.

THE DETERMINANTS OF THE RESPONSE

The determinants that shaped the Reagan Administration's response to the CPP/NPA insurgency were varied. However, as in Central America, the interests at stake and the agencies involved greatly determined, and to some extent themselves were influenced by, the developing nature of this low intensity guerrilla war.

US Interests

In the 1980s, the primary motivation for US opposition to the insurgency in the Philippines was broadly consistent with earlier administrations and the long-held Cold War global objectives of US foreign policy: to maintain and further US economic and national security interests. Within the Philippines these interests were significant.

Of considerable importance to Washington were the US bases provided for under the Military Bases Agreement, signed in Manila on 14 March 1947.[1] Excluding associated sites, five major American military installations of different size and significance were located in the Philippines: the Subic Naval Base in Zambales and Bataan, the Clark Air Base in Pampanga and Tarlac (by far the most important bases outside of the US mainland), the San Miguel Naval Communications Complex in Zambales and Tarlac, the USAF Wallace Air Station in San Fernando, La Union, and the Camp John Hay Leave and Recreation Center in Baguio City.[2]

As one foundation of America's Cold War forward defence policy in Asia, the bases played a significant role. They provided a strategic springboard into mainland Asia for military forces to protect US access to resources and markets, as well as being an obstacle to further expansion of Soviet influence into Southeast Asia and the Pacific. They allowed Washington to maintain regional power balances and access to the major sea passages between the Pacific and Indian Oceans. And, moreover, they provided storage centres for nuclear weapons. All in all, in the post-Vietnam era of 'selective containment', the Philippines was of critical strategic importance as a major pillar of US influence in the region. Situated along the Jakarta-Taipei-Tokyo-Seoul axis running along the Pacific rim, the bases were an important link in the network of alliances, naval installations and other military bases Washington could use to combat not only further 'communist expansionism', but also maintain 'stability' in the region. Hence, the maintenance of these facilities was a primary US foreign policy goal.

The economic stability of the Philippines was also important, as US economic interests in the country were extensive. As far back as the early 1970s, US interests in the Philippines were valued at $1.5 billion and US investment was greater than in any other country in Southeast Asia. A number of major US corporations, including Caltex, had considerable investments in the Philippines especially in mining, agribusiness, chemicals, pharmaceuticals, beverages and cosmetics. As political stability ensured economic stability, many of these corporations strongly supported the Marcos government, which in turn ensured they had tax havens and cheap labour for their operations.[3]

The United States also had important political interests at stake in the archipelago. Manila had long been Washington's closest ally in Southeast Asia, and the Philippines' membership of the Association of Southeast Asian Nations (ASEAN) reinforced US links to other states in this regional organisation. A former US colony, the Philippines was also strongly tied to the United States historically, culturally and even institutionally with its political system modelled on the American system. If this 'showpiece' of democracy in Southeast Asia was 'lost' to revolutionary nationalism, the blow to US credibility would have been more damaging than the 'loss' of Vietnam.[4]

The Threat

In the early 1980s, both legal and revolutionary nationalist forces in the Philippines threatened America's extensive interests in that country. While the 'democratic opposition' to President Marcos consisted mainly of left-wing groups, included within it were also many nationalists of the Filipino elite and lobby groups strongly opposed to the US bases. Operating within legal limits, these opposition groups were effectively restrained by the Marcos government. The revolutionary opposition, however, was not. Consisting mainly of the CPP/NPA, this force represented the most extreme manifestation of the long-enduring Filipino nationalist movement, and as such it posed the greatest threat to US interests in the Philippines and as a consequence (in global terms) US 'national security'.[5]

The CPP/NPA waged an armed insurgency against the Marcos government with increasing ferocity during the early 1980s. Estimates of the New People's Army strength varied through this period, though the minimum was put at approximately 17,000 combatants in 1985.[6] The United States actively assisted Marcos's counterinsurgency campaigns aimed at destroying this revolutionary movement, but after the assassination of opposition leader Benigno Aquino in 1983, the Reagan Administration began to pay even closer attention to the growing political instability in the Philippines which the CPP/NPA embodied. In particular, Washington was alarmed by the NPA's rapid growth both in strength and confidence.[7] The US Assistant Secretary of Defense for International Security Affairs, Richard Armitage, for example, reported that in 1983 the New People's Army initiated approximately 60 per cent of the 2,400 reported contacts with government forces. In 1984, this increased to 75 per cent and a total of more than 3,500 incidents. Armitage argued that this increase in activity was consistent with an expansion of the NPA's armed strength to a possible 15,000 armed troops.[8] As a consequence, the Reagan Administration was increasingly concerned that with the insurgency unchecked a communist victory in the Philippines might be a very real possibility. This would mean the forced closure of the US bases allowing the Soviets to increase their influence and military presence in the region. A CPP/NPA takeover of the Philippines would also threaten the unity and pro-US policies of the ASEAN nations. Hence, along with other US interests, the maintenance of the bases was considered imperative.[9]

Marcos Losing Control

The Reagan Administration's fears of a communist victory were also accentuated by a growing perception that the Marcos government was losing control and unable to contain the insurgency. There were various reasons for this conclusion, some relating to the nature of Marcos's rule itself: extensive government corruption and cronyism, for example, was increasingly apparent during the 1980s. Marcos appeared to have lost his ability to control the political agenda in the Philippines, manifest in the consequences of the politically disastrous assassination of Senator Aquino, widely regarded as the work of government (and military) agents on Imelda Marcos's orders.

More than any other factor, the Aquino assassination destroyed Marcos's remaining popularity and credibility among urban Filipinos who identified strongly with US electoral politics and middle-class values.[10] Importantly, the assassination also destroyed Marcos's support base among a Filipino elite well-tuned to participating in the revolving political power-sharing game, long an informal tradition in Philippine politics. Within the Filipino business community, the government's documented human rights abuses, corruption and now apparent policy of eliminating its opponents rendered Marcos 'bad for business'.

The Reagan Administration recognised that this deteriorating domestic political situation was also a product of the rapidly worsening Philippine economy, traceable in part to the regime's corruption. More importantly, Washington concluded that Marcos was failing to combat the insurgency politically, in the sense that the regime had weak support at the grassroots level. One reason for this was that it was failing to address the falling living standards of the people, a factor which was specifically fuelling the insurgency. On the other hand, however, the CPP/NPA's political activities were proving very effective. The CPP/NPA was building impressive local support organisations in and among the Filipino people in contrast to the seemingly endless abuses perpetuated by the military in the countryside compounded by the government's unpopularity in the cities.[11]

The United States also recognised that Marcos had heavily politicised and corrupted the Filipino military. In particular, he had stacked its highest levels with officers from his own ethnic Ilocano group from Northern Luzon, who were personally loyal to both him and General Fabian Ver (Marcos's cousin and Army Chief of Staff).[12] Moreover, Marcos had rendered much of the Armed Forces of the Philippines (AFP) ineffective against the insurgency because at least eight of the AFP's crack battalions were used merely to 'protect the palace' against potential opposition to Marcos from within the military itself.[13] General Ver had restructured the AFP to ensure Marcos's total control, as such the Presidential Security Command (PSC) was the strongest unit in the military. With the AFP's priorities thus skewed towards 'palace' defence, these crack PSC units were unavailable for counterinsurgency operations. Worse, the distortion and draining of military resources to serve palace security and the President's superstitions, denied the AFP adequate leadership in the provinces.[14] As a consequence, the AFP suffered from declining morale and effectiveness while the New People's Army continued to gain ground, exacerbating even further discord within the AFP. Military factions such as the 'Reform the Armed Forces Movement' (RAM) became increasingly disgruntled with Marcos's rule. RAM was a network of disgruntled lieutenant colonels and other junior officers, which spread throughout the AFP in 1984 and 1985. Anxious to concentrate more effectively on counterinsurgency, these officers wished to revitalise and professionalise the AFP by eliminating corruption from its ranks and reforming its leadership.

On the battlefield itself, it was more than apparent that the military were failing to contain the CPP/NPA. Despite a build-up of the AFP during the late 1970s, extensive US military aid and massive counterinsurgency campaigns, the most prominent of which was Oplan Katatagan in 1983, the CPP/NPA insurgency gathered in intensity throughout 1984 and 1985.[15]

Launched in 1983, Oplan Katatagan was significant because it embraced some elements of low intensity conflict. The campaign was devised after US military advisers studied the counter-guerrilla operations of former governments in the Philippines. Similar to the successful campaign waged against the Huks by the Magsaysay regime in the 1950s, foremost within the objectives of Oplan Katatagan was a 'hearts and minds' approach to win over the local Filipino population. Implicit in this approach was recognition of the importance of the political dimension in counterinsurgency, and particularly the struggle at the grassroots level, to gain the political allegiance and loyalty of the people. Included also in Oplan Katatagan were civic action programmes, psyops and an increased emphasis on intelligence and other activities. Pursued in conjunction and together with military counterinsurgency activities, this approach paralleled the pattern of LIC emerging in Central America at this time.

However, Oplan Katatagan was generally inconsistent with the overall nature of the Government's counterinsurgency campaigns that it had waged since the late 1960s and continued to use against the New People's Army. To combat the surge of NPA activity in 1984 and 1985, the AFP and the Philippine Constabulary (PC) in fact persisted with counterinsurgency actions in close accord with the unsuccessful strategy of 'attrition' developed and applied by the US military in Vietnam. This conventional approach was intensified after 1978 because of Marcos's failing health and impending elections. Described as a 'big unit' strategy, the AFP sought to crush the New

People's Army with military firepower and used search-and-destroy tactics, strategic hamletting, zoning, food blockades, free-fire zones and widespread death-squad activity, or 'salvaging' (summary killing) operations, against specific targets to terrorise the population into compliance.[16] In specific areas of NPA activity, a war against the people was waged in which everyone was considered and thereby written off as a 'communist'.[17]

However this big unit approach proved extremely counterproductive, causing heavy civilian casualties which only alienated much of the population and further fuelled the insurgency.[18] As Larry Niksch observed, even though the government considered adopting a broader counterinsurgency strategy that included dialogue with civilians, civic action and economic development programmes, approaches of this nature occurred only sporadically (as had Oplan Katatagan). Instead, the regime retained a reactive strategy applied to areas only after there was evidence of CPP/NPA activity within.[19] The Marcos government, it seemed, was prepared to ignore the political dimension of the conflict in which it was engaged.

THE NEED FOR A NEW APPROACH

As early as 1984, the Reagan Administration recognised that a new approach to the insurgency in the Philippines was needed which could address the political dimension of the conflict. However, any change in approach was resisted by both Marcos and General Ver. Marcos and his close allies feared that the adoption of reforms would result in challenges to their monopoly on power. Though US Defense Department officials worked with the AFP to try to introduce reform, they achieved meagre results, not altogether surprising given that most of the military's top leaders were Marcos's political cronies. Many of these highly politicised generals had overstayed their natural tenure, provoking resentment from the lower ranks and particularly from the RAM faction. Richard Armitage thus argued that the AFP's leadership posed a significant problem and that a change in command was needed to provide the Philippine military with 'vigorous' leadership.[20]

As indicated by various US observers and official reports, the Reagan Administration was aware that military reform was also badly needed to prevent a continued prolific abuse of the civilian population by the AFP, the Constabulary, the Police and the Civilian Home Defence Forces (CHDF),[21] a paramilitary group under the control of the Constabulary.[22] Abuses, including corruption, drunkenness, torture and indiscriminate killings particularly by the CHDF were an ongoing problem in the Philippines and had accelerated in the five years after Marcos lifted martial law in 1981.[23] As the top ranks of the military continued to swell with Marcos loyalists rendering the military increasingly corrupt, factionalised and inefficient, growing use was being made of the CHDF in counterinsurgency actions in the provinces. While this practice made the CHDF a much more active arm of the military, it also exacerbated the problem of civilian abuse,[24] and enhanced the transformation of some provincial units of the CHDF into private armies of many pro-Marcos 'warlords'. Local politicians, businesspeople or other powerful members of the elite (usually members of Marcos's ruling New Society Movement) in the countryside and provincial cities would often arm, dress and feed these forces and thereby exert command over them in pursuit of their own political ends.[25]

Reform of the AFP and the CHDF was needed at many levels. The Reagan Administration regarded an increase in training, professionalism and pay, and the provision of better equipment and food resources for the AFP as essential. Only through the introduction of such measures could problems like poor morale and internal corruption be addressed, and relations between the military and the general population improved.

By the beginning of 1985, Washington had also recognised that the regime's intolerance of democratic opposition had isolated it from other organisations and individuals wielding political power in the Philippines. These included wealthy and influential businesspeople, the Catholic Church, middle-class professionals and opposition groups with which the regime would have to align itself if it was to combat effectively the united front tactics of the CPP/NPA.

THE REAGAN ADMINISTRATION RESPONDS

Recognising the growing crisis in the Philippines, Reagan responded in a manner that replicated the conflict profile emerging in Central America at that time. Evidence suggests that as early as 1984 the Administration attempted to influence the nature and fortunes of the counterinsurgency conflict. For example, a US National Security Study Directive (NSSD) was issued in November of that year virtually prescribing the adoption of low intensity conflict in the Philippines, and in January 1985 it was officially adopted as policy. The NSSD directed that US forces place an emphasis on propaganda and psychological warfare, civic action, training and assistance in battlefield communications and logistics. As Armitage observed, the directive implicitly stressed that 'Counterinsurgency strategy must involve the entire Philippine Government in a coordinated program of political, social and economic measures.'[26] In effect, the directive was a compromise between the US State Department and those in the Department of Defense who could not agree on an appropriate policy. The compromise was forged by a loose 'interagency group' headed by Admiral William Crowe that was set up after the Aquino assassination.[27] However, the conflict prescription embodied within this compromise was not adhered to by the Marcos Government.[28]

By early 1985, the Reagan Administration had recognised that the Marcos regime's refusal to implement military and other reform in the Philippines held out the unpalatable post-Vietnam prospect of the United States being directly involved in a protracted conflict with the CPP/NPA, should the regime become too destabilised by the insurgency. Washington faced the unpleasant dilemma of having either to abandon its interests in the archipelago or become involved militarily. Neither option was particularly attractive or feasible. The Vietnam experience clearly militated against notions of US military intervention in Southeast Asia, particularly in a state where a pro-American government was publicly proclaimed as stable and democratic. Such an intervention would also exacerbate anti-US nationalist sentiments in the Philippines and further feed the flames of insurgency.[29] These factors therefore necessitated a covert response from official US foreign policy agencies, aided by private organisations which, as in Central America, would pursue their own anti-communist agenda in concert with the Reagan Administration.

THE THIRD WAY – THE LIC RESPONSE

By the end of 1985, President Marcos and his closest associates, particularly General Ver, were perceived as the greatest obstacle to reform.[30] As a consequence, the Reagan Administration (under particular influence of the State Department) determined that the Philippine government should be pressured into adopting the more politically oriented counterinsurgency approach as outlined in the previously cited LIC profile directive.

The first requirement of this approach was the political reform of the Marcos Administration itself. As noted in the report prepared for the US Senate by the Congressional Research Service, two basic ingredients were needed to deal with the insurgency: leadership and resources. Reform of both the government and the military was also needed so that a greater emphasis could be placed on adopting a political approach to what was primarily a political conflict.[31]

In 1985, Reagan enforced political reform initially by applying pressure on Marcos to hold elections. Though there were obvious disagreements as to the best method of achieving such reform, to undercut the appeal of the revolution the democratic third way had to be established in the Philippines. The result was the election of February 1986 and the 'people power' revolution which installed Cory Aquino as president.

LIC CHARACTERISTICS

A number of major themes and LIC characteristics can be identified in the changing nature of the counter-revolutionary conflict that was evident in the Philippines by 1985, as well as in the actual process of the regime change that occurred in 1986. Following Marcos's overthrow, the new Aquino government placed a greater emphasis on the political/psychological dimension of counter-revolutionary warfare. Though there was a major intensification of military operations against both the NPA and the Muslim insurgency in the south led by the Moro National Liberation Front (MNLF), in 1986 there began an extensive civilianising and to a lesser extent privatising of the counter-revolutionary conflict against the CPP/NPA. Many of the same LIC agencies already operating in Central America were involved.

The US agencies implementing this covert response included all branches of the US armed services operating in the Philippines headed by the Joint United States Military Advisory Group (JUSMAG), and US Special Operations Forces (SOFs) stationed at Clark and Subic bases and elsewhere. Official US civilian agencies included, as in Central America, the United States Information Agency (USIA), the United States Agency for International Development (USAID), and the Peace Corps.[32] Moreover, the omnipresent CIA was also strongly involved, as indicated by the large increase of its budget and presence in the Philippines in 1986.[33] Related quasi-official US bodies also included the National Endowment for Democracy (NED). Private or unofficial agencies contributing to the privatisation of the conflict in the Philippines included the Heritage Foundation, the WACL and CAUSA among others.[34] Also active were representatives of the Enterprise, including John Singlaub and Ray Cline,[35] while foreign conservative religious groups involved included John Whitehall's Christian Crusade.

The Philippine Government and all branches of its armed services were among the agencies involved in this changing conflict, including the Philippine Constabulary, the Integrated National Police and many civilian paramilitary groups, generally defined as CHDF, that were originally formed and used by Marcos as a major counterinsurgency tool. However, the most prominent agencies in terms of civilian involvement in the conflict were the 'vigilantes'. Similar to the Contras, the vigilantes should be considered as 'civilianising' agents of the conflict. Many of them owed much of their organisation, support and direction to service and civilian agencies of the Reagan Administration and private organisations also pursuing US foreign policy objectives. Like the Contras, the vigilantes occupy a special category in any analysis of the conflict.

At this point it is prudent to note that on first examination much of the evidence linking the vigilantes with the US Administration does appear tenuous and even circumstantial. However, when the role of the vigilantes is analysed within the conceptual framework of the counter-revolutionary strand of LIC (as I do in the next chapter), a strong case can be made that the Reagan Administration exerted significant if indirect influence over the formation and role of many of the vigilante groups in the conflict.

While it is true that vigilante groups existed in the early 1980s, and historically were a common phenomenon in the Philippines, in the latter half of 1986 a wave of vigilante activity suddenly swept the nation. Beginning first in the south of the archipelago, vigilante groups led by the 'Alsa Masa' rapidly formed and began to conduct their own private war against the CPP/NPA. Known also by such names as 'the Nagasaka' and the 'Tad Tads',[36] these civilian groups were usually made up of strongly religious anti-communist fanatics, criminal elements or members of local politicians' private armies.[37] Their activities included murdering suspected communists as well as human rights workers, anti-US activists and members of progressive organisations working for reform among the poor.[38] After the

Alsa Masa had proved effective in virtually eliminating the NPA from in and around Davao City (on the southern island of Mindanao), once an area of heavy insurgent activity and for that reason a test case for the formation of these groups elsewhere, vigilantism rapidly spread throughout the archipelago, and even into Manila itself. By the end of 1987, over seventy vigilante groups were reported to have formed in the Philippines. The Aquino government and military officials subsequently presented the paramilitary groups as 'spontaneous' formations of totally autonomous civilian groups banding together to fight communism and, in the local and international press, as a further manifestation of Cory Aquino's 'people power' revolution.

Agency Coordination and Control

In the Philippines, as in Central America, it is apparent that the Reagan Administration through its own agencies influenced not only the activities of vigilante groups but also those of the Philippine government and other agencies and organisations combating the CPP/NPA. US influence could be exerted over the Philippine Government and its armed services through many conduits, ranging from historical and colonial ties and common cultural traits and strong emotional bonds that accompany shared historical experiences,[39] to more tangible avenues for the exercise of influence and power. The latter included military treaties and agreements, diplomatic channels where political pressure and influence could be exerted directly, and economic channels through which trade, aid and other agreements could be used as leverage to influence the government's counter-revolutionary approach.

Military Control

The US exerted considerable influence over the Armed Forces of the Philippines (AFP) through long-standing agreements and US-dominated military supervision and advisory bodies. Of these, the two major tools were the Military Assistance Agreement (MAA) and the Joint US Military Advisory Group (JUSMAG) with its headquarters in Quezon City.

The United States – Republic of the Philippines (US-RP) Military Assistance Agreement (MAA) was the main mechanism of US control over the Philippine military. The MAA dictated the conditions under which the US provided military assistance to the Philippines (MAP) so that its armed forces could fulfil any obligations and commitments arising from international agreements and be able to maintain internal peace and security.[40] This assistance included all forms of military equipment and supplies, training and advice.[41] By exerting this military influence, the MAA also served to forge close political ties between the two countries and to politicise the Philippine military with pro-US values.

The MAA also provided for the operation of the JUSMAG, the military advisory group consisting of high-ranking US Army, Navy and Air Force officers. The JUSMAG was officially attached to the US diplomatic mission to the Philippines and thereby under the authority of the US Ambassador. Though this body officially had an advisory role with the AFP, it exerted considerable control via its military advisers who extended direction, logistics, training and intelligence coordination to the AFP. From the time of its inception, the JUSMAG exerted influence over the actions of the Philippine military to such a degree that many considered the AFP to be merely a surrogate force of the United States.[42] Moreover, it also had a considerable role in training and directing the Philippine Constabulary. The JUSMAG also assisted the implementation of the 'Country Plan', an outline of US foreign policy objectives to be achieved in the Philippines. The team responsible for the implementation of a Country Plan at the highest level in a target state usually includes the heads of the USIS, USAID, the Peace Corps, the local CIA station and military attachés, all of whom are headed by the US Ambassador. In the Philippines, the JUSMAG directed the AFP's use of US military aid and ensured that the purposes of the MAA, in accordance with the Country Plan, were accomplished.

Other mechanisms of influence and control were the US-RP Mutual Defense Treaty (a Pacific expression of the US containment policy) signed in August 1951,[43] the Mutual Defence Board (MDB) which was designed to ensure smooth military relations between the United States and the Philippines, and the International Military Education and Training (IMET) programme, also managed by the JUSMAG, through which many Filipino soldiers were trained. Further, USAID administered 'Security Supporting Assistance' which provided the Philippines with non-lethal equipment such as helicopters, trucks, tractors and jeeps, as well as training. Such USAID programmes were under the jurisdiction of the US State Department.

Economic Control

The Reagan Administration also used considerable economic assistance to exert influence over the Philippine government. Much US economic assistance was channelled through the US-RP Military Bases Agreement which ostensibly was a two-way mechanism through which the Philippines could also exert pressure on the United States, as Marcos often did during the early 1980s (generally to secure increased aid rather than agitate for the removal of the US bases). Economic aid under the heading of 'foreign assistance' was also channelled through the MAA, USAID, the 'Food for Peace' programme and the Peace Corps.[44] Indirect influence was exerted through international organisations that were heavily supported and influenced by the United States such as the International Monetary Fund, the World Bank and the Asian Development Bank.[45]

Vigilante Control

There is very little, if any, direct evidence linking the Reagan Administration to the formation of the vigilante groups, or at least there is none that compares with that linking the US to the Contras. Nevertheless, significant circumstantial evidence exists to suggest that the Administration did indeed influence the formation and the nature of the activities of many of these groups. This is strongly evident, for example, in the known activities in the Philippines of several of those organisations identified earlier as agencies of US foreign policy, both in creating vigilante groups and then directing their pursuits.

In the first instance, abundant evidence links the formation, support and direction of many vigilante groups in the mid-1980s to the AFP and the Aquino government. Much of the initial stimulus for the government and the military's assistance in creating vigilante groups in 1986 stemmed from the continuing factionalism within the highly centralised AFP General Headquarters (GHQ) in Manila. Conflict between the RAM forces, Marcos's supporters and the pro-Ramos faction of the military had diverted GHQ's attention away from the CPP/NPA, thereby rendering its response to the insurgency ineffective. Armed Forces Chief of Staff Fidel Ramos had resisted those reforms that, while increasing the AFP's effectiveness in combating the CPP/NPA insurgency, would also diminish his own grip on military power. In response, to combat the NPA, local military commanders and political elites mainly in the insurgent strongholds of the Visayas and Mindanao were forced to devise *ad hoc* tactics based upon earlier AFP counterinsurgency tactics. Paramilitary groups were recruited from NPA returnees, criminals, religious fanatics and others to assist the local military in gathering intelligence and rooting out CPP/NPA suspects and perceived sympathisers from the local population. At times they even assisted in combat against the New People's Army. It was from these elements that vigilante groups such as the Alsa Masa grew. Ultimately, however, once General Ramos had consolidated his grip on power, he acknowledged the efficacy of the vigilante groups in counterinsurgency operations. The AFP then vigorously sponsored and even forced the formation of further groups throughout the Philippines.[46]

The evidence that implicates both the AFP and the government in the creation of the vigilantes is most compelling in relation to the Alsa Masa.[47] In 1987 and 1988, Philippine and international human rights groups, including Amnesty International and the Ramsay Clarke Team, investigated the Alsa Masa seeking to determine the nature and origins of the vigilante phenomenon.[48] The evidence obtained indicated that the AFP and in many cases local governments, directly armed, trained and funded the Alsa Masa and other groups.[49] The most notorious example of this was the role Lt Colonel Franco Calida, Commander of the Metropolitan District Command (METRODISCOM) in Davao City, and his command played in forming, arming, training and directing the Alsa Masa. The Philippine Alliance of Human Rights Advocates (PAHRA) extensively investigated this case as did other human rights groups based in Davao. PAHRA charged that the METRODISCOM and the local Philippine Constabulary unit armed and supported the Alsa Masa, and in response Lt Colonel Calida, on behalf of his command, openly admitted such activities.[50] Moreover, Calida's considerable role in organising and leading the Alsa Masa was evident in the recorded minutes of Alsa Masa meetings, indicating his command had an extensive and ongoing role in directing this group's activities.

At different times, the Aquino government and AFP officials also publicly expressed support for these multifarious groups. President Aquino, for example, publicly endorsed the formation of 'Nakasaka' (Nagkahiusang Katawhen Alarig Sa Kalinaw – United People for Peace) as a form of 'people power' and an effective weapon against communism. The Secretary of Local Government, Jaime Ferrer, openly campaigned in 1986 for the organisation of vigilante groups throughout the country. The Minister of National Defence, Rafael Ileto, also openly admitted his support for the more notorious Alsa Masa.[51] Moreover, the Department of Local Governments ordered all Governors in Mindanao to set up vigilante-type self-defence community-based units modelled on the Nakasaka by 31 May 1987.[52] Failure of the Governors to do so meant risking their positions. The Ramsay Clarke Team was also able to establish through interviews with military and government officials and testimonies from human rights organisations, that Philippine military officers and some government and business leaders had not only endorsed, but armed, organised and funded vigilante groups to form a nationwide vigilante movement.

It is also evident, however, that Aquino did not support the proliferation of the vigilantes to the same extent as the military. This suggests perhaps that the Reagan Administration and the Philippine military were closer in agreement over questions of counter-revolutionary strategy than either of them were with the new Government. This lack of consensus over the vigilantes was clearly demonstrated after Aquino's endorsement of the new Philippine Constitution in 1987. The Aquino government attempted to implement Article XVIII, Section 24, which sought the dismantling of the vigilante and other paramilitary groups in the wake of the much publicised human rights abuses attributed to these groups by such organisations as Amnesty International. The ban was followed by a second order providing for the formation of a single national police force (that would include the CHDF). However one month after the ratification of the Constitution, the Aquino government, under pressure from the military, backed down and endorsed the vigilantes. Further, the AFP Chief of Staff, General Fidel Ramos, sought an expanded role for these groups. Ramos justified their proliferation by invoking Marcos's Presidential Decree 1016, which had created the CHDF. He also authorised the arming of the vigilantes so they could 'support' the military's counterinsurgency activities. Other military officials also reacted strongly against Aquino's presidential directive. They believed the vigilantes were a key weapon in the fight against the CPP/NPA and were reportedly offended by Aquino's stance.[53] In the face of such pressure, President Aquino subsequently claimed that the directive did not aim for the immediate disbandment of the vigilantes. Shortly after she publicly endorsed the Nakasaka and approved military plans for special Nakasaka patrols in most villages throughout the archipelago. Moreover, the Philippine Departments of National Defence and Local Governments endorsed both the Nakasaka in Davao del Sur and the Alsa Masa in Davao City.

The government's backdown suggests two related realities about Philippine politics in the post-Marcos era. First, though Aquino may have intended to express some degree of autonomy in the handling of the insurgency, real power within the Philippines lay with the Ramos-led AFP. Second, the nature of the AFP's counter-revolutionary strategy in the post-Marcos era was strongly influenced by the United States via the extensive links the US retained with the Philippine military.

Aquino's subsequent attempts to woo the support of the military and importantly Ramos' 'pro-Constitution' faction thus ensured the continued existence of the vigilantes. The Government's endorsement of the vigilantes was a political trade-off for Ramos's support against the threat from within the armed forces posed by the increasingly alienated RAM and the lingering pro-Marcos factions.[54]

The Direct US Role

While the US could exert little direct control over the vigilantes once they were formed, considerable circumstantial evidence nevertheless suggests that US agencies not only assisted the formation of the vigilantes but even attempted to guide their activities. For example, the US-Philippine Fact Finding Mission to the Philippines in its May 1987 report argued that the establishment of a CIA branch of seventy agents in Mindanao in 1986, the increased spending of $10 million, and the appointment of twelve new agents for CIA covert operations in the Philippines, were all activities conducted in association with the formation of vigilante groups and these activities thus deserved further investigation. Moreover, evidence suggested that the CIA also assisted the CHDF's counterinsurgency operations. Ralph McGehee, a former CIA operative who participated in the notorious 'Operation Phoenix' in Vietnam (responsible for some 20,000 Vietnamese lives), claimed that distinct parallels existed between the counterinsurgency operations of the vigilantes and those conducted by the US during the Vietnam War. The vigilantes were 'like the provincial reconnaissance units which were actually assassination teams sent to "purify" villages of alleged Communists'.[55] Officers of the NPA General Staff also claimed that both the CIA and US Special Forces were directly involved in forming vigilante groups.[56] Other fact-finding missions similarly claimed that the CIA played an extensive role in forming these groups in 1986 and 1987. The director of PAHRA at that time, Arnel de Guzman argued:

The circumstantial evidence of CIA involvement was simply too big to be ignored. For example in Davao del Sur, ... Governor General Douglas Cagas who admitted [sic] and some American officials ... have signified their intention to finance the Nakasaka projects. In Davao del Sur, Governor Cagas and Provincial Commander Colonel

Magno started another vigilante group called 'Nakasaka' it stands for United Movement for Peace,' and it is supposed to be unarmed ... But you will see here in this picture [picture of three men with severed heads] that they are fully armed.[57]

Further, Lt Colonel Calida admitted he was trained by US Special Forces at one of the US bases in the Philippines and that he had retained links with these forces. He also claimed to have participated in two training courses in the United States, one at Fort Lee in Virginia, and the other at Fort Bragg in North Carolina. Calida boasted that he had met with US Embassy officials to discuss the 'similarities' between the formation of the Alsa Masa and the counterinsurgency strategies used in Central America. Reports of frequent meetings of a USIS representative, William Parker, with Calida in Davao City further indicate that direct links existed between US Administration officials and organisers of the vigilantes.[58] At different times the US Embassy also expressed its support for the growing vigilante movement. For example, before leaving his post in Manila, the US Ambassador Stephen Bosworth actually endorsed these groups as 'one of the fine ingredients of an effective counterinsurgency'.[59] Even Secretary of State George Shultz is reported to have given them his personal endorsement.[60]

Private Group Involvement

Many of the aforementioned private US and international organisations also contributed to civilianising the conflict in the Philippines by helping to form and train vigilante groups (as often claimed by the NPA and others).[61] After 1985 these private organisations, many identified earlier as LIC agencies in Central America, began to appear in the Philippines with increasing prominence. They included the Heritage Foundation, CAUSA International, the AAFLI (an arm of the AFL-CIO and claimed by many to be CIA supported)[62] working with its Philippines Trade Union Counterpart – the Trade Union Congress of the Philippines (TUCP), and the WACL.[63] Another 'Christian Front' group which worked with the TUCP and the AAFLI in organising vigilante groups was the 'Anti-Communist Crusade'. The 'Crusade' was sponsored by the Christian Anti-Communist Crusade, a Christian fundamentalist group allied with CAUSA. It conducted anti-communist seminars and, in cooperation with the Philippine Defence Ministry, helped forge a coalition group of vigilantes known as the 'National Coalition Against Communism'. Many of these private organisations, while involved in vigilante organising and recruitment activities, also cooperated with US Administration agencies such as the CIA, USAID and USIA. For example, in February 1987 the CIA reportedly sponsored a national conference of anti-communist groups at the TUCP's headquarters in Manila.[64]

Finally, the omnipresent, retired US Major-General John Singlaub, a prominent figure in the WACL and a familiar participant in the secret war in Central America, also appeared in the Philippines in 1986 and actively organised counterinsurgency activities from then onwards. To train the vigilantes, Singlaub recruited mercenaries as well as special warfare personnel on 'sheepdipping' operations. Moreover, he reportedly acted as a 'contract agent' in what the US Fact Finding team regarded as CIA operations.[65]

THE COLLECTIVE RESPONSE

To show that agencies previously identified as developing LIC elsewhere also operated in the Philippines does not prove that a coherent counter-revolutionary strategy was pursued in this country. Also, to demonstrate that the US exerted control over these agencies is one thing, but to establish that control was exerted in a way that reflects the emergence and operation of LIC is quite another. We must also not necessarily accept at face value the claims made by the NPA and others that LIC was 'applied' in the Philippines because of the obvious question of the reliability and objectivity of these sources. Nationalist opponents of the Philippine Government and the United States stood to increase their credibility and even popular support by arguing that the government was controlled by the US, which was actively and covertly intervening in the Philippines in pursuit of its own interests.

What can be established at this point with a minimum of extrapolation, however, is that similar determinants or preconditions existed in the Philippines to those from which LIC emerged in Nicaragua. Foremost among these was the significant threat to US interests posed by revolutionary nationalist forces, in this case by the CPP/NPA. US intervention in some form or another was a necessity due to the failure of the pro-US forces (the Marcos regime) to contain this threat. Nevertheless, as in Central America, the Vietnam Syndrome was an underlying, or at least implicit, constraint on direct US military intervention, as was rationalising and legitimising the defence of a corrupt regime which had distorted its defence capacity to protect the self-interest of the head of state. Other preconditions included the existence of civilian elements that could be shaped into paramilitary forces, as some already were, to combat the CPP/NPA and thereby civilianise the conflict. Further, many private US and other agencies similarly interested in combating the CPP/NPA were also present in the Philippines organising and working with these indigenous paramilitary groups to achieve this end. However, there existed still another major precondition, as yet to be examined. This was the presence of a legal opposition within the Philippines, led by Cory Aquino, which could be moulded into the 'democratic alternative', or to use LIC jargon the 'third way'. In the next chapter, I explore this opposition in the context of the political dimension of LIC's operation in the Philippines.

So far I have established the existence of similar conflict determinants in the Philippines to those in Nicaragua. However the most effective means of determining whether or not LIC developed in this 'target state' is to examine whether the collective activities of Reagan's 'agencies' formed a coherent conflict profile that conformed to the conceptual profile or footprint of LIC outlined earlier. My next chapter is devoted to this task.

8   THE COUNTER-REVOLUTIONARY PROFILE

Reagan's counter-revolutionary strand of LIC did in fact emerge in the Philippines by the end of 1987. In this chapter, I demonstrate this by tracing the profile of the US and Philippine governments' response to the CPP/NPA guerrilla insurgency and show how it replicates LIC's characteristic 'footprint'. Within this analysis, I examine the activities of those organisations identified earlier as US foreign policy agencies and measure how much they fitted in with the nature of LIC.

On balance this comparison of actions with blueprint reveals that Reagan's response to the threat of revolutionary nationalism in the Philippines was markedly similar to the way the Administration responded to the Sandinistas in Nicaragua. In the Philippines, as in Central America, Washington's emergent multidimensional approach was significantly privatised and civilianised. It also possessed a strong political/psychological theme with a marked reliance on initiated and self-initiating psyops. All the activities pursued by US agencies in the Philippines ultimately served the common LIC objective of the political/psychological defeat of the insurgency and the achievement of popular support for the US-backed 'third way'. In this case, it was the new government of Cory Aquino that was presented to the world as the democratic alternative to the extreme right and the insurgent forces of the extreme left (the CPP/NPA).

As suggested earlier, the activities of the US and its allied agencies in the Philippines, like in Nicaragua, can be loosely categorised into distinct but closely interrelated political/psychological, economic, military and civic action dimensions. As such, this analysis follows the same analytical framework, beginning with the political/psychological dimension of Reagan's response to the CPP/NPA insurgency.

THE POLITICAL/PSYCHOLOGICAL DIMENSION

In an attempt to politically discredit the revolutionary forces during the 1980s, US foreign policy agencies often portrayed the Philippines under both Marcos and Aquino as a fledgling Third World democracy besieged by Marxist terrorism. The Reagan Administration reinforced this view by arguing that the CPP/NPA forces were Soviet-backed and equatable to the Khmer Rouge.[1] Concomitantly, in official announcements, press releases and in publications of such groups as the Heritage Foundation and the Committee on the Present Danger (through the CPD's journal *Commentary*), the case was thereby made for expanded US military and economic aid.

Within the Philippines, however, the Reagan Administration's political/psychological approach to defeating the insurgency was far more complex. As noted earlier, after Benigno Aquino was assassinated, Washington pressured Marcos to implement reform and in particular hold elections to revitalise the regime's image and credibility and thus enhance its capacity to combat the 'hearts and minds' campaign waged by the CPP/NPA. Led by the movement's political arm, the National Democratic Front (NDF), the CPP/NPA was using Maoist united front tactics in a very effective political campaign to win support for the revolution. However, the Reagan Administration believed that a significant proportion of the movement's rank and file actually lacked an ideological commitment to communism and that presidential elections would undercut support for the insurgency. Richard Armitage argued, for example, that a 'free and fair election' would blunt the momentum of the CPP/NPA, which thrived on the argument that the 'political situation' and the 'environment' were both repressive under the Marcos regime.[2] Moreover, if the Filipino people considered the elections to be fair and democratic, the CPP/NPA would be delivered a telling blow. If Marcos could demonstrate his democratic credentials, the credibility of the revolution would be damaged, and the CPP/NPA would be denied 'a major element in their proselytising campaign'.[3] If, on the other hand, the elections were popularly perceived to be corrupt and unfair, this would be of enormous advantage to the insurgency. This latter scenario was to be avoided at all costs.

Pressure on Marcos to hold presidential elections in 1985 came from both the US Congress and the Reagan Administration, using US aid as leverage. For these elections to be popularly recognised as honest and legitimate, Washington believed that the AFP would have to refrain from intervening. It would have to project the image of being 'non-partisan' and merely concerned with providing 'the environment of security which allows the Philippine people to express their will'.[4]

President Marcos ultimately accommodated the United States by holding elections on 6 February 1986, a concession that was the result of the 'reform or else' pressure applied by Washington. However, military reform was not undertaken, with Marcos intent on maintaining his support base within the military's higher ranks.[5] Without this compliance, Washington's attempts to achieve stability in the Philippines and the question of continued US support for the Marcos Government thus depended heavily on whether the election would be fairly conducted. If the election was ultimately proven to be corrupt, the Reagan Administration would be under pressure to re-examine its options to achieve acceptable political, military and economic reform. Some of this pressure would stem from the US military itself, which was convinced that the insurgency would continue to grow if Marcos stayed in power. If this were to occur, one possible option open to Reagan was to abandon Marcos altogether.

The Installation of the Aquino Government as the 'Third Way'

As it transpired, Marcos attempted to distort the election results and hold onto power illegally in the face of widespread public and international opposition. In response, the US, to ensure that the CPP/NPA or a nationalist and hence possibly anti-US regime did not seize power as a result of the ensuing domestic backlash, pursued the LIC tactic of promoting a palatable democratic alternative. The Reagan Administration withdrew its support for Marcos (despite lingering personal ties between President Reagan, Mrs Reagan and the Marcoses that delayed this action),[6] and thus swung its full support behind the installation of Cory Aquino. The new president would head a new 'democratic' government that would actively engage in 'nation building'.

While it is not suggested that the US was primarily responsible for the Aquino government's assumption of power, it is clear nevertheless that Aquino's victory did result in part from US pressure on Marcos to democratise the country. In the wake of the Benigno Aquino assassination and the exposure of the regime's determination to hold on to power at any cost, Washington had distanced itself somewhat from the Marcos Government. Soon after the assassination, Reagan abruptly and pointedly cancelled a scheduled presidential visit to the Philippines, a move recognised by many as the beginning of the deterioration of relations between the two governments.

When viewed from an LIC perspective, it can be argued that the pressure Washington exerted on Marcos to introduce democratic reforms was an integral part of an enduring campaign to establish a 'legitimate and viable alternative' to the revolution in the Philippines; this campaign constituted an essential strand of the nation-building component of low intensity conflict.

The timely defection of General Ramos, Defence Minister Juan Ponce Enrile and the 'pro-reform' RAM forces, not only assisted the change of government, but can also be construed as serving LIC objectives. While Enrile and Ramos were obviously pursuing their own political agendas, both their destinies and the pursuit of US objectives coincided for a short period, thereby ensuring the demise of President Marcos in the relatively bloodless military coup of February 1986.[7] Importantly, however, this defection also enabled the Armed Forces of the Philippines (AFP) to establish its popular image as a force for democracy in the initial post-Marcos years, an image considered essential for waging LIC.

Pressure for the Adoption of an LIC Approach?

Once Corazon Aquino was in power, it is clear the Reagan Administration pressured the new government to pursue LIC activities that at times conflicted with the notions of democratic reform that Aquino and others in her government believed to be necessary. Richard Armitage, for example, argued that the Aquino Government had to accept 'the need for a total integrated counterinsurgency package' which included political, economic, social and military components.[8] According to Armitage, the government's counterinsurgency plan also had to integrate military operations 'with the programs of civil authorities',[9] which reflected Washington's desire for the counter-revolutionary forces in the Philippines to place an emphasis on civic action. Further, supported by the more pro-American and pro-'constitutional' elements of the military under Ramos's leadership, the US pressured Aquino to exclude all left-wing elements from her government. While President Aquino achieved a high media profile in the United States and enjoyed strong support within the Philippines, the US exerted diplomatic pressure and used economic and military aid in a 'carrot and stick' approach to achieve its ends.[10] The Reagan Administration was worried about the centre-left forces behind Aquino which continued to agitate for labour rights and opposed the presence of the US bases. As a consequence, it embarked on a propaganda campaign to generate anti-communist hysteria and rumours about a coup in order to isolate these elements. Some of the individuals involved in this 'psyops' were connected to LIC in Central America including John Singlaub and Ray Cline (who had a long association with the CIA). Among other activities these individuals, prior to the aborted November 1986 coup attempt, were involved in incessant 'coup talk' with Enrile and Ramos in what amounted to an exercise of coercive diplomacy, threatening the Aquino Government with destruction unless it complied with US wishes.[11] Simultaneously, the Philippine military pressured Aquino to adopt a more hard-line, anti-guerrilla campaign; in part, the emergence of the vigilante groups was a further manifestation of this pressure. In this manner, the 'democratic alternative', underscored and prodded by an aggressive military, steadily implemented the LIC approach recommended in the Reagan Administration's National Security Study Directive that was completed in November 1984 and adopted as policy in January 1985.

Aquino's introduction, with US backing, of immediate political reforms to establish the democratic credentials of her government was also a fundamental part of the LIC operation within the Philippines. A Constitutional Commission was formed and a new provisional constitution was designed to protect civil rights and make all presidential legislation subject to review. Moreover, the Government sought to depoliticise the Supreme Court and restore basic democratic processes including the writ of habeas corpus and due process. In March 1986, Aquino announced a timetable to return the country to full constitutional government, and on the 18th of that month she emphasised the preservation of human rights by appointing a 'Presidential Committee on Human Rights' (PCHR) with powers to investigate abuses committed by the military and to recommend actions as a result. This committee was headed by Senator Jose Diokno and included representatives from the military and major human rights organisations such as Task Force Detainees of the Philippines (TFDP) and the Free Legal Assistance Group (FLAG).[12] In addition, a significant number of political prisoners were released, reported by Amnesty international to be as many as 563.[13] Later, in accordance with the 1987 Constitution, a Constitutional Commission on Human Rights (CHR) was established (the PCHR was formally dissolved by Executive Order No. 163 on 5 May 1987). The CHR was given a large mandate to investigate alleged abuses by both the military and opposition, though, like the PCHR, the CHR was empowered only to investigate these allegations with the prosecution of human rights violations left to either civil or military courts. While these measures appeared to be aimed at 're-democratising' the Philippines, from an LIC perspective collectively they served to legitimate and enhance the appeal of the democratic alternative.

The Ceasefire

Even Aquino's own attempt to pursue a genuine peace initiative that could accommodate all sides was thwarted by LIC. In 1986, the Aquino Government entered into negotiations with the National Democratic Front and forged a 60-day ceasefire agreement with the NPA beginning on 10 December. However, while President Aquino desired to end the insurgency and somehow accommodate the CPP/NPA, the ceasefire received only mixed backing from the Reagan Administration. It was also opposed by many hardliners in the Philippine military, as well as officials in the Philippine Ministry of Defence who perceived that a CPP/NPA influence in the new democratic process would threaten any attempts to politically discredit the insurgency. It is in this context that the military's involvement in the Mendiola Bridge massacre of 22 January 1987 should therefore be viewed.[14] In this incident, soldiers fired on unarmed peasants protesting about the lack of progress on land reform programs. The peasants were generally supporters of a peasant organisation known as the Kilusang Magbubukid ng Pilipinas (KMP), and 78 of their number were wounded and 19 killed. The incident, which effectively destroyed the ceasefire, elicited the following comment from an NPA cadre: 'We, the Filipinos will observe that Aquino does not really mean change. She just continues Marcos rule [sic] – I think she had no choice because of the Army. The Mendiola Bridge massacre turned many against her ... it showed she was just like Marcos.'[15]

Considering the views of the ceasefire's opponents, this apparently premeditated massacre was an attempt by the military to rekindle the insurgency and thereby end the ceasefire negotiations.[16] The CPP/NPA at the time of the ceasefire was gaining positive press coverage, even 'cult' status among the Filipino middle class, and achieving significant political gains. This made the CPP/NPA harder to discredit as its growing association with the Aquino Government saw it increasingly perceived by the public as part of the 'democratic alternative'. The ceasefire thus threatened to isolate the military's hardliners. It also held out the prospect of a political settlement of the conflict, which in making concessions to Philippine nationalism might again place US interests in the country at risk.

The ceasefire question posed quite a dilemma for Reagan. The US State Department was generally supportive of the Aquino strategy as it underlined the reformist image of the new government, but the Department of Defense and close supporters of President Reagan considered a negotiated settlement dangerous.[17] In this respect the Mendiola Bridge massacre fortuitously resolved this dilemma by effectively destroying any prospect of negotiations.

Despite disagreement over the ceasefire question, the short-lived ceasefire itself can nevertheless be construed to have actually served LIC political objectives. Like the Duarte Government in El Salvador, the Aquino Government, by negotiating with the insurgent forces, demonstrated that it was open to reconciliation and further reform. When the ceasefire collapsed on 30 January 1987, and President Aquino subsequently declared (in familiar LIC rhetoric) 'total war' against the insurgency, it was apparent that the Government's initial pursuit of negotiations had seriously eroded support for the revolution – again one of LIC's fundamental goals.[18]

Self-Initiating Psyops

Close analysis of the counter-revolutionary conflict in the Philippines in the 1980s also reveals the operation of many self-initiating psyops, including the ceasefire itself. These activities presented the target population with a desired positive image of the new government and a negative image of the CPP/NPA. In this respect, perhaps the major self-initiating psyops within the Philippines was the rapid formation of the vigilantes. The proliferation of these groups appeared a manifestation of mass popular support for the Aquino Government, and an example of an ongoing mobilisation of the Filipino people in a 'people power' revolution, this time against the CPP/NPA.

Other groups and professional organisations which conducted self-initiating psyops both during and after the Marcos period included elements of the Philippine trade union movement. For example, the Asian American Free Labour Institute (AAFLI), funded by both the US Agency for International Development (USAID) and the National Endowment for Democracy (NED) (and an arm of the AFL-CIO, a major LIC agency active in Central America), conducted programmes through the Trade Union Congress of the Philippines to organise anti-communist trade union groups and organisations 'in an effort to sustain their faith in the democratic center'.[19] Emphasis was placed on encouraging free trade unionism and organising workers and farmers in areas of communist activity into anti-communist groups to counteract leftist union groups, in particular the trade union front known as the May First Movement (KMU). Producers' and consumers' collectives were also organised and assisted in these areas.[20] The AAFLI identified its programmes as more than just traditional trade union activities. Charles Gray, Director of the AFL-CIO, openly admitted that the AAFLI's grassroots activities had political implications in that its programmes were 'conducted in just those areas where the Communists are most active' and were designed to give workers an 'immediate alternative to despair and violence'. Gray argued that the AAFLI's programmes demonstrated that democratic institutions could 'change the dismal status quo within a stable social and cultural framework'. This was considered important in combating the left-wing trade union fronts that would, for example, exploit the problem of landless agricultural workers. Gray argued that if these landless elements were armed with new skills with which to earn a living they would form democratic unions and organisations to 'defend their homes and their livelihood from NPA shakedown artists posing as tax collectors'.[21] Gray was in a sense admitting that the AAFLI used political and economic development programmes, which in reality were psyops, to convince the local people to reject and combat communism. Moreover, while admitting that its programmes were not a substitute for a 'full-fledged' economic development programme, the AAFLI, by claiming to be directly assisting the trade unions, farmers' organisations and consumer cooperatives in the 'front line of the democratic struggle in the Philippines',[22] also revealed that its major objectives were political rather than economic.

Initiated Psyops

US foreign policy agencies also conducted initiated psyops in the Philippines and, as could be expected, waged an anti-CPP/NPA propaganda campaign both internationally and within the United States. Moreover, many of the psyops practices developed in Central America were used in the Philippines (particularly after Marcos's downfall in 1986) to generate popular support for the Manila Government and a negative image of the CPP/NPA. The propaganda campaign had two basic messages, both of which obscured other more complex and relevant issues such as the need for land reform. First, the insurgency was reducible to godless communism that threatened Aquino's fledgling democracy. Second, the Filipino people were rising up *en masse* against this terrorist organisation.

Within the US, agents of this 'perception management' campaign were first the Executive itself and the USIA through which the Administration pursued anti-CPP/NPA propaganda, and second, many private US organisations such as the CPD through its journal *Commentary*, and the Heritage Foundation through its regular publications. Other organisations agitating against the CPP/NPA included the AFL-CIO and international lobby groups and activist movements such as the Christian Anti-Communist Crusade, the World Anti-Communist League and many others.

Collectively, these agencies presented Aquino as the real democratic alternative in the Philippines and sought US public support for the Government's struggle against this 'dire' communist threat. At the forefront of this campaign, the White House itself claimed that the Aquino Government had 'made progress restoring democracy and laying the foundation for economic growth' but that it also faced 'major political, security and economic challenges'. The Administration declared it would use all its available 'tools' to help this 'important Pacific ally' counter the threat of a 'virulent internal communist insurgency' and strengthen the operation of democratic government.[23]

US agencies also attempted to discredit all active and possible sources of support for the revolution. The Heritage Foundation and the Christian Anti-Communist Crusade, as in Nicaragua, waged a strident campaign against Church and other organisations deemed sympathetic to the insurgent movement. Their targets included the Nobel Prize-nominated Task Force Detainees in the Philippines, which they accused of being a communist front. The Heritage Foundation also demanded a Congressional investigation of US organisations it claimed were working for the CPP and the NDF, and claimed that the latter organisation was trying to gain influence within the European Parliament.[24]

Other familiar initiated psyops waged by these groups within the US included efforts to dispel the popular image the NPA had gained as the 'Nice People Around' by portraying them as a repeat performance of Pol Pot's Khmer Rouge. This propaganda campaign subsequently formed the basis for extensive public lobbying within the US for increased military aid for Aquino.

Though the vigilantes propagated their own anti-communist propaganda, these groups were themselves an effective tool in the 'perception management' campaign pursued both in the US and the Philippines. Presented locally and internationally as a popular expression of the people's power revolution, the vigilantes were proclaimed by some of these agencies to be the Philippine equivalent of 'freedom fighters for democracy'.[25] Using the vigilantes as an example, the Filipino people were presented as spontaneously rising up against the CPP/NPA, a claim reinforced by Aquino's attempts to popularise the Nakasaka as a group upholding the 'EDSA' (February uprising)[26] tradition of pursuing political change peacefully (even though the Nakasaka was armed and had been involved in many violent incidents).

Propaganda was thus an essential component of initiated psyops conducted within the Philippines. Organisations waging direct propaganda campaigns in the cities and rural areas of the archipelago included CAUSA, the Heritage Foundation and the CIA. Film nights, conferences and other presentations were conducted propagating the message that the CPP/NPA were foreign backed, anti-Christian, and terrorist.[27] US agencies also recruited for the vigilantes forming anti-communist networks that included businesspeople, media figures, academics, journalists, military officers, planters, trade unions, religious groups and others. At this point, the activities of the omnipresent John Singlaub deserve special mention. In cities near the US bases, Singlaub was heavily involved in organising right-wing business groups to oppose leftist labour unions and activists and public demonstrations against the bases. Using the cover of hunting for General

Yamashita's lost treasure, he held many meetings with Defence Minister Juan Ponce Enrile and Luis Villareal, Chief of the National Intelligence Co-Ordinating Authority (NICA). Singlaub was trying to sell arms and equipment that was useful in counterinsurgency operations and even offered financial support to anti-communist sugar planters on the island of Negros.[28] Many rightist politicians, military officials and business leaders admitted to meetings with Singlaub: Alberto 'Magg' Maguidad, a prominent vigilante leader from Tuguegaroa, admitted that his group had the backing of Singlaub and the World Anti-Communist League.[29]

The US Information Service (USIS) was also heavily involved in propaganda activities within the Philippines, sponsoring anti-communist lectures and distributing literature of the same tone to top-ranking students who were then encouraged to also form anti-communist organisations. To popularise the US presence in the Philippines, the USIS executed a mass public relations campaign through the printed media and the Voice of America.[30] It disseminated printed audio and visual materials to influential persons and groups, as well as schools and libraries throughout the country.[31] The major theme of its campaign was that the Philippines was threatened with 'Soviet aggression' and in the absence of the US bases it would face economic ruin and a communist takeover. The USIS reported secret visits of foreign submarines and deliveries of arms for the NPA while virulently attacking anti-base activists, politicians and organisations generally opposed to the US presence. It also assisted the AFP's own propaganda campaigns in which the military presented films and conducted 'dialogue sessions' pursuing the familiar 'Khmer Rouge' theme to shatter any romantic notions about the CPP/NPA struggle among the Philippine urban middle class, especially the young.

CAUSA – the Confederation of the Associations for the Unity of the Societies of the Americas – was particularly active in these operations, combining humanitarian aid and construction programmes with its own intensive propaganda exercises. These paralleled US government activities in Central America, which, as the Clarke Report argued, suggested covert US funding. CAUSA materials were freely available from the USIS and similar literature was distributed through the USIS library.[32] The Clarke Fact Finding Team also had evidence linking the activities of General Singlaub, the CIA, the NED, the Philippines Military, the TUCP (formerly linked to Marcos), media personnel and radio stations (such as DYCA) with CAUSA activities in forming vigilante groups and waging anti-communist psyops. All in all, such evidence suggested that these activities were part of a larger coordinated effort to build a nationwide, right-wing network covertly supported by the United States, as was also claimed by a Filipino presidential adviser.[33]

Sectors of the Philippine media were essential to this mass propaganda campaign and under close supervision by either the military or various vigilante groups. Major newspapers and radio stations disseminated anti-communist articles while downplaying military and vigilante atrocities and human rights abuses. For example, much publicity was given to 'discoveries' by the military of mass graves of alleged victims of NPA atrocities (later rumoured to be vigilante victims). [34] NPA guerrillas were also labelled in media reports as 'criminal elements', or in familiar LIC jargon as 'terrorists'. In contrast, the vigilantes were often referred to as 'God-fearing freedom fighters' promoting democracy. Many employees of local media organisations were themselves often prominent members of vigilante groups, such as the high-profile radio announcer Jun Pala who continually waged a pro-Alsa Masa campaign on Radio DXOW in Davao City. [35]

The CIA's role in these psyops was extensive. The Clark Report claimed that the agency was heavily involved in massive media and propaganda operations centered around a cadre of recruited members of the country's media. This network of media people worked closely with 'agents of influence' within the military and in political, labour, academic, religious and cultural organisations to generate anti-communist hysteria among the Filipinos. The report also claimed the CIA used stories of Soviet ships 'depositing weapons at isolated beaches', claims of NPA assassination lists, and details of purported NPA massacres to spread panic and forge public acceptance of the adoption of repressive counterinsurgency legislation and operations. [36]

Still other agencies were involved in these initiated psyops. The Asia Foundation, considered a CIA and State Department funding conduit, financed the electronic media, and particularly the Catholic-run Radio Veritas, which played a key role in organising the mass demonstrations that toppled Marcos. [37] US conventional military forces actually waged what amounted to initiated psyops themselves by conducting war games and joint exercises in the Philippines during the national elections in 1987. With over 20,000 US naval personnel on Philippine soil, these 'shows of strength' paralleled similar demonstrations of US force in the Nicaraguan context. [38] In addition, the US military pursued initiated psyops in other forms by undertaking civic action programmes in the areas around the bases and elsewhere in the Philippines (this US role will be examined separately below).

Religion

In the Philippines, the claim that the CPP/NPA was a 'godless' movement was a particularly important rallying point around which many vigilante groups formed. [39] Such accusations were indicative of the way religious beliefs and values were injected into the conflict in ways reminiscent of the Central American experience. In the Philippines, religion was used extensively as a psyops tool with which to mobilise the population against the revolution. Bimboy Penaranda of EPIC claimed, for example, that the military 'has been able to win over the fanatical religious grass roots cults in the Philippines by talking about the godlessness of communism ... They were able to create a fanatical response from these groups – of which there are many ... and so the NPA has to deal with these groups.' [40]

Operating inside the predominantly Catholic Philippines, the military and other counterinsurgency agencies sought to erode the movement's mass support base particularly by targeting people who were perhaps more 'religious' than 'politicised'. Moreover, the military encouraged the vigilantes to attack sympathetic or pro-revolutionary elements within the Church, as well as Church-based organisations and other groups attempting to reform the living and working conditions of the poor. Because they generally challenged the status quo, these reform groups were deemed subversive and therefore supporters of the NPA. In Davao for example, Lt Colonel Calida accused three prominent religious congregations: the Assumption Sisters, the Redemptorist Fathers and the Carmelite Sisters of stockpiling arms for the New People's Army. These groups were subsequently harassed by the Alsa Masa and persecuted by the local press.

Terror

Counterinsurgency agencies in the Philippines widely used terror tactics as part of their psyops to try and destroy the mass base of the insurgency. A NPA cadre claimed, 'In Davao, the first area they set up the vigilantes ... our sources said that if you do not join this vigilante group your house will be crossed [a cross marked on the door], which means that you are a communist or a communist supporter of the NPA and you will be liquidated.'[41]

The vigilantes waged large-scale terror campaigns in both urban and rural areas against suspected communists. Progressive elements of the Church and Church-related agencies, union members and labour leaders, aid, relief, and other community workers were regularly harassed, tortured and even executed (often by such grossly inhuman means as beheading) with what appeared to be the tacit approval of the military.[42] Human rights organisations, including the Philippine Alliance of Human Rights Advocates and the Ecumenical Movement for Justice and Peace (EMJP), investigated the gross abuses committed by vigilante groups. The Presidential Committee on Human Rights which many of these groups petitioned in 1987, subsequently recommended to President Aquino that the vigilante groups be 'strictly restricted to their respective neighborhoods ... unarmed, and their recruitment ... clearly voluntary'.[43] However, in an apparent public relations manoeuvre to foster the impression that the groups were being disbanded, the Government kept them in existence by merely renaming them.

By waging what was little more than a campaign of terror, the military, assisted by the vigilantes, was thus able to adopt a total war approach in areas of strong CPP/NPA influence. This campaign allowed no neutral ground. Lt Colonel Calida was reported as saying at a meeting of the Alsa Masa on 6 March 1987 that the war in Davao was a war between communism and democracy: 'If they want communism, they should be in Russia! Neutrality is not accepted here!'[44] Whole populations were directed either to support or join vigilante groups such as the Alsa Masa to 'protect themselves' from communism, or be branded as communist sympathisers and be dealt with accordingly. Other means were also used to discredit the insurgent movement, including using alleged NPA 'surrenderees' to denounce the CPP/NPA,[45] and blaming the insurgent forces for the often forced evacuation of civilians from their *barrios* (villages). This tactic, Calida claimed, was designed 'to move the people to join us and reject the enemy, the Commie rebels'.[46] Moreover, the military also encouraged bounty hunting as further incentive for civilians to expose, capture or eliminate supporters of the revolution.[47]

The vigilantes' and the military's terror tactics, quite apart from indiscriminate killings, also involved death-squad activities. Following their rapid proliferation in 1986, the vigilantes effectively replaced the AFP and the discredited CHDF as the major vehicle for the physical elimination of prominent targets among the legal opposition as well as potential opponents of the Government, a widespread practice under Marcos known as 'salvaging'. A number of observers and human rights organisations claimed that some vigilantes were trained in assassination techniques by the CIA and as well as other 'private' agencies.[48] Such assassination operations were often publicly justified as necessary to combat the CPP/NPA's 'godless terrorism' manifest in many attacks made by NPA 'Sparrow' units, the revolutionary movement's own assassination squads.

Psyops in LIC 'Total War' Strategy

What is quite significant when we examine the counter-revolutionary conflict in the Philippines is that the initiated psyops pursued in this country collectively were aimed at mobilising the population to actively oppose the CPP/NPA insurgency, a fundamental element of the 'total war' tactic of LIC. President Aquino articulated this total war policy in March 1987, and it was vigorously pursued by the military, the vigilantes, and right-wing groups and religious organisations ranging from the Opus Dei to fundamentalist anti-communist groups. Emulating aspects of Maoist 'people's war', these groups sought to mobilise popular support for the democratic alternative. Military victory would be easier to achieve if the mass support base of the CPP/NPA revolution was eroded. Human rights abuses were also easier to justify if portrayed as a consequence of a popular people's war against the terrors of communism. Further, vigilante operations served the military purpose of driving the CPP/NPA fighters and organisers into the countryside away from their bases in the urban areas and local town centres. It was thought that with the 'fish' thus separated from the 'sea', the CPP/NPA insurgents would prove easier targets for large-scale military operations.

After 1985, the civic action undertaken by the AFP was an initiated psyops tool to win the local people's support in contested areas and hence create a total war environment. While the military pursued other psyops to foster political allegiance to the government, the AFP's role in these 'special warfare' activities, however, should also be interpreted, in part, as an expression of the factionalism and continuing power struggle within the military's high command during this period. The struggle was primarily between Enrile, RAM supporters, pro-Marcos forces and the Ramos faction (mainly drawn from the Constabulary). And it was often manifest in periodic coup attempts, which subsequently rendered the AFP ineffective in waging conventional operations in the provinces.[49] As indicated earlier, Chief of Staff General Ramos's grip on power depended on the continued existence of a highly centralised GHQ and his control of the more politicised Constabulary. Ramos thus actively encouraged the military to pursue special warfare against the insurgency while resisting attempts by his rival, Secretary of Defence Rafael Ileto, to decentralise the AFP and conduct more conventional search-and-destroy operations against the NPA in the provinces.[50] This issue was finally resolved in January 1988 when President Aquino forced Secretary Ileto's resignation and General Ramos was appointed in his place. However, even in his new role, Ramos kept his factional favourites in place in the GHQ and maintained his control of counterinsurgency operations. Ramos continued to resist committing his resources to conventional military campaigns against NPA main-force formations as this required loosening his political hold over the AFP. Instead he pursued a small-unit civic-action cum paramilitary programme that actually added legitimacy to the spread of local vigilante organisations.

Nevertheless, in pursuing these small-unit tactics against the New People's Army, the small Special Operations Teams (SOTs), often supported by vigilantes, attacked the insurgent movement's mass base by occupying many pro-NPA *barrios* and then implementing a combination of civic action and law-and-order campaigns. In this manner, these forces attempted to win the hearts and minds of the people while simultaneously eliminating NPA regulars and prominent supporters through death-squad activities similar to LIC operations conducted elsewhere such as in El Salvador.

THE ECONOMIC DIMENSION

Analysis of the Philippine counter-revolutionary conflict profile also reveals an economic dimension that closely accords with LIC. With Aquino as the democratic alternative in place, the third way, if considered in LIC terms, had to be made economically viable to maintain its credibility. Reasoning that poverty bred communism, the Reagan Administration increased its aid programs to the Philippines and pressured Aquino to implement both economic and land reform as a way of reinforcing the government's legitimacy and undercutting support for the insurgency.[51] The US Administration, along with the expanded involvement of the US Export-Import Bank and the Overseas Private Investment Corporation, also attempted to invigorate the Philippine private sector with trade and investment measures including new agreements on the Generalised Trade System preference and textile quotas.[52]

In 1986, the United States granted a supplemental aid package to the Philippines that was $150 million above normal levels of assistance to offset the severe economic crisis facing the Aquino Government. The aid took the form of increased economic and security assistance to support economic reform and recovery in the country. In total, this meant some $500 million of economic assistance and $100 million in military assistance, 90 per cent of which was made available on a grant basis to avoid further strain on the country's external debt.[53] This aid recovery programme was implemented mainly through USAID which coordinated its operations with several international funding agencies and donor groups, many of whom were involved in Central America.[54] As the Deputy Assistant Secretary of State for East Asia and Pacific Affairs observed, the US recovery programme was only one part of a multilateral effort which included the International Monetary Fund, the World Bank, the International Finance Corporation, the Asian Development Bank, Japan and other donor countries.[55] The economic package contained several key components, including an additional $100 million in Economic Support Funds (ESF) in addition to that provided via the 1983 US-Philippines Bases Agreement review, and separate from the overall five-year pledge of ESF assistance made as a consequence of that review.[56] It also included provisions for increased food assistance and an increase in 'people to people' programmes for health, infant care and food assistance.

USAID translated much economic assistance into electrification and rural projects, which were part of its Integrated Development Strategy that included credit support infrastructure, farm extension, legal assistance and the development of rural industries. These aid and assistance programs were concentrated in the areas of most revolutionary unrest, indicating that USAID priorities were determined more by political than economic considerations, though the two are usually closely related. For its part, the Aquino government promised land reform but was hindered in part by squabbling among government administrators. In July 1987, Aquino signed Executive Order No. 229 on land reform, committing her government to a five-year programme to redistribute the ownership of much of the Philippines' agricultural land. However these measures, which covered all private and public agricultural lands regardless of tenurial arrangements or type of crop, were vigorously opposed by conservative landowners, some of whom were represented in the Philippine Congress.

THE MILITARY DIMENSION

It is difficult to assess the extent of LIC's development in the Philippines purely by determining the extent to which the United States responded militarily to the insurgency. The strategy certainly incorporated military action, but then so do most revolutionary and counter-revolutionary strategies. More decisive indicators of LIC are the relative priority given to military action, the nature of the military objective sought in terms of political and psychological impact on the enemy, and the nature of the agency pursuing that objective. To be expected in the Philippines, the major agency pursuing military objectives was the AFP. Close examination of the AFP's role in the conflict and the transformation the military underwent after Marcos's fall indicates that by the end of 1987 it was fully engaged in LIC.

The Reform of the Armed Forces of the Philippines

After Marcos's overthrow, the AFP was reformed into a more professional and effective military force to combat the insurgency. This in itself may not appear unusual, but the nature of this reform and the AFP's consequent military initiatives, as well as those of Reagan's other agencies in the Philippines, exhibited several characteristics in common with LIC military initiatives in Central America.

The Reagan Administration was aware that the AFP was badly in need of reform as early as 1984. Under Marcos, the AFP had degenerated into a force with little interest in fighting the revolution. It was too preoccupied with internal factional power struggles and had accommodated Marcos's apparent security paranoia too well. In March 1985, Richard Armitage argued that the AFP needed to be professionalised if it was to defeat the insurgency. The battlefield approach of the AFP therefore had to be reformed because, as Richard Armitage argued, at 'the end of the day' the New People's Army would still have to be defeated on the battlefield.[57] More emphasis had to be placed on training, even though the US had already been providing considerable funding for training purposes since 1981. High standards of discipline needed to be reinstated, adequate leadership developed, pay levels increased to eliminate corruption, and troop morale improved, particularly following the military's embarrassing involvement in the Aquino assassination. Armitage also observed that in order to improve its image among the population, the AFP needed to reduce civilian abuse and engender closer cooperation with the Church. The counterinsurgency effort also needed to be integrated at provincial and regional levels and the AFP's procurement procedures needed reform. Failure to implement such reforms would enable the insurgency to 'end democracy in the Philippines, force the removal of our defense facilities, and seriously damage our regional interests in Asia'.[58]

With Marcos's departure in February 1986, military reform was undertaken in a number of key areas. The AFP was renamed the New Armed Forces of the Philippines (NAFP) in an attempt to improve its image. However, those more substantial reform measures undertaken included removing pro-Marcos politicised elements from the NAFP leadership to increase the military's professionalism. Though Minister of Defence Juan Ponce Enrile and Chief of Staff 'Eddy' Ramos retained their positions in 1986, all previous deputy ministers and 24 'overstaying' generals were replaced by officers whose professionalism and leadership were widely respected. NAFP officers previously assigned to the management of commercial activities, a widespread practice during the Marcos era, were returned to military units. Attempts were also made within the military to generate greater loyalty to the nation, and on the instigation of Ramos and Enrile, military panels began investigations of military corruption and abuse. Other reform measures included placing a greater emphasis on the training of the NAFP's rank and file, and the other 'official' security forces (including the CHDF). Supporting this retraining process, in 1986, US Military Training Teams (usually composed of Special Operations Forces) focused on training the Philippine military in the use of helicopters and armoured vehicles. The Green Berets and other SOFs, comprising three MTTs permanently stationed in the US bases, also conducted training in counterinsurgency, weapons, demolition, intelligence, communications and medicine.[59] Discipline was enforced, which enhanced the NAFP's pride and improved its reputation and image. Attention was also paid to lesser questions of military bearing, including the wearing of 'crisp' uniforms and the adoption of a business-like approach to routine duties. Similar attention was devoted to eliminating the corruption that was widely acknowledged to exist in the CHDF, and to improving its discipline and image and, importantly, curbing its human rights abuses. Moreover, on General Ramos's direction, the CHDF was reduced in strength and its command transferred from local authorities to the NAFP.

An increase in military aid and funding, via the Military Assistance Program (MAP), was essential in reforming the Philippine military into an effective instrument with which to combat the insurgency. In 1986, the Philippines received a total of US $105.1 million in military assistance, more than double the amount granted in 1985. A sum of US $2.25 million was also allocated to the International Military Education and Training (IMET) programme, through which NAFP officers were trained at Fort Bragg and elsewhere in the United States.[60] As Armitage argued, these funds were not to be used for 'expensive high tech weapons systems', but for weapons and equipment that could enhance the basic ability of the Philippine armed forces to combat the insurgency. The procurement thus concentrated on communications, transportation and logistical requirements, to enhance the military's ability to 'shoot, move and communicate' and thereby enable the NAFP to wage 'counter-guerrilla' warfare more effectively.[61] This meant that the military would pay less attention to preparations for repelling 'invaders' and more to increasing internal security. In addition, a greater emphasis was placed on engineering equipment and the procurement of bulldozers for the 'NAFP's Civic Action programme'. However, increased attention was also given to the needs of the individual soldier, including new uniforms, boots, and medical equipment. For FY 1986, the Reagan Administration offered an additional US $50 million in MAP and proposed 'that the military component of the FY.87 aid request be converted to all MAP funding, for a total of $100 m [million]. And ... all FMS credits for FY.85 and FY.86 be converted to MAP [approximately $29 million].' The Administration argued, '... we believe that the additional $50 million for FY.86 will be a good first step toward helping the NAFP achieve a reasonable state of combat effectiveness'.[62] In FY 1987, the US Congress, in response to requests by the Reagan Administration, removed restrictions on 'lethal equipment' that could be delivered to the NAFP. Over the course of that year, US $64 million, the highest volume of security assistance delivered in five years, reached the Philippines.[63] Among other initiatives, the USAID's Office of Public Safety also continued efforts to increase the ability of the police force to cope with urban unrest. In short, the Reagan Administration's emphasis on military aid in 1986 and 1987 was designed to improve markedly the Philippine military's capacity to counter the NPA's guerrilla war.

Military Action

As regards actual military action against the New People's Army, the NAFP and the Constabulary, assisted and advised by the Joint US Military Advisory Group (JUSMAG), continued to play the major role. A whole gamut of other agencies were also involved, however, including US SOFs, US conventional forces, the CIA, the CHDF and importantly the vigilantes with their battlefield involvement providing still further evidence of LIC's emergence in the Philippines. Following their rapid growth during 1986, the vigilante groups played a prominent and increasing role in military action against the NPA, significantly civilianising the conflict by the end of 1987. The vigilantes' part in this dimension was also enhanced by the NAFP placing a greater reliance on local 'intelligence' and covert operations that reflected the military's attempts to locate the conflict more firmly within the civilian population and thereby foster total war against the revolution.

In 1987 after the failed ceasefire, more units of the NAFP were also redeployed to country areas for 'the protection of the Filipino people'.[64] The military pressured the Government to take a tougher approach and in accordance with Aquino's consequent 'unsheathing the sword' against the insurgency, the NAFP was able to intensify its military activities against the NPA.[65] It subsequently reinvigorated its peasant relocation programmes and increased conventional operations that included bombings, artillery and search-and-destroy campaigns. As part of this actual intensification of military operations, US SOFs and some conventional US military units assisted the NAFP in training, logistical support and even participated in some combat operations.[66]

For its part, the US military has a long history of involvement in counter-insurgency conflict in the Philippines ranging from the JUSMAG's Military Assistance Program and its advising all levels of the Philippine military, to actually documented cases of the involvement of US SOFs (from advisers to full US units) in combat.[67] US Air Force planes also reportedly provided reconnaissance for the NAFP. A declassified US Government report indicated that in 1984 and 1985, two aircraft of the US Air Force's 1st Special Operations Squadron based at Clark Air Force Base were damaged by groundfire while on routine low-level, terrain-following missions over northern Luzon where the NPA was active. One observer noted that it was possible such reconnaissance 'training missions' were used to gather intelligence on the NPA.[68]

Intelligence and Covert Action

Increased conventional actions notwithstanding, however, within this military dimension there was substantial evidence of LIC's emergence in the greater emphasis placed on gathering intelligence and waging covert action to exploit it. Beginning in 1986, the NAFP and the CIA significantly increased their intelligence activities within the Philippines and redirected Marcos-organised military intelligence operations, used previously against the domestic legal opposition, to target the insurgency's rural support base. Concomitantly, the capability of these agencies to conduct effective intelligence operations was significantly enhanced. The number of CIA personnel in the Philippines, for example, was rapidly expanded in early 1987 with Washington authorising a 10 per cent increase in CIA personnel attached to the US Embassy in Manila, as well as a $10 million budget for surveillance and covert action.[69] The Clarke Report argued that a Presidential Finding of early 1987 directed the CIA to 'conduct low intensity operations' against the CPP/NPA. These activities included overflights:

... probably with heat measuring cameras and the scattering of motion censors, both with the goal of locating and targeting guerrilla camps and movements; teams of advisors [probably Special Forces under civilian cover]; CIA up-country advisers, improving the record keeping ability of the Philippine armed and intelligence services through the provision of computers and computer technicians ...[70]

The Finding was the result of Reagan's alarm over the continued growth of the CPP/NPA in 1987, and unconfirmed reports the movement was receiving arms and training from Soviet-backed countries.[71] As a consequence, this two-year plan for increased CIA involvement in the conflict included provisions for more technical intelligence assistance to the NAFP and greater involvement in covert political action.

The Presidential Finding and the CIA's subsequent increase in resources revitalised the agency's capacity to gather effective intelligence and feed it to the NAFP after Marcos's departure. Previously, the CIA had failed to develop a significant intelligence capacity in the country due to its close relationship with the Philippine National Intelligence and Security Authority (NISA), which had been rendered largely ineffective after the departure of its commander, General Ver, and other pro-Marcos officers involved in military intelligence.[72] The CIA also found that by dealing directly with NAFP provincial commanders in Mindanao and elsewhere, it was able to circumvent the costly factionalism in the higher echelons of the NAFP, most evident in the attempted coups against the Ramos faction in Manila.

The enhanced access to effective intelligence improved many facets of the Government's military effort. Against the civilian population, it enabled CPP/NPA sympathisers to be identified, kidnapped and eliminated by the military's own intelligence units. Against the NPA itself, it proved even more effective. Enhanced intelligence enabled the military to infiltrate the NPA and even its high command with 'deep penetration agents' (DPAs), or 'zombies' as they were known. These operations proved so effective that in 1986, for example, the Davao front (in Davao City, Mindanao) of the CPP/NPA collapsed.[73]

Paramilitary Action

Vigilante military action can be loosely divided into two forms of activity. The first was direct or indirect military support of the NAFP and Constabulary against the NPA in the field. For example, the vigilantes played a useful role as 'civilian volunteers' in actual combat against the insurgents in a number of operations in Mindanao. Also in many urban areas and *barrios*, the vigilantes conducted operations against NPA Sparrow units. The second vigilante activity was military action waged against the perceived civilian support base of the revolution under the rubric of defending 'democracy'.[74] This comprised the major part of the vigilantes' activities. As noted previously, the vigilantes harassed, terrorised and liquidated suspected communist sympathisers including members of the Church and legal left organisations such as the KMU (May First Movement), BAYAN (New Patriotic Alliance), the KMP (Philippine Peasants Movement) and even some reform organisations. In this manner, many potential centres of anti-government opposition were either suppressed or destroyed. The vigilantes also aided the military by setting up checkpoints and gathering intelligence, and even participating in some search-and-detain operations conducted by the Constabulary.[75]

The vigilantes also served another valuable role. By eliminating sympathisers and suspected communists among the local population, a task formerly performed by the armed forces and the CHDF in the Marcos era, these agencies effectively deflected away from the military subsequent community outrage at such atrocities. The military, by blaming human rights violations on either criminals or over-zealous elements associated with the vigilantes, could thus blur and even sidestep ultimate responsibility for such counterinsurgency tactics.[76] The vigilantes therefore proved to be instrumental in protecting the new image being so assiduously cultivated for the NAFP.[77]

THE CIVIC ACTION DIMENSION – COMPLETING THE PICTURE

After 1986, the Philippine military's increased emphasis on pursuing civic programmes to win the hearts and minds of the people completes the full conflict profile of LIC's operation. The military's increased involvement (both the NAFP and the Integrated National Police) in civic action programmes which, as in Central America, were identified with the notion of nation building, was integral to the self-promotion of the military's image as a 'people's army', working to improve the harsh socioeconomic conditions that lay at the core of the insurgency.

From the onset of the Reagan Administration's initial alarm at the growth of the CPP/NPA insurgency, both US forces and the Philippine military stepped up their involvement in civic action in that country. Between October 1984 and May 1987, the Pentagon transported over 358,000 pounds of 'surplus, non-lethal military goods' donated by private-aid groups, to the Philippines – an amount of 'humanitarian civic assistance' second only to that received by the Contras in Honduras.[78] US conventional forces and SOFs also participated in civic action campaigns funded under the provisions of the US-RP Military Bases Agreement of 1983. These forces conducted year-round nationwide civic action programmes in coordination with the Philippine military and other Philippine Government agencies.[79] Robert Wolthus, the director of the Pentagon's Humanitarian Assistance Office, noted that such action was a 'tool in helping people feel better about the US military presence and local military forces'.[80] These programmes were conducted not only around the US bases to diffuse the NPA presence in these areas, but also in other areas of heavy insurgent activity.[81] After the fall of Marcos, the US forces stationed in the Philippines increased their involvement in local civic action projects, and the civic action component of joint US-RP military exercises was enlarged such as those incorporated in the annual 'Tangent Flash' manoeuvres. One prominent example was the visit of the US Navy hospital ship *USS Mercy* to seven ports in the Philippines in April and May 1987 to distribute free medical and dental treatment not only to military personnel but the local civilian population as well. This medical mission was a combined US-RP manoeuvre coordinated by the JUSMAG to improve the public image of the US and NAFP forces. It was also assisted by Americares, already noted for its previous activities in Central America, which provided considerable stocks of medicine for the project. Major General William P. Winkler, Head of the Academy of Health Science, effectively underlined the worth of these missions when he noted pointedly that 'Military medicine is the least controversial, most cost-effective means of employing military forces in support of US national interest in low intensity conflict situations.' From an LIC perspective, these visits proved to be particularly valuable 'psyops operations' in that they displayed US military strength in critical ports such as Davao where NPA activity was strong. Further, such visits served to deny the insurgency potential future base areas among the local population. Lt Colonel James Taylor, Chief of SOUTHCOM's Humanitarian Services Division, noted for example that such operations called for military doctors to enter 'preselected target population areas in conjunction with engineers, signals, civil affairs, psychological operations and intelligence personnel before the tactical situation can deteriorate to open conflict',[82] or to put it differently in order to target and undercut local support for the revolution.

In increasing its own participation in civic action after 1986, the NAFP provided medical care, engineering and other rural project assistance to build popular support as a 'people's army' in areas where formerly it had abused and alienated the local population. The code name for the NAFP's overall civic action programme was 'Oplan Mamamayan', superseding the former government's Oplan Katatagan. This plan was based on three basic objectives: national reconciliation, security and development. In 1986 and 1987, the program aimed to impose peace by conducting 'security operations and thereby ensure the protection of the people against atrocities and inimical acts of the local communists'. It sought to maintain and strengthen 'the people's faith in the NAFP and the new government', and to upgrade morale and discipline within the NAFP and improve its operational effectiveness.[83]

The NAFP thereby became heavily involved in 'image-building' activities such as medical immunisation campaigns among the local people, distributing food and toys, entertaining, and sponsoring sporting events and other community affairs. The US also upgraded the NAFP's engineering battalions with bulldozers and other equipment to help it build more roads and bridges and further contribute to the Government's effort to revitalise the rural economy.

Other Agencies

To complete this survey, it should be said that many civilian and private US agencies were also directly involved in civic action. Prominent among these was the US Peace Corps, overseen by the US Embassy. In areas of concentrated revolutionary activity, the Peace Corps was often actively engaged in civic action activities such as family planning campaigns, sanitation and well-building projects, bridge building and other programmes. Similarly, USAID, by virtue of its charter, implemented an extensive programme, which included health and sanitation projects, the development of agricultural marketing infrastructures, workers' cooperatives and relief work such as food and medicine hand-outs in poverty-stricken areas.

A CHARACTERISTIC LIC RESPONSE?

Considering the above analysis of the conflict in the Philippines, it seems apparent that LIC was being waged there by the end of 1987, given the close similarity that exists with LIC's footprint elsewhere. As in Central America, Reagan's approach to the threat posed by revolutionary nationalism was multidimensional, with a heavy emphasis on political/psychological operations. There was also a strong emphasis on privatising and civilianising the conflict, as evidenced by the rapid formation of vigilante groups and the activities of varied organisations and individuals, many of whom were also active in Central America.[84] Overall, the similarities between the Philippines and El Salvador are most striking. It is possible, for example, to draw direct parallels between the Filipino vigilante groups and the operations of the anti-communist Salvadoran death squads. In both states there were attempts to establish the 'Third Way', to reform the armed forces, and wage total war against the revolution assisted by massive propaganda and psyops 'hearts and minds' campaigns. In both conflicts, pro-US forces were also assisted by US military and civilian advisers through covert operations, military training, logistics and hardware.

The CPP/NPA itself observed that an operational strategy of this nature had emerged and was pursued in practice by agencies of the Reagan Administration. Officers of the NPA General Staff argued that there was a definite and significant change in the nature of the counterinsurgency strategy pursued in the Philippines following Aquino's installation. Detecting a greater emphasis on political/psychological tactics, they viewed with alarm the distinct reversal their movement suffered as a result.[85] Figures are impossible to obtain, but the CPP/NPA hierarchy recognised that the revolution had lost significant support. In particular, the movement's boycott of the 1986 election campaign was identified as a major tactical error. Many within the leadership argued that the CPP/NPA should have participated in the election in order to be seen as part of the 'democratic alternative' and thereby counteract the 'LIC political offensive sponsored by the Reagan Administration'.[86] For their part, key US policy makers were also aware of the relative success of these activities, claiming that the change of government seriously weakened support for the CPP/NPA revolution.[87]

Deviations

There are elements of the conflict profile in the Philippines, nevertheless, that do not closely accord with what I have identified as LIC. For example, there was considerable reliance on conventional military action with the reformed and reinvigorated New Armed Forces of the Philippines (NAFP) and various paramilitary groups applying continual pressure on the insurgency and its support base. In addition, not all the agencies involved in the conflict were controlled or managed by the Reagan Administration, nor were all agencies willing to pursue the same objectives. This became evident when various factions of the NAFP ultimately refused to accept the legitimacy of the Aquino Government and attempted to install their own version of the 'democratic alternative' in its place.[88] With the pro-'constitutional' Ramos faction maintaining support for Aquino, paradoxically, it was the RAM faction led by Colonel Gregario 'Gringo' Honasan (previously Enrile's chief aide) which proved an ongoing obstacle in the way of efforts by the Reagan Administration and the Aquino Government to achieve political stability in the Philippines. General Ramos made it clear, however, that he appreciated the nature of LIC and saw the necessity of actively pursuing it:

... insurgency is primarily political and only incidentally military ... We need to coordinate the middle forces, civilian authorities, religious and civic groups in our anti-insurgent campaigns; reform the social, political, and economic systems;

improve intelligence and combat capability; and intensify action and public information programs.[89]

On the other hand, the Reform the Armed Forces Movement (RAM) faction, made up of highly disciplined and professional but also extremely authoritarian officers, instead emphasised the need for a predominantly military approach to the insurgency. It also desired to politicise the military by installing a military junta in power to eradicate the ongoing corruption it perceived the Aquino Government was fostering. None of these objectives was congruent with the nature of low intensity conflict and this suggests one major reason why the Reagan Administration maintained its support for Aquino.

Within the Reagan Administration itself, there were also strong disagreements over which tactics to pursue at different times, indicating yet again that in the Philippines as elsewhere LIC gradually developed, rather than being mechanically applied from outside. There is evidence that pragmatic elements within the State Department were apprehensive about backing the vigilantes.[90] Moreover, the often distinct difference of views between the State and Defense Departments, the CIA and other agencies, reflected quite different perspectives on the conflict. Whereas the CIA and the Defense Department tended at times to emphasise the somewhat 'traditional' counterinsurgency approach, the State Department, perhaps indicative of its charter, placed more emphasis on more political-economic measures to undermine the insurgency.[91] As indicated, these differences were manifest in the responses to Aquino's attempts to pursue the ceasefire. While the ceasefire was supported by the State Department, a number of Pentagon officials criticised the policy as naive and a waste of time, and even when Aquino reverted to a hardline approach they still criticised the posture as inadequate.[92]

Though this divergence of views may suggest that the Reagan Administration's response to the insurgency did not constitute a coordinated or coherent strategy, a different and more credible conclusion is also possible. The lack of consensus at different levels within the Administration did not necessarily reflect a lack of consensus within the National Security Council (NSC), the arm of the Executive ultimately responsible for LIC. Indeed, such divergence as existed between the various policy-making levels reflected the nature of LIC itself; in any case, the divergence was symptomatic of the long maturation process within which the LIC strategy was conceptualised and implemented. Over time a consensus emerged within the NSC on foreign policy ends and means. By the end of 1987, this consensus was reflected in the similarity of the developments in the Philippines and Central America. In contrast to the notion of the existence of a 'laboratory' for LIC and then its determined application elsewhere, only as the success of the natural wedding of LIC elements in a total war approach became more apparent in these cases so too did a readily identifiable conflict profile.

It is therefore reasonable to argue that the counter-revolutionary strand of low intensity conflict did emerge in practice in the Philippines. However, in taking such a position a number of qualifications must still be made. To claim that the conflict was intentionally civilianised by external agencies which created, supported and assisted vigilantism in the Philippines, and to draw too many parallels with the role of the Contras in Nicaragua would be to 'strain' such a comparison. It is clear the Contras were, in the main, a US creation. However, vigilantism in the Philippines has a long history. By the same token, it is clear the Reagan Administration with the aid of private agencies was able to use a variety of channels through which it exercised considerable influence over the resurgence and general development of this phenomenon and the particular role played by vigilantes in the archipelago in the 1980s. It is therefore legitimate to argue that these private agencies, and by extrapolation the Reagan Administration, significantly contributed to the civilianisation of the conflict.

It remains, of course, extremely difficult to judge with any great precision the exact extent to which LIC's implementation in the Philippines was driven by 'external forces'. One runs the risk of assuming that a 'passive' military existed in the Philippines and of negating its wealth of experience, independent initiatives and long history of waging counterinsurgency. What is clear, nevertheless, is that the LIC approach that developed in the Philippines was the result of similar factors that helped to forge the nature of Washington's response to revolutionary nationalism in Central America. Many of the same or similar agencies were directly or indirectly involved, and in each case the United States was in a position of enormous influence and thereby possessed the capacity to shape the nature of the conflict. However the timing, the manner and the means by which LIC emerged indicates that, while influenced by US interests and strategic priorities in combating revolutionary nationalism elsewhere, in the Philippines at least, LIC's development was still characterised by a degree of independence or autonomy grounded in the particular social and political conditions of that country. Nevertheless, this is an expected reality of any conflict.

One indisputable fact, however, also remains common to the case studies I have reviewed so far in this book and unquestionably supports the argument that a new US approach to revolution had emerged during the Reagan era. This was the Administration's reprehensible inclusion of the US people as a target of its pysops war to generate support for its intervention-ist foreign policy objectives. Above all, the Administration was determined to crush once and for all the Vietnam Syndrome, the ongoing determination of so many American citizens to resist such interventionism, which in response saw the Reagan Administration resort to a new civilianised and privatised foreign policy strategy with which to hoodwink the US public.

9   LIC CONTINUED?

It is clear that during the Reagan years there emerged a predominantly covert and selective foreign policy strategy which the United States used to combat revolutionary nationalism in the Third World. In particular LIC was fully developed and pursued in all its interrelated dimensions in Nicaragua and the Philippines by both official and private US agencies and allied organisations. As initially an *ad hoc* approach pursued separately in each of these countries, the strategy steadily gained coherence and, after being legitimised by the Reagan Doctrine, assumed the status of a *de facto* national security strategy by the end of 1987. As such the Reagan Doctrine reflected the Administration's need to justify its actions after the public exposure of the covert activities of several security agencies in Central America. The Doctrine was symbolic of the Administration's realisation that faced by significant domestic opposition to an interventionist foreign policy, it needed to civilianise conflicts and enlist the assistance of private US and international 'anti-communist' organisations to achieve its foreign policy objectives in target states. As a consequence, the Reagan Administration's development and subsequent pursuit of LIC challenged the assumption that a heavy reliance on military power was necessary to combat Third World revolutionary nationalist movements. In contrast, LIC seemed well suited to the intensely political complexion of the low intensity warfare environments within which these movements predominantly operated.

The emergence of low intensity conflict during the 1980s represents both continuity and discontinuity in the evolution of US foreign policy: continuity because LIC represented a reassertion of interventionism in foreign policy as the 'militarist' persuasion regained its dominance in Washington, but discontinuity in terms of the means used to achieve US objectives which had remained broadly consistent since the end of the Second World War, namely to contain and combat communism and revolutionary nationalism which could threaten US interests. As a further expression of US coercive diplomacy, LIC emerged as primarily a political strategy. Military action was only a minor dimension of a multidimensional approach designed to achieve US foreign policy objectives by politically discrediting and undercutting the support base of target revolutionary movements and governments.

Low intensity conflict as it emerged was also a mix of old and new. It was old in the sense that it relied on many tactics borrowed from earlier US and various European powers' counterinsurgency and unconventional strategies used against revolutionary movements and governments in the Third World. But LIC was also new in terms of its coherence and the degree to which the Administration and its agencies sought to mobilise American society and gain domestic support for the pursuit of its foreign policy objectives, which in some cases were 'illegal'.

The key words I have used in much of this book have been 'emergence' and/or 'development', rather than 'application'. LIC, far from being a strategy carefully formulated and then systematically applied to a target state, tended instead to emerge or develop in situ as part of a complex but recognisable pattern, 'footprint' or 'profile' of activities. To talk of 'application' is to infer the conscious application of a coherent strategy. To use the term 'development' is to indicate more clearly the emergence of a reactive and basically ad hoc approach, which tended to produce similar outcomes in similar circumstances. To this extent there is some evidence of a common conflict scenario in many Third World states. It is more appropriate, then, to understand LIC not so much as a new strategy but more as a developing practice associated with the manifold activities pursued by US agencies executing an ongoing commitment to combating revolutionary nationalism. Practice preceded precept: the enunciation of the Reagan Doctrine and the restructuring of the National Security Council, among other measures, merely formalised an approach to which several official US agencies were already committed in different parts of the Third World.

LIC EMERGENT

By the end of 1987 the full conflict profile of LIC (in both its revolutionary and counter-revolutionary forms) was identifiable in all its dimensions within Nicaragua and the Philippines. As I have also suggested, it was also fully evident in El Salvador and to lesser extents in Afghanistan, Cambodia and Angola. In other words, LIC essentially evolved into a strategy operating across a wide regional and political spectrum. However, within this spectrum the full LIC picture could emerge only in those states in which certain determining factors or preconditions existed, which was certainly the case in Nicaragua and the Philippines. Moreover, though LIC ostensibly emerged as a US global strategy to combat communist aggression, albeit with a Third World focus, in reality its emergence was conditioned more by the threat of revolutionary nationalism (though admittedly many movements of this ilk were communist-backed or inspired).

Although LIC attained ideological legitimacy and the status of a national security strategy through the articulation of the Reagan Doctrine, this strategy itself was never fully or formally enunciated. While a number of LIC's overt activities designed to support democratic forces in the Third World were openly described at different times, most prominently in the 1988

National Security Strategy of the United States report, the character and role of many of its covert activities were not articulated. These included psyops activities pursued by US Special Forces (SOFs), the CIA and private organisations not directly accountable to Congress and therefore not sanctioned by US legislative processes. Moreover, while LIC ostensibly targeted communist forces in the Third World, one other major target was not disclosed: the 'collective mind' of the US public. Reagan's claimed intention of assisting democratic revolution in the Third World disguised his Administration's attempts to civilianise covertly those conflicts and to camouflage its role not just in assisting 'democratic forces' but also actually creating them. In this sense, the Reagan Doctrine may itself be considered a LIC psyops tool designed both to legitimise US intervention in foreign conflicts and to minimise domestic and international opposition to such intervention. Further, during the Reagan years the American public itself was both a primary target and indeed victim of LIC.

LIC was also a *de facto* strategy in the sense that it was implemented to a significant extent by private American militarist but principally neo-conservative organisations which were not politically accountable to the American people. LIC thus emerged more as an expression of the foreign policy approach of the neo-conservative persuasion in the United States rather than policy sanctioned by Congress as the representative body of the American body politic. As such, the emergent strategy strongly reflected the anxieties of neo-conservatives concerned with the retraction of US hegemony and power and their resentment at the many related humiliations the US had experienced in the Third World, particularly its defeat in Vietnam. From the neo-conservative and broader militarist perspective, the resultant Vietnam Syndrome necessitated the development of an alternative strategy to direct intervention to ensure the political feasibility of Reagan's interventionist objectives in the Third World. The importance of the US domestic opposition as a factor in LIC's emergence, therefore, cannot be overstated, which is not to discount the significant role of the international opposition that existed to such an interventionist foreign policy.

While economic considerations were obviously an important factor in LIC's emergence, in particular the cost of direct military intervention, they do not compare in importance with the issue of public support. The United States convincingly demonstrated in Grenada in 1983, when there was little prospect of serious public opposition because preparations for an impending foreign intervention (or even the intention to intervene) were kept secret and the operation itself achieved its objectives quickly and with minimum cost in human lives, the financial cost of such an operation proved a relatively minor (though still significant) constraining factor on US actions. Further, as in the case of Iraq and Operation Desert Storm in 1990–91,[1] when there existed extensive domestic as well as international support for military intervention, the massive cost of this very public operation was still a lesser factor than public opinion in determining whether it was to proceed or not.

In a sense, therefore, the emergence of LIC in the 1980s was indicative of the US's weakened capacity to project its military power in the Third World to achieve somewhat questionable foreign policy objectives. The crucial factor in foreign policy equations was now first and foremost the question of establishing ongoing public support. In the case of Nicaragua, for example, because the Sandinistas stressed their democratic and nationalist credentials, revolutionary nationalism proved a difficult force for the United States to combat through calls for holy crusades against communism, particularly when the largest such crusade had been so recently and severely discredited in Vietnam. The lack of sufficient public support thus posed a dilemma for an Administration seeking to reassert US power and hegemony in its own backyard. When considering dubious national security goals that smacked of the Vietnam nightmare, Reagan's National Security Council was forced to pursue more indirect means of foreign intervention, including the possible assistance and involvement of private organisations 'on the ground' in target states. It also prompted the Administration to pursue an extensive propaganda campaign at home, which included appeals to the American people's religious beliefs and their abhorrence of terrorism to generate popular domestic support for its objectives. The collective outcome was the emergence of LIC a strategy which grew out of the collective experiences of the US approach to revolution in Nicaragua and the Philippines, a strategy that was intellectually honed by the continuing debate within the US military over the most appropriate means to intervene in low intensity wars.

LIC's emergence, however, did not herald a reassertion of US power and influence throughout the Third World to contain or even roll back anti-US forces everywhere. Nor did the Reagan Doctrine, which justified LIC, have graded objectives as some of its supporters have argued.[2] In practice, the Administration's objectives proved far less ambitious than its rhetoric would suggest. Even though the Reagan Doctrine signalled that the US was seizing the initiative against pro-Marxist revolutionary regimes, thereby challenging the widespread perception that Marxist revolutions in the Third World were irreversible, in practice US foreign policy was far more limited in scope. Instead of being universally interventionist, it appeared intent only on recouping, where possible, some of the losses the US had incurred in its battle against revolutionary nationalism in the 1970s, while at the same time shifting the terms of the superpower rivalry in the Third World back in Washington's favour.

LIC's emergence and its somewhat selective operation thus indicates considerable difference between the rhetoric and perhaps intention of the Reagan Administration and its foreign policy practice. Similarly, it reflects a considerable degree of tension and disagreement between the 'realists' within the NSC, and the 'neo-conservatives' within the Administration and those supporters of the Reagan Doctrine outside of government over different perceptions of what foreign policy initiatives were necessary to further US interests. The NSC, it is clear, operated on a case-by-case approach while justifying its activities by reference to a neo-internationalist doctrine. Significantly, the Reagan Administration, for example, apart from a small amount of funding refrained from supporting insurgent forces in Ethiopia, while it supported the Contras in Nicaragua.[3] Similarly, in 1986, the US was reported to be aiding revolutionary movements to significant (though varying) degrees only in Nicaragua, Angola, Cambodia and Afghanistan. This therefore suggests two possible and not necessarily mutually exclusive realities about the development of LIC during the Reagan years. First, Washington had more to gain by pursuing a selective approach, concentrating on countries where its interests were severely threatened rather than by opposing revolutionary nationalism across the board. Second, by 1986, the Administration was adopting a more realist rather than neo-conservative approach to foreign policy in light of the obvious constraints on pursuing the latter and perhaps also because of its inability to do so.

I have argued that the Reagan Administration's foreign policy is more clearly understood if one considers that a national security strategy evolved during Reagan's tenure which, in certain target states, could achieve US foreign policy goals without resorting to more costly forms of direct intervention. As an inexpensive low-profile approach to combating revolutionary nationalism, LIC, which correctly posited that LIW environments were primarily political, sought to channel people's war against either revolutionary nationalist movements or regimes. In so doing, LIC filled a strategy vacuum left after the US policy of containment was discredited in Vietnam.

By the end of its tenure, the sum total of the Administration's responses to revolutionary nationalism in Central America made up the conflict profile of low intensity conflict. LIC's emergence in this region attracted so much attention that Central America was regarded by many as the LIC laboratory. Nicaragua in particular became the linchpin in the controversy over US involvement in the region eventually resulting in the articulation of the Reagan Doctrine, which legitimated LIC. Moreover, as the focal point of the perceived success of revolutionary nationalism in the Americas (outside of Cuba), to many observers Nicaragua soon represented both a litmus test and a catalyst for LIC's development. However, LIC activities were being simultaneously pursued elsewhere and, given ideological coherence by the Reagan Doctrine, LIC evolved conceptually from these different operations, despite the Doctrine's emphasis on justifying US support for the Contras, which gave the strategy the appearance of being born in Nicaragua.

By the end of 1987, LIC had emerged as a coherent, national security strategy for rolling back revolution (albeit selectively). Largely a synthesis of former counterinsurgency and unconventional warfare tactics in the Third World, LIC had two major targets: revolutionary nationalism in the Third World and the Vietnam Syndrome at home. Both were perceived by neo-conservatives as inimical to US national security. LIC avoided direct involvement of US troops and instead promoted the use of local 'democratic' forces, while at the same time it aimed to rebuild domestic consensus for the re-establishment and forward projection of US military power in the Third World. It was, and is, thus quantitatively and qualitatively different from earlier US national security strategies. Based on the assumption that the cause of revolutionary nationalism in the Third World was both external and internal, the strategy on a theoretical level could deal with both.

It could also accommodate both the foreign policy goals of the neo-conservatives and the constraints of US domestic opposition. In this sense, LIC's emergence may be best understood as a consequence of the Reagan Administration's strategic reorientation in the aftermath of the collapse of military containment in the Third World. Reagan's January 1988 report to the nation on national security strategy thereby formalised in broad outline LIC's emergence as a substitute for direct US military intervention.

In this book I have placed President Reagan's 'secret war' in Nicaragua within the overall context of this emerging and mainly covert US foreign policy strategy, which was only partially exposed during the Senate investigations into the Iran-Contra affair. While indeed LIC embraces elements of counterinsurgency long waged by the United States and indeed many of its allies at least since the Second World War, as I have argued LIC is not simply counterinsurgency under another name – it was and is a new strategy. While many observers have noted this approach, some fundamental facets of its nature have been overlooked. The extent to which it was predominantly political/psychological (and not military) in nature and its activities privatised and civilianised make it different to traditional counterinsurgency tactics pursued by earlier administrations, at least in terms of emphasis. It was also not intentionally or systematically developed in the first instance, but emerged in the wake of desperate and at times unconnected attempts by official and private US agencies to combat revolutionary nationalism in selected target states, all constrained however by a domestic political climate which was anti-interventionist (at least in military terms).

It is this last facet of LIC which is perhaps the most chilling and serious in terms of its impact on the operation of democracy, freedom of political expression and thought in America itself. The major target of LIC via its psyops component, a euphemism for a campaign of deliberate deception to mask US involvement in foreign conflicts, has been and remains the US people themselves. At the beginning of the twenty-first century, it is difficult to gauge exactly how much the development of LIC during the Reagan era has had lasting implications for democracy in the US. By conducting illegal foreign policy activities and defying the wishes of Congress, the Reagan Administration clearly set a precedent for future Administrations which also might wish to circumvent public and Congressional opinion by justifying US foreign policy actions as necessary to protect 'democracy' in target states. By equating either the promotion of democracy or its defence in such states with US national security interests, ironically, the Reagan Administration might well have placed the future functioning of the US democratic process itself in jeopardy. Time is still out on that one.

THE SUCCESS OF REAGAN'S LIC?

What remains an important undertaking is an evaluation of LIC's success in achieving its goals as defined during the Reagan era. With relation to the US global strategic goal of combating the Soviet bloc, many can argue it was successful. As we know, the immediate years following the Reagan era were marked by massive and indeed unexpected geopolitical change. At the end of the 1980s, the 'Old World Order' was transformed: the Cold War ended, marked by the disintegration of communist Eastern Europe. And, in the early 1990s, the Soviet Union itself collapsed. The triumph of the West appeared complete, a triumph that can be argued was part attributable to, and a legacy of, Reagan's LIC.

Though President Gorbachev adopted *perestroika* and *glasnost* in the late 1980s, these wide-ranging economic and political reforms occurred much too late to save the Soviet Union's demand economy, strained as it was by so many ailments. One essential factor contributing to the Soviet economy's downfall, however, was the economic strain of Moscow's continued support for Marxist governments in the Third World, particularly Afghanistan. By the end of the 1980s, the retraction of the Soviet empire that Reagan so resolutely pursued was thus fully in train. In short order, Moscow distanced itself from such firm allies as Nicaragua and Castro's Cuba. Both were simply too much a heavy economic burden, as were Ethiopia and Angola. With the withering of Moscow's economic power, internally the Soviet Union also rapidly disintegrated as its many republics sought their independence. As a result, America's neo-conservatives celebrated as the Reagan Doctrine's foreign policy objectives appeared to have been achieved.

In the Third World, many regimes formerly allied with Moscow but now deprived of Soviet aid soon collapsed. In Afghanistan, Kabul fell to the Mujahideen.[4] In Nicaragua, LIC proved ultimately victorious. The Sandinistas, after enduring a decade of US aggression and a state of economic siege, lost power in the 1990 elections to a US-backed 15-party coalition. Paradoxically, one of its members was the Nicaraguan Communist Party, revealing to the world the absurdity of former President Reagan's proclaimed anti-communist stance in Central America. Cuba, also, entered its 'Special Period in a Time of Peace',[5] a euphemism for a period wherein the US-strangled Cuban economy was collapsing and Castro was now facing significant internal and external opposition.

Success of the 'Third Way'

As successful in global strategic terms as it may have been, in terms of establishing democratic and economic reform otherwise known as the 'third way', LIC's long-term success is much more questionable in states where this strategy achieved its initial objectives (as in the case of Nicaragua, El Salvador and the Philippines). Low intensity conflict, after all, as a strategy to combat revolutionary nationalism ostensibly offered Third World target states the chance to establish the 'democratic alternative' and by implication Western modernisation and development. However, in the 1990s, it offered very little in terms of concrete plans for durable economic and political development (at least this was certainly so in the three cases just cited). Instead, Reagan's foreign policy was predicated on the assumption that once LIC succeeded and 'democratic' forces were victorious, 'real' democracy and neo-liberal development based on the operation of free market forces, Western aid and capital investment (as well as notions of wealth 'trickle-down') would ensure that the oppressive socioeconomic and political conditions that originally spawned revolutionary nationalism would be a thing of the past.

How valid was such an assumption? Would an LIC victory in a given state set the stage for a new direction of development? Or might it merely lead to the reinstatement or protection of political and social structures that though democratic in name (as with the Marcos and Somoza regimes) might in practice assume repressive, authoritarian and exploitative rule? After the initial victory, LIC, while appearing to offer democracy and Western development (by simple extrapolation), may simply have offered 'more of the same' – the consolidation of structures that produced revolutionary nationalism in the first place. The important question thereby arises: has the 'democratic alternative' embodied first by the Aquino and then the Ramos, Estrada and now the Arroyo governments in the Philippines, and the Chamorro and subsequent governments in Nicaragua, and those in El Salvador, provided the basis for real democracy and genuine economic development in these societies? At the beginning of the twenty-first century, the verdict is still not conclusive. While representative democracy at least in name appears to operate in these states, there appears no such progress in economic development. Indeed, for the elites and the deprived in these countries, it seems to be 'business as usual'. Moreover, with regard to those opposition forces temporarily vanquished by LIC, ongoing revolutionary struggle remains an alternative, and in the case of the NPA in the Philippines – a reality.

AN ONGOING STRATEGY

Given that many LIC operations were covert, other important questions need to be investigated. Primary among these are: has and is LIC still being waged today? To what extent has low intensity conflict been appropriated and waged by other states throughout the world? And, to what extent has this strategy been continued by subsequent US administrations since the Reagan years?

A Relevant LIW Climate

To assess the likelihood of LIC continuing to be waged in the post-Reagan era, a measure of its relevance to the post-Cold War world order must be first gauged. When so doing, it soon becomes apparent that even the most cursory examination of the nature of the current international order reveals that LIC remains as relevant today as in the 1980s.

Over the last decade, the world has witnessed a considerable proliferation of LIW environments and not exclusively in the Third World. Since the collapse of the Soviet Union, the international regime has been dominated by only one superpower – the United States. However, throughout the 1990s and at the beginning of the twenty-first century, instead of offering relative harmony and an easing of international tensions, this unipolar regime continues to be plagued by considerable conflict and instability. During the Cold War the international community, though divided roughly into two blocs, nevertheless knew some sense of order forged by the bonds of common ideology, underpinned as they were by military and economic alliances. This provided the world community with a crucial, albeit fragile, stability that offset the continued threat of nuclear war. The enduring Cold War antagonisms actually imposed a sense of order and stability in the world that in the 1990s rapidly disappeared. Without the oppressive lid imposed by the Cold War rivalry, the pot has been boiling over. While for some the process of globalisation has been a unifying force within the world community, it has been more than countered by the divisive force of revolutionary nationalism, particularly that which is primarily ethnically driven. While the world has witnessed some large-scale conventional conflicts since 1990 involving the United States and the major powers including Operation Desert Storm and the campaign waged against Milosevic's Serbia, the majority of conflicts have been civil or intra-state, revolutionary nationalist in nature (and not necessarily Marxist flavoured) and markedly in LIW environments. As such, LIC remains extremely relevant.

While democracy has been triumphant in world politics, achieved as it was in some states by LIC, as a phenomenon itself it has proven simply not enough to instil a new sense of order in international politics. With many different interpretations of what democracy really means and with the disappearance of overarching Cold War alliances, many states and indeed peoples within states formerly within colonial, or neo-colonial relationships, or within a powerful neighbour's sphere of influence, are now being embroiled in LIW environments. This is not restricted to the Third World as it includes those in regions formerly under the most heavy-fisted rule of the Cold War world, as in the former Yugoslavia and the Balkans, and in parts of the former Soviet Union such as Chechenya. In these regions in the 1990s, ethnic nationalist conflicts emerged with frightening intensity, usually over scarce resources, historic differences (including religion) and contested borders. However, similar conflicts have also erupted or gained in intensity in states formerly ruled by Western-backed dictatorships or corrupt democracies as in the case of the Moros in the Philippines, and many ethnic groups struggling for self-determination in Indonesia. In the latter case, as elsewhere, the cultural nationalism of some threatened ethnic groups has transformed into political nationalism and demands for sovereignty as pursued, for example, by the OPM (Free Papua Movement or Organisasie Papua Merdeki) in Irian Jaya (West Papua) and the Free Aceh Movement in Aceh. Further east, the story is similar with the Bougainville Revolutionary Army (BRA) in Papua New Guinea. In some states, conflict spawned by economic recession has seen populations divide along ethnic lines, and victimisation and brutalisation of minorities take place such as that endured by the ethnic Chinese in the Indonesian riots in 1998. Flashpoints fed by revolutionary nationalism are thus manifold: in Indonesia (Timor, Aceh, Ambon, West Papua), in the former Yugoslavia (Croatia, Bosnia-Herzegovina and Kosovo), and in Ireland and Chechenya to name just a few, without even mentioning those in Africa or Latin America. In many parts of the world at the beginning of the twenty-first century, ethnicity and religion now appear the major elements of ideological currency causing the legitimacy of so many states to be challenged. As such, the case can be made that revolutionary nationalist struggles in low intensity warfare environments are now the most predominant form of conflict in our time and perhaps the major threat to future world stability.

In sum, as so many national and subnational groups worldwide have entered into armed conflicts for self-determination and/or scarce resources, the reality of the post-Cold War world order is a disordered community of crisis and conflict, an international climate wherein low intensity warfare environments predominate. At the core of these conflicts, the political battle for the hearts and minds of the people remains the common essential factor. As such, it is these people, be they Basque, Moro, West Papuan or ethnically other, and be they combatant or supporter, in all cases they remain the primary targets of such conflicts. It is in this respect, therefore, that LIC as a strategy for engaging in this form of conflict maintains its relevance and utility for those powers seeking, or forced, to do so.

LIC and Other States

It has not been my intention to fully overview the use of LIC by other states since its emergence. I intend to leave that complex task to other observers at least for the present. However as a starting point for other scholars, evidence does suggest that many other states have adopted LIC or at least elements of this form of warfare in order to combat revolutionary nationalism.

Indeed, when one looks past the sensationalism of recent or current conventional conflicts, LIC's footprint can be identified in many places around the world. Whenever governments embarking on either international or domestic intervention (usually against sub-nationalist forces) lack ideological legitimacy and/or popular support and need to manufacture it, there is a tendency to use low intensity conflict or at least many elements of it. Again, these include attempts to civilianise and/or privatise the conflict, attempts to create the appearance of total war, and to fight revolution with revolution, usually masking such interventionist activities or oppressive 'internal' actions with a smoke-screen of pysops disinformation. The conflicts in the former Yugoslavia with the extensive use of Serb paramilitaries and the brutal activities pursued by the Jakarta regime as Indonesia continues to disintegrate are two major cases in point. Overall the means remain the same, as do the targets – the support base of the revolutionary nationalist threat. In the former Yugoslavia and Indonesia, for example, it has been the support bases of the independence movements or governments. In the latter, paramilitary forces or 'the militias' have been particularly relied on to disguise the extent of state involvement. In East Timor, for example, the local militias with army support forcefully attempted to stamp out any support for independence before and after the 1999 plebiscite and at the time of writing still conduct cross-border raids. Also, in West Papua, the OPM and its supporters are now facing similar paramilitary action, with the Jakarta regime behind the emergence of militias attempting to destroy any support for the popular separatist movement. As such, in these and other similar conflicts waged against revolutionary nationalist movements and post-revolutionary nationalist states the mark of LIC is proving identifiable time and again.

LIC and the US: Identifying the Footprint

Does the US itself still pursue LIC? Yes it does. While my intention in this book has been to focus mainly on the emergence of LIC in the 1980s, some commentary, however, on LIC in the post-Reagan years is warranted. Reagan's legacy indeed lives on. While the conceptual basis of this strategy may have faded with the discrediting of many of its proponents whose collective actions during the Reagan years defined this strategy, the broad LIC thrust, or approach, remains relevant to the conduct of US foreign policy. Moreover, the detection of at least its operative footprint indicates that it is still pursued as an element of continuity in US foreign policy.

Within the post-Cold War Order or 'New World Disorder' that I have described earlier, a considerable and continuing foreign policy dilemma has faced Presidents Bush and Clinton in turn, and now also faces the former's son President George W. Bush. In this era the United States has continued to have global interests that have had to be maintained in many regions enduring LIW environments. And while it has remained the sole economic and military superpower, many in the world community have continued to expect it to play the role of 'world policeman' maintaining these and allied interests. However, with the collapse of communism, the ideological justification for such a role is now gone, particularly for its involvement in LIW environments, as the US is no longer considered the 'ideological' superpower. In the 1980s, the United States had the option of direct conventional intervention into LIW environments, constrained as it was by the Vietnam Syndrome, and it had LIC. However, with the overlying structure of the bipolar world and the constraints of Cold War alliances and confrontational relationships removed, in the post-Cold War years the major ideological justification for the US to intervene into LIW conflicts to restore or alter the status quo (in terms of maintaining its interests) disappeared. Apart from such recalcitrant states as Castro's Cuba, the US has no longer been able to pursue rhetorical 'anti-communist' crusades against 'maverick' states to justify either direct intervention and/or covert action and the operation of many if not all dimensions of LIC. The dilemma for the United States in the post-Cold War years has therefore been how to maintain its sphere of influence and defend its far-flung web of economic and strategic interests without ideological legitimation. Without such legitimation, US involvement in regional conflicts to protect its interests however defined runs the risk of appearing quite starkly as typical Great Power, imperial behaviour. Moreover, this is in an era where revolutionary nationalism in the Middle East, in the Pacific, in Asia, and in Latin America still poses the greatest threat to US interests. Further, it proves a difficult force to combat when many of these movements are, or have been, inspired by desires for real democracy and self-determination. It is in this sense that LIC has remained relevant and in lieu of taking a case-by-case approach, in a general sense elements of its conflict profile are still readily identifiable.

In the 1990s to the time of writing, apart from more traditional and peaceful means of diplomacy, the options for the United States to enforce its foreign policy agenda in the post-Reagan years have remained conventional military force and elements of LIC. While Reagan's LIC might not exist in the form of the exact package that emerged in the 1980s, the preconditions and political imperative to wage total war using political/psychological means still do, so much so that in recent years there has been an observable shift in the fundamental way the US now wages even conventional war. This shift is away from ground war to America's current reliance on massive 'air wars' hopefully to achieve its objectives with a minimum of body bags returning home, as was more than evident in Operation Desert Storm and the more recent bombing campaigns directed against President Milosevic's regime in Belgrade. Without a convincing and sustainable ideological rationale, successive US administrations simply have not been able to risk enflaming the long-enduring Vietnam Syndrome with heavy military casualties. Thus while the 'most public' form of large-scale conflict in the post-Reagan years has continued to be conventional in nature, the nature of waging these conflicts has changed.

LIC, therefore, remains a major strategy for achieving US foreign policy objectives albeit perhaps less 'publicly' than in the Reagan years and certainly less sensationally. While LIC and particularly its targeting of the US public was exposed with the Iran-Contra scandal – the emphasis nevertheless placed by subsequent US administrations on waging total war with a primary focus on the political remains.

While LIC might not be pursued publicly or even consciously in terms of an articulated strategy, it is still pursued as a matter of course. Successive administrations have understood the necessity of winning the political war at all costs to achieve public support for often dubious foreign policy objectives. LIC has always been about winning the political conflict before the military – about winning the total war for the minds of the people in terms of shoring up US domestic and international support and destroying the support base of the target movement or government. In the post-Cold War years, it has proven a necessary national *de facto* security strategy with which to combat nationalism, demands for self-determination and sometimes demands for democracy, where these demands within a target state might conflict with US interests. Military force alone cannot win; psyops as well as other aspects of LIC must be used.

Low intensity conflict, or major elements of this strategy, has thus remained a viable foreign policy option, and one that has indeed been pursued. Even cursory observations of the conduct of US foreign policy in the post-Cold War years indicate that the determinants for pursuing LIC still exist.

In the post-Cold War years, the Vietnam Syndrome has remained a major constraint on direct intervention and a trigger for the pursuit of LIC. Indicative of this, throughout the 1990s, the US was hamstrung by domestic opposition to direct military involvement in foreign conflicts even when obvious transgressions of international law occurred. Subsequently, Presidents Bush and Clinton were both forced to wage extensive campaigns to woo public and international support for direct military intervention via the UN and America's NATO allies into Iraq and the former Yugoslavia despite the obvious aggression and abuse of human rights attributable to these regimes. It is thus clear that the Vietnam Syndrome, or variants of it, has now become a near-permanent feature of US political culture, a reality that US foreign policy makers must continue to accommodate.

With regard to combating revolutionary nationalism or post-revolutionary governments in the post-Cold War era in places like Cuba, or in LIW environments in which US interests are threatened, ideological legitimation continues to be fundamental to US political crusades in these LIC or 'neo'-LIC cases. Unable to continue to credibly pursue anti-communist crusades, particularly when the US has been forging relationships with China and Vietnam, the United States tends to rely on two other ideological justifications for foreign interventionist activity. The first is the prevention of 'instability', which is often promoted as a major justification for action and is used as a pysops weapon assisting US foreign policy activities. It is continually inferred that the maintenance of stability in target states or regions furthers the development of democracy, as the latter can only flourish in stable economic and political conditions. The second ideological justification is that of combating terrorism. Successive US administrations in the 1990s, similar to other governments in the West, found that it suited their cause to label ideological opponents as terrorists to achieve public backing for their policy objectives. By using such an emotive label, domestic support against foreign political opponents is far more readily attainable than for vague ideological crusades. Moreover, by equating foreign revolutionaries with terrorism, these elements could be stripped of any ideological legitimacy and their activities rendered little more than common criminal acts. In this manner, for example, the left-wing elements who opposed and even attempted to assassinate General Pinochet in Chile in the late 1980s were regarded by the Bush Administration as merely irrational 'terrorists', as also were the PLO or Hamas guerrillas in the Middle East from time to time, and even the Serb paramilitaries in Yugoslavia. As such, the use of these ideologically contestable terms, particularly when considering according to whose interests is such instability considered threatening, demonstrates that elements of LIC in the pursuit of US foreign policy still exist.

When looking for the most prominent example of the continuation of LIC by the US in the post-Reagan years, one need look no further perhaps than the continued campaign by successive US administrations to overthrow the Castro government in Cuba. Cuba remains a post-revolutionary nationalist regime which the US has long considered antagonistic to its interests, and Castro a perpetual foreign policy irritant. So intense is this dislike for Castro's Cuba some US administrators have developed an almost 'pathological' hatred for the ageing leader. As Wayne Smith argued, 'Cuba has the same effect on American administrations that the full moon has on werewolves; they just lose their rationality at the mention of Castro or Cuba.'[6]

Indicative of this, the United States has long pursued many if not all elements of LIC against Castro. Least of these has been the military option in the last few decades given Castro's domestic popularity and tight grip on the island state, memories of the Bay of Pigs fiasco, and the potential international ramifications of US military intervention, not to mention US domestic opposition as well. Covert action including assassination attempts aside, most prominent among activities long pursued by the US to destroy Castro has been the psyops war conducted both within Cuba and the US itself, and also that waged internationally targeting the regime's support base.[7] For many years Castro has been portrayed as a brutal totalitarian dictator imposing his whims on the Cuban people with no regard for democracy or human rights. As such, successive US administrations have long expressed varying degrees of support for the Cuban American National Foundation (CANF), what many consider to be the basis of a Cuban 'democratic' government in exile.[8] More telling however has been the ongoing economic embargo the US has pursued as a major correlated LIC tactic designed to break Cuba economically and force change from within. As a result, Cuba was almost economically suffocated during the 1990s following the collapse of the Soviet bloc and subsequent termination of its economic lifeline.[9] Nevertheless, despite such harsh conditions, the regime endures, fuelled and propped up by extreme nationalism which US actions have actually strengthened contrary to their objectives. As such the regime survives and at the time of writing appears to have weathered the storm, with President Clinton having slowly relaxed the US position. As opposed to Nicaragua and the Philippines, the strength of Cuban nationalism thus appears to have so far thwarted LIC in the Caribbean.

In this book I have outlined the origins and nature of LIC as it emerged during the Reagan years. At the beginning of the twenty-first century, LIC appears to be waged by many states as this strategy/approach retains its relevance in an era dominated by LIW environments wherein civic and ethno-based nationalism fuels many internecine or intra-national conflicts. As such, the military forces of those states consumed by such conflicts are generally committed more against their own people than external aggressors. Such states thereby have difficulty arguing an acceptable rationale for such action, both to their home communities and the world at large. In short, this has led to a continued use of LIC or major elements of it. Whenever governments lack popular support and need to manufacture it, there is a tendency to use low intensity conflict to engage in LIW environments. In all cases, the primary target remains the same – the support base of the revolutionary nationalist threat.

As regards the United States, while developed as a necessity during the Reagan era, LIC remained, and still is, an option for later administrations which appear to have adopted elements or the full thrust of this strategy as a matter of course. In the post-Cold War years, it is possible to identify the signs of LIC in a number of conflicts in which the US has either been involved or influenced. But certainly this area is worthy of more study. This much is certain, however. In the post-Cold War years, the United States no longer faces an international communist threat, nor are there perceptions of the umbilical theory stalking the minds of those in the National Security Council. Moreover, the wave of democracy that recently swept the world makes an interventionist foreign policy by any state much harder to justify – hence the increased need, or necessity, to rely on covert actions and psyops. The Vietnam Syndrome (or its modern-day variant) has continued to plague subsequent US administrations as a factor in foreign policy formulation, rendering the political battle much more important to win in overcoming revolutionary nationalism and 'other forces' considered threatening to US interests. It is thus clear that LIC still exists, and major international conflicts notwithstanding, it appears to be the predominant form of conflict the US will continue to pursue at least in these early years of the unfolding twenty-first century. For the United States, LIC's continued importance today is underlined by the fact that America's global military muscle remains just as irrelevant in LIW environments as it did in the 1980s. LIC therefore remains both America's most effective alternative, or precursor, to conventional military intervention. The United States has finally learned the lesson which old guerrilla war-horses such as Mao Tse Tung and General Giap underlined in their historic victories – the importance of the total war approach embodied in LIC. Central to this approach is the political dimension of winning the hearts and the minds of the people not just those in target states but the American people themselves.

At the beginning of the twenty-first century, when confronted with the necessity to intervene in LIW environments, LIC thus remains a pervasive and dominant approach to warfare in which hearts and minds are considered more important than battlefield victories. The United States now pursues wars for the 'political headspace' of target populations as matter of priority to avoid but yet also pave the way for military intervention if needed as a last resort. For the US, the major lesson of Vietnam still rings true: military victories alone cannot decide the outcome in a LIW or total war environment – all they do is prolong it.

NOTES

INTRODUCTION

1. For an analysis of this syndrome see Michael Klare, *Beyond the Vietnam Syndrome, US Interventionism in the 1980s* (Washington, DC: Institute for Policy Studies, 1982), p. 1.

2. The War Powers Act required the President to consult with Congress before military forces were committed to a conflict. For an overview see Colonel Harry Summers, *On Strategy: The Vietnam War in Context* (US Army War College, Carlisle Barracks, Pennsylvania: Strategic Studies Institute, November 1983), p. 18.

3. See Fred Halliday, *Cold War, Third World, An Essay On Soviet-American Relations* (Sydney: Hutchinson Radius, 1989), p. 29.

4. See Statement of Secretary of Defense Caspar Weinberger, in his report to Congress in February 1984, also quoted in 'America's Secret Soldiers: The Buildup of US Special Operations Forces', *Defense Monitor* (Washington, DC: Center For Defense Information, 1985), p. 2.

5. This is the same criterion the noted LIC theorist Dr Samuel Sarkesian uses to measure coherence. See Samuel Sarkesian, 'Low Intensity Conflict: Concepts, Principles, and Policy Guidelines', *Air University Review*, Vol. XXXVI, No. 2 (January–February, 1985) p. 12.

6. For one overview of the decline of American economic power since 1960, see Walter La Feber, *America, Russia and the Cold War 1945–1992* (New York: McGraw-Hill, 1993), pp. 255–87.

7. They were considered threatening because such movements and regimes often seek to nationalise their economies, as in the case of Chile and Nicaragua, threatening US or allied economic interests in the process.

8. Interview with former Captain John Zindar, School of Army Intelligence, Center For Defense Information, Washington, DC, 25 May 1988. See also William Leogrande's critique of Sarah Miles' assessment of LIC in William Leogrande, 'Central America: Counterinsurgency Revisited', in *NACLA Report on the Americas*, Vol. XXI, No. 1 (January/February 1987), pp. 3–5.

9. For some aspects of this lengthy debate see Alan Nairn, 'Low Intensity Conflict One Hit, Two Misses', in *NACLA*, Vol. XX, No. 3 (June 1986), pp. 4–7, also see in this same volume Peter Kornbluh and Joy Hackel, 'Low-Intensity Conflict, Is It Live Or Is It Memorex?', pp. 8–11.

10. This can include counterinsurgency, counter-revolution, terrorism, counterterrorism, peacekeeping, anti-narcotics campaigns and a host of other operations including psychological, sociological and political activities.

11. This is generally the position of Klare and Kornbluh in Michael Klare and Peter Kornbluh (eds), *Low Intensity Warfare* (New York: Pantheon, 1988). See also Sarah Miles, 'The Real War: Low Intensity Conflict in Central America', *NACLA*, Vol. XX, No. 2 (April/May 1986), pp. 17–25. It also the position of such military strategists as Sarkesian, see for example Sam Sarkesian, 'Organizational Strategy and Low-Intensity Conflicts', in Frank Barnett, Hugh Tovar and Richard Shultz (eds), *Special*

Operations in U.S. Strategy (Washington, DC: National Defense University Press, National Strategy Information Center, 1984), pp. 271–89.
12. For further clarification of its scope see Sarkesian, 'Low Intensity Conflict', p. 2.
13. The White House, *National Security Strategy of the United States* (January 1988).
14. Charles Krauthammer, 'The Poverty of Realism', *The New Republic* (17 February 1986), p. 14.
15. See Miles, 'The Real War', p. 19.

CHAPTER 1

1. Interview with Charles Salmon, Director of the Philippines Department, Bureau of East Asian and Pacific Affairs, State Department, Washington, DC, 26 May 1988, hereafter known as 'Salmon interview'.
2. See the statement of General Paul F. Gorman, US Army (Ret.), Chairman, Regional Conflict Working Group, Commission on Integrated Long Term Strategy, to the Senate Committee on the Armed Services on the 28 January 1987, in *National Security Strategy: Hearings Before the Committee on the Armed Services*, United States Senate, 100th Congress, First Session: 12, 13, 14, 20, 21, 27, 28 January; 3, 23 February; 25, 30 March; 3 April 1987 (Washington, DC: US Government Printing Office, 1987), p. 766, hereafter cited as *Hearings 1*.
3. See Colonel Kenneth Alnwick (USAF), 'Doctrine Overview', in David Dean, Lt Colonel, USAF (ed.), *Low Intensity Conflict and Modern Technology* (Maxwell Air Force Base: Air University Press, Center for Aerospace Doctrine, Research and Education, June 1986), p. 266.
4. 'Joint Low-Intensity Conflict Project Final Report: Executive Summary' as presented in *Department of Defense Authorization for Appropriations for Fiscal Years 1988 and 1989: Hearings Before the Committee on the Armed Services*: United States Senate, 100th Congress, First Session on S. 1174 (Washington, DC: US Government Printing Office, 1988), p. 3691, hereafter cited as *Hearings 2*.
5. *Hearings 2*, p. 3691.
6. See Summer's definition cited in Col. Kenneth Alnwick (USAF), 'Doctrine Overview', in Dean, *Low Intensity Conflict*, p. 266.
7. See W. Robinson and K. Norsworthy, *David and Goliath: Washington's War Against Nicaragua* (London: Zed Books, 1987), p. 29. These authors argue that the case of Grenada supports this view.
8. See The White House, *National Security Strategy of the United States*, January 1988, hereafter known as *National Security*.
9. *National Security*, p. 8.
10. *National Security*, p. 24.
11. *National Security*, p. 34.
12. Three prominent LIC theorists and their respective works includes Sarkesian, 'Low Intensity Conflict: Concepts, Principles, and Policy Guidelines', *Air University Review*, Vol. XXXVI, No. 2 (January–February 1985), S. Miles, 'The Real War: Low Intensity Conflict in Central America', *NACLA*, Vol. XX, No. 2 (April/May 1986) A. Nairn, 'Low Intensity Conflict One Hit Two Misses', *NACLA*, Vol. XX, No. 3 (June 1986) and Kornbluh in M. Klare and P. Kornbluh (eds), *Low Intensity Warfare* (New York: Pantheon, 1988).
13. General Gorman supported this interpretation of LIC's nature when he appeared before the US Senate Committee in 1987. See Gorman in *Hearings 1*, pp. 753–4.
14. Interview with John Zindar, former Captain, School of Army Intelligence (Center for Defense Information, Washington, DC, 25 May 1988) hereafter cited as 'Zindar interview'.
15. For a comprehensive account of people's war, see Mao Tse Tung, *Selected Military Writings of Mao Tse Tung* (Peking: Foreign Language Press, 1963).

16. For a definition of FID, see Dr Richard Shultz, 'Low Intensity Conflict and US Foreign Policy: Regional Threats, Soviet Involvement, and the American Response', in Dean, *Low Intensity Conflict*, p. 91.

17. The Reagan Administration's response to low intensity warfare has often been interpreted as incorporating a third anti-terrorist strand. However, in terms of the US's response to combating revolutionary nationalism in the Third World, it is not directly relevant for my purposes in this study.

18. For the citation of this quote see Nairn, 'Low-Intensity Conflict', p. 6. For an excellent analysis of military operations to defeat revolutions within the parameters of LIC, see Sarkesian, 'Low Intensity Conflict', pp. 4–5.

19. See Sarkesian, 'Low Intensity Conflict', p. 5.

20. Zindar interview.

21. While at times the US did undertake direct military intervention during the Reagan years in places like Grenada, these were not LIW environments in which the US faced a strong risk of involvement in protracted Third World revolutionary conflicts.

22. See Saul Landau, *The Dangerous Doctrine – National Security and U.S. Foreign Policy* (London: Westview Press, 1988), pp. 83–4.

23. See 'Right Wing Vigilantes and US Involvement', *Report of a US-Philippines Fact Finding Mission to the Philippines, May 20–30, 1987* (Manila: Philippine Alliance of Human Rights Advocates, July 1987), p. 40. This report is also known as the 'Ramsay Clarke Report'.

24. See Sarkesian, 'Low Intensity Conflict', p. 2.

25. Carl Von Clausewitz, *On War* (Princeton: Princeton University Press, 1984), p. 605.

26. For example, Lt General Gordon Sumner argued, 'The objective of negotiations is to protect our national security and our national interests.' See Lt General Gordon Sumner (Ret.), 'Negotiating with Marxists in Central America', *Address to International Security Council Forum* (Washington, DC: 21 March 1985).

27. Caspar Weinberger, 'US Defence Strategy', *Foreign Affairs*, Vol. 64, No. 4 (Spring 1986), p. 686.

28. *National Security*, p. 35.

29. *National Security*, p. 10.

30. Larry Pratt, 'The Reagan Doctrine and the Third World', *Socialist Register* (London: Merlin Press, 1987), p. 70.

31. Noam Chomsky, 'The Fifth Freedom', *Listener* (23 March 1989), p. 9.

32. Chomsky, 'The Fifth Freedom', p. 9.

33. For an example of the LIC tactic of portraying everything in opposition to US foreign policy as an act of terrorism, and equating Marxism to terrorism, see 'American Survey: With Foreign Policy, Reagan Advises, Congress Consents', *The Economist* (3 August 1985), pp. 29–30.

34. These included the attack on the liner *Achille Lauro*, and the hijacking of TWA flight 847.

35. For one analysis of the militarist argument on terrorism see Charles Townshend, 'With What Right, and to What End?', *Politics* (29 August 1986), p. 928.

36. President Reagan described the Soviet Union as the 'evil empire' on numerous occasions, see for example the USIS press release, 'Reagan's Legacy, New Era For The US and World' by Alexander M. Sullivan, USIA White House correspondent (18 January 1989), p. 4.

37. Interview with Father Miguel D'Escoto, Foreign Minister, Government of Nicaragua, Managua, 14 February 1985.

38. Sarkesian, 'Low Intensity Conflict', p. 4.

39. Major Donald J. Bruss, US Army, 'The Emerging Role of US Military Health Care in Low Intensity Conflict', in Dean, *Low Intensity Conflict*, p. 232.

40. For an outline of MEDCAP in operation and the role of USAID in supplying health care to the local population, see Bruss, 'The Emerging Role', pp. 223–35. For a

discussion of the considered usefulness of US forces using military medicine in such ways see Gorman in *Hearings 1*, p. 753.

41. See Bruss, 'The Emerging Role', p. 226.
42. Sarah Miles, revised draft of 'The Real War: Low Intensity Conflict in Central America' (January 1986), p. 47, hereafter cited as Miles, 'Revised Draft'.
43. Zindar interview.
44. See Major Andrew Pratt (USMC), 'Low Intensity Conflict and the United States Marine Corps,' in Dean, *Low Intensity Conflict*, pp. 296–7.
45. Pratt, 'Low Intensity Conflict', p. 297.
46. *National Security*, p. 12.
47. As General Gorman observed, see Gorman in *Hearings 1*, pp. 767–8.
48. See Statement of General John R. Galvin, Commander in Chief, US Southern Command in *Hearings 1*, 23 February 1987, p. 95. Often considered America's 'secret soldiers', SOFs are effectively military commando units trained for unconventional warfare, covert action and counterinsurgency. SOFs range across all US service branches. For a full description of their operations, see 'America's Secret Soldiers: The Buildup of U.S. Special Operations Forces', *Defense Monitor*, Vol. XIV, No. 2 (Washington DC: Center for Defense Information, 1985), pp. 1, 4–8, hereafter cited as 'America's Secret Soldiers'.
49. Statement of General Duane H. Cassidy, USAF, Commander in Chief, Military Airlift Command, in *Hearings 2*, p. 3570.
50. The Center for Defense Information argued that MTTs not only helped to improve the armed forces of allies, but also provided a means for the US to maintain troops in troubled regions and support 'friendly' governments while intimidating unfriendly ones. See 'America's Secret Soldiers', p. 12.
51. Sarkesian outlines the importance of indigenous civilian groups in destroying the political base of the revolutionary forces in Sarkesian, 'Low Intensity Conflict', p. 6.
52. William Bode, 'The Reagan Doctrine', *Strategic Review* (Winter 1986), p. 25.
53. For the argument of the costs that a Soviet-supported client regime would have to bear to combat an insurgency, see Bode, 'The Reagan Doctrine', p. 25.
54. *National Security*, p. 10.
55. Interview with Andrew Semmler, Senator Richard Lugar staff member, Washington DC, 31 May 1988.
56. See later chapters dealing with the pursuit of 'revolutionary' LIC in Nicaragua.
57. 'The Low Intensity Conflict', *AMPO*, Vol. 18, No. 1, pp. 73–4. Israel, Taiwan and South Korea were also often involved in supplying hardware and training, see later notes in Chapter 5.

CHAPTER 2

1. For a discussion of these influences see Charles Kegley and Eugene Wittkopf, *American Foreign Policy: Pattern and Process* (London: Macmillan, 1987), pp. 11–12, 17, 21–3, 25.
2. The internationalist tradition has taken several forms. It has embraced a willingness to exercise power, to intervene economically, politically and even militarily in the affairs of other societies, to pursue a global profile diplomatically and to attempt to impose American lifestyles and value systems upon others.
3. For interesting perspectives see Michael Hunt, *Ideology and U.S. Foreign Policy* (London: Yale University Press, 1987), pp. 5–8, 14–15.
4. For a seminal work on realism, see Hans J. Morgenthau, *Politics Among Nations* (New York: Knopf), ch. 1.
5. See Chapter 5 for discussion of the 'Project Democracy' initiative.
6. See Saul Landau, *The Dangerous Doctrine – National Security and U.S. Foreign Policy* (London: Westview Press, 1988), pp. 41–7.

7. In 1950 NSC-68 directed that all communist, hence Soviet, expansionism be combated globally by all means short of initiating war. It advocated the massive nuclear and conventional build-up of US armed forces and the formation of strong anti-communist alliances.

8. The underlying assumptions of NSC-68 appeared confirmed when North Korea attacked the South. As a result, the US Congress accepted the broad principles of this, then secret, document. For one account see Thomas McCormick, *America's Half Century* (London: Johns Hopkins University Press, 1989), pp. 99–106.

9. Though bipartisan, the CPD was derived predominantly from the Republican Party and in particular its 'big business Eastern Wing'. See Jerry Sanders, *Peddlers of Crisis* (Boston: Southend Press, 1983), pp. 14, 66–75.

10. For the CPD's extensive publicity campaign to achieve its objectives and outmanoeuvre its opponents, see Landau, *The Dangerous Doctrine*, pp. 48–51.

11. As a way of reducing military expenditure while still providing a credible counterweight to Soviet conventional strength, President Eisenhower presided over a major build-up of US nuclear forces and a corresponding reduction in US non-nuclear ground and naval strength.

12. The National Security elite saw the possible invasion of China as too risky, see McCormick, *America's Half Century*, pp. 100–6.

13. For one extensive account of US intervention in Central America, see later editions of Walter La Feber, *Inevitable Revolutions* (New York: Norton, 1983).

14. For an extensive coverage of the CIA operation in Guatemala in support of US economic interests, see Stephen Schlesinger and Stephen Kinzer, *Bitter Fruit* (London: Sinclair Browne, 1982).

15. For an outline of early US covert activities aimed at overthrowing revolutionary nationalist governments, see John Prados, *President's Secret Wars – CIA and Pentagon Covert Operations From World War II through to Iranscam* (New York, Quill, 1986).

16. For the successful containment operations of Third World revolutions in this era, see Fred Halliday, *The Making of the Second Cold War* (London: Verso, 1986), pp. 84–5.

17. US elite consensus on military containment effectively ended with the Tet offensive in 1968, see John Spanier, *American Foreign Policy Since World War II* (New York: Holt, Rhinehart & Winston, 1985), pp. 147–51.

18. For an analysis of the factors causing the decline of US economic power since 1960 see Walter La Feber, *America, Russia and the Cold War 1945–1942* (New York: McGraw-Hill 1993), pp. 267–8.

19. For extensive notes on the War Powers Act, see Colonel Harry Summers, *On Strategy: The Vietnam War in Context* (US Army War College, Carlisle Barracks, Pennsylvania: Strategic Studies Institute, November 1983), p. 18.

20. During Nixon's presidency, the Bretton Woods agreement disintegrated and the United States lost its economic hegemony over the Western world.

21. The influential Trilateral Commission consisted of key US, Western European and Japanese decision makers from the world of politics, business, and academia sponsored by the Rockefeller family. For one overview, see Kegley and Wittkopf, *American Foreign Policy*, pp. 164, 264, 265–7.

22. The New Right was regarded as the right-wing internationalist faction supporting global anti-communism. See 'The Reagan Doctrine and Counterrevolution', *NACLA*, Vol. XX, No. 4 (July/August 1986), p. 16, hereafter known as *NACLA*, 'The Reagan Doctrine'.

23. See Halliday, *The Making of the Second Cold War*, p. 15.

24. Officially reforming in 1976 after two years organising, the CPD went public on 11 November 1976. The CPD's founding statement 'Common Sense And The Common Danger' made its debut on Veteran's Day, 1976, three days after Carter's victory. For this document see C. Tyroler and M. Kampelman, *Alerting America: the Papers of*

the Committee on the Present Danger (Washington, DC: Pergamon Brassey, 1984), pp. 3–9.

25. This rejuvenated organisation had grown out of the 'Team B' group of foreign policy experts formed to research and provide an alternative appraisal of Soviet foreign policy to that of the CIA. Its report emerged as a virtual update of the major tenets of NSC-68 stressing that the Soviet Union remained the greatest threat to the United States. For the Team B Report, NSC-68 update, see Sanders, *Peddlers*, pp. 198–204.

26. For the list of the founding members of the Board of the reformed CPD and their former positions see Tyroler and Kampelman, *Alerting America*, pp. xxi, pp. 5–9. Norman Podhoretz's work, *The Present Danger* (Touchstone, 1966), became the manifesto of the movement and *Commentary* became its monthly bulletin – see Christopher Hitchins, 'A Modern Medieval Family', *Mother Jones* (July/August 1986), p. 76.

27. Tyroler and Kampelman, *Alerting America*, pp. xv–xvi.

28. Among others there was also the Centre for Strategic And International Studies (CSIS) at Georgetown. For these groups see Hitchens, 'A Modern Medieval Family', pp. 74–6.

29. Many of the firms associated with this complex also supported the American Security Council. They included the Honeywell Corporation, General Electric, Lockheed and McDonnell-Douglas, as well as firms like Motorola who also depend on military production for their existence. See Sanders, *Peddlers*, pp. 223–6. For a description of the operation of the military-industrial complex see Kegley and Wittkopf, *American Foreign Policy*, pp. 268–77.

30. See Harold Relyea, 'The American Security Council', *Nation* (24 January 1972), p. 114. The firms which were acknowledged to support the Council, together with those actually interlocked with it through corporate relationships, ranked among the top defence contractors in the country.

31. The CPD charged that the Soviets were outstripping the US militarily and that Carter's human-rights based foreign policy was playing into the Soviets' hands. For an overview of the groups in this campaign see Tyroler and Kampleman, *Alerting America*, p. xix. For a CPD paper urging a string of US military build-up measures, see pp. 178–83.

32. Stansfield Turner was appointed by the Carter Administration to purge the CIA of its militarists and to limit its covert action capability.

33. Landau, *The Dangerous Doctrine*, p. 127.

34. See Tyroler and Kampelman, *Alerting America*, p. 172.

35. See 'What Is The Soviet Union Up To?' in Tyroler and Kampelman, *Alerting America*.

36. The New Right sought to downplay the focus on Europe and instead redirect US attention to the Third World where they saw the decisive conflict was to be fought. See Peter Binns, 'Understanding the New Cold War', *International Socialism*, I.S.J. 2:19 (1983), p. 21.

37. The Carter Administration's increasingly militarist foreign policy was reflected particularly in the debate over the role of human rights versus military interventionism within Washington, much publicised in the Young, Vance and Brezinski differences. The debate reached a climax over the SALT II issue.

38. For the close parallels of the Carter Doctrine and NSC-68, and the subsequent collapse of the 'centrist' position within the Carter Administration, see Sanders, *Peddlers*, pp. 238–40.

39. As part of this doctrine, Carter created the Rapid Deployment Force. See Michael Klare, 'The New US Strategic Doctrine', *Nation* (28 December 1985/4 January 1986), pp. 711–12, hereafter cited as Klare, 'Strategic Doctrine'.

40. After the Nicaraguan revolution in Central America, Carter reversed his policy of Third World caution by increasing aid to the military regime in El Salvador.

41. Other CPD members appointed to prominent positions included Richard Allen (National Security Coordinator), Richard Pipes (considered the Chief Kremlinologist in the Reagan Administration), Jeane Kirkpatrick (US ambassador to the United Nations), Richard Stillwell (Undersecretary for Defense), John Lehman (Secretary of the Navy), George Shultz (Secretary of State) and William Casey (Director of the CIA).

42. See Sanders, *Peddlers*, pp. 280–90, pp. 341–2, see also Arthur Macy Cox, *Russian Roulette: The Superpower Game* (New York: Times Books, 1982).

43. This group prepared a policy guideline for Reagan in 1980 entitled *Committee of Santa Fe, A New Inter-American Policy for the Eighties* (Washington, DC: Council for Inter-American Security, 1980). The Committee called for immediate action to install 'a revitalised Monroe Doctrine' in which no hostile foreign power was to be allowed military or political influence in the region thereby preventing new 'Cubas', see Allan Nairn, 'Endgame – A Special Report on US Military Strategy in Central America', *NACLA Report on the Americas*, Vol. XVIII, No. 3 (May/June 1984) p. 24.

44. Secretary of State George Shultz demonstrated such moralistic sentiments within the Administration when he claimed: 'America has a moral responsibility. The lesson of the postwar era is that America must be the leader of the free world; there is no-one else to take our place,' Kegley and Wittkopf, *American Foreign Policy*, p. 74.

45. See Morris Morley, *Washington, Somoza and the Sandinistas* (New York: Cambridge University Press, 1994), pp. 19–23.

46. The US Congress is part of the exceedingly complex process which is US foreign policy making, however the President's resources are clearly more formidable than those available to Congress. Nevertheless, Congress has significant powers to affect foreign policy making as in the National Commitments Resolution (1969), the repeal of the Gulf of Tonkin Resolution (1970), the Case Act (1972) and the War Powers Act (1973).

47. President Johnson duped Congress over the Gulf of Tonkin Resolution by arguing it gave him the power to wage war in Vietnam. The meaning of this resolution was strongly debated as the US involvement in Vietnam deepened. However, it is generally accepted now that Congress was deceived by a president who controlled the information, and hence the policy.

48. Carter's human rights pledges were encumbered by Congressional restraints as soon as he became president. There were numerous instances of both the Ford and Carter Administrations flouting the War Powers Act and conducting missions of force abroad. Later, it was also flouted by Reagan in the invasion of Grenada and the sending of advisers to El Salvador.

49. See Kegley and Wittkopf, *American Foreign Policy*, p. 117.

50. The White House, *National Security Strategy of the United States*, January 1988, p. 3. See also statement of Secretary of Defense Caspar Weinberger in *Hearings 1*, p. 11 (for full reference, see Chapter 1, note 2).

51. See *National Security*, p. 5.

52. See Richard Pipes, *Survival is not Enough: Soviet Realities and America's Future* (New York: Simon & Schuster, 1986), pp. 243–4. Noam Chomsky observed that supporters of economic nationalist goals in foreign states which denied supply of local resources to the United States were also considered threats to US national security. See Chomsky, 'The Fifth Freedom', p. 8.

53. *National Security*, p. 3.

54. See Statement of Secretary of Defense Caspar Weinberger in *Hearings 1*, p. 21.

55. See Klare, *Beyond The Vietnam Syndrome: US Interventionism in the 1980s* (Washington, DC: Institute for Policy Studies, 1982), p. 81.

56. Both Klare and Kornbluh infer that LIC was a readily formulated strategy, as does Bello in the context of the Philippines. See Michael Klare and Peter Kornbluh (eds), *Low Intensity Warfare* (New York: Pantheon, 1988), pp. 3–20, 158.

57. As claimed by Colonel Waghelstein, former head of the US military group in El Salvador, see Klare and Kornbluh, *Low Intensity Warfare*, p. 6.

58. This position is outlined in Peter Kornbluh and Joy Hackel, 'Low Intensity Conflict, Is It Live Or Is It Memorex?', *NACLA*, Vol. XX, No. 3 (June 1986), pp. 8–11. Charles Silver of the United States Information Agency also took this view (interview with Charles Silver, United States Information Agency, Washington DC, 24 May 1988).

59. This strategy also included the 'new villages' programme, later termed 'strategic hamlets' when the Americans tried to imitate the programme in Vietnam. See for example Thomas Mockaitis, 'The Origins of British Counterinsurgency', *Small Wars & Insurgencies*, Vol. 1, No. 3 (December 1991), pp. 209–25.

60. Interview with former Captain John Zindar, School of Army Intelligence, Center for Defense Information, Washington, DC, 25 May 1988. For a review of counter-insurgency in Malaya, see Maj. Daniel S. Challis, 'Counterinsurgency Success in Malaya', *Military Review* (February 1987), pp. 56–69.

61. Zindar interview.

62. For a further discussion of the Algerian conflict see Alistair Horne, 'The French Army and the Algerian War, 1954–62', in Ronald Haycok (ed.), *Regular Armies and Insurgency* (London: Croom Helm, 1979), pp. 69–83.

63. See Waldon Bello, *Creating The Third Force: US Sponsored Low Intensity Conflict in the Philippines* (San Francisco: Institute for Food and Development Policy, 1987), p. 3. For a full analysis of the Huk (Hukbo ng Bayan Labal sa Hapoaon – The National Army against the Japanese) rebellion, see Benedict Kerkvliet, *The Huk Rebellion* (Los Angeles: University of California Press, 1977).

64. US Colonel Edward Lansdale was a CIA operative working out of the Civil Affairs Office in Manila. He also worked with the Joint United States Military Advisory Group (JUSMAG) and the United States Information Service.

65. For propaganda campaigns against the Huks, see *Right Wing Vigilantes and US Involvement, Report of a US-Philippine Fact Finding Mission to the Philippines, May 20–30, 1987* (Manila, Philippine Alliance of Human Rights Advocates (PAHRA), July 1987), pp. 12–13, 45–6.

66. *Right Wing Vigilantes*, pp. 12–13. For an extensive analysis of LIC elements used by Lansdale and the CIA in the Philippines against the Huks, see Renato Constantino, *The Philippines: The Continuing Past* (Quezon City: The Foundation for Nationalist Studies, 1978), pp. 226–302.

67. For an excellent case study which documents many elements now identified as components of LIC strategy that were used in Vietnam, see Jeffrey Race, *War Comes To Long An* (Berkeley: University of California Press, 1972).

68. See Landau, *The Dangerous Doctrine*, pp. 78, 79–80.

69. For example, see John Ranelagh, *The Agency: The Rise and Decline of the CIA* (New York: Simon and Schuster, 1987).

70. For these extracts see Sanders, *Peddlers*, p. 25, see also p. 94 for the urgings of Bill Donovan, the former chief of the Office of Strategic Services (OSS), whose strategy recommendations included advocating internal subversion to roll back communism in foreign countries.

71. LIC was considered by some of its proponents to be a kind of 'American Leninism,' see Fred Halliday, *Cold War, Third World* (Sydney: Hutchinson Radius, 1989), p. 71. For Shultz's description of LIC see Chapter 3.

72. See William M. Leogrande, *Central America and the Polls: A Study of U.S. Public Opion Polls on U.S. Foreign Policy Toward El Salvador and Nicaragua under the Reagan Admin-istration* (Washington, DC: Washington Office on Latin America, 1984), pp. 3–5, and Grant Hammond, 'Low Intensity Conflict: War By Another Name', *Small Wars & Insurgencies*, Vol. 1, No. 3 (December 1990) pp. 226–38.

73. For an overview of many of these earlier covert and other strategies, see Prados, *President's Secret Wars*.

74. Donald Morelli and Michael Ferguson, 'Low-Intensity Conflict: An Operational Perspective', *International Defense Review*, 9 (1984), p. 1219.

75. For Pipes' view on strategic opportunities for the United States, see Pipes, *Survival*, pp. 222–4.

76. For a pro-Administration analysis of the opportunities provided to the US and explanations for the rise of resistance in such countries as Afghanistan, see Maggie Gallagher and Charles Bork, 'The New Freedom Fighters', *Commentary* (September 1985), p. 58.

77. For the argument that the selective application of the Reagan Doctrine did pay off, see Stewart Eizenstat and Robert Hunter, 'Defense Lessons for Democrats', *Washington Post* (19 June 1988), C2.

78. For the Reagan Administration's actions in Angola, see Prados, *President's Secret Wars*, p. 385.

79. See Jeane Kirkpatrick, 'Dictatorships and Double Standards', *Commentary*, Vol. 68, No. 5 (November 1979).

80. Kegley and Wittkopf, *American Foreign Policy*, p. 77.

81. Kegley and Wittkopf, *American Foreign Policy*, p. 77.

CHAPTER 3

1. Statement of Colonel Harry Summers, Jr, Contributing Editor, *US News & World Report* (27 January 1987), in *Hearings 1*, p. 716 (for full *Hearings 1* reference, see Chapter 1, Note 2). Paradoxically, Summers was an advocate of strong military responses to low intensity war, see Colonel Harry Summers, 'Principles of War and Low Intensity Conflict', *Military Review*, Vol LXV, No. 3 (March 1985).

2. For example see Colonel Harry Summers, *On Strategy: The Vietnam War in Context* (US Army War College, Carlisle Barracks, Pennsylvania: Strategic Studies Institute, November 1983). This influential analysis of Vietnam had an enormous impact on the US military.

3. Sam Sarkesian, 'Organizational Strategy and Low Intensity Conflicts', in Frank Barnett, Hugh Tovar and Richard Schultz (eds), *Special Operations in U.S. Strategy* (Washington, DC: National Defense University Press, National Strategy Information Center, 1984), p. 274.

4. See the 'Kissinger Commission: Report on Central America' (January 1984), which guided US foreign policy thinking; for an extract see Robert Leiken and Barry Rubin (eds), *The Central American Crisis Reader* (New York: Summit Books, 1987), pp. 556–62.

5. Nairn attributes this position to such Administration officials as Under-Secretary of Defense for Policy, Fred Ikle and the then Secretary of State, Alexander Haig, see Allan Nairn, 'Endgame – A Special Report on US Military Strategy in Central America', *NACLA Report on the Americas*, Vol. XVIII, No. 3 (May/June 1984) p. 32.

6. Summers, *On Strategy*, pp. 48–9, 117.

7. One of the most influential works on which proponents from the LIC school based their post-Vietnam analysis was Richard A. Hunt and Richard H. Shultz, Jnr (eds), *Lessons From An Unconventional War: Reassessing US Strategies For Future Conflicts* (New York: Pergamon Press, 1981).

8. See Raymond Copson and Richard Cronin, 'The Reagan Doctrine And Its Prospects', *Survival*, IISS (January/February 1987), p. 43.

9. 'The Low Intensity Conflict', *AMPO*, Vol. 18, No. 1, p. 74.

10. See Michael Klare, 'The Interventionist Impulse: U.S. Military Doctrine for Low-Intensity Warfare', in Michael Klare and Peter Kornbluh (eds), *Low Intensity Warfare* (New York: Pantheon, 1988), pp. 60–3.

11. Interview with former Captain John Zindar, School of Army Intelligence (Center for Defense Information, Washington, DC, 25 May 1988).

12. See 'Joint Low Intensity Conflict Project Final Report: Vol. 11, Low Intensity Conflict Issues and Recommendations' (Fort Monroe, Virginia: US Army Training and Doctrine Command, August 1986), pp. c3–2, c3–3.

13. See *Right Wing Vigilantes and US Involvement, Report of a US-Philippine Fact Finding Mission to the Philippines, May 20–30, 1987* (Manila: Philippine Alliance of Human Rights Advocates (PAHRA), July 1987), p. 43.

14. For the argument that both the Kennedy and Johnson Administrations believed the US could win a 'cultural' war in Vietnam without knowing the language, customs, or history of the people, see Saul Landau, *The Dangerous Doctrine – National Security and U.S. Foreign Policy* (London: Westview Press, 1988), p. 95.

15. Zindar interview.

16. W. Robinson and K. Norsworthy, *David and Goliath: Washington's War Against Nicaragua* (London: Zed books, 1987), p. 32.

17. Summers, 'Principles', p. 49.

18. See Summers, *On Strategy*, p. 3.

19. Caspar Weinberger, 'US Defense Strategy', *Foreign Affairs*, Vol. 64, No. 4 (Spring 1986), p. 685.

20. Weinberger, 'US Defense Strategy', p. 686.

21. Reported conversation in Hanoi, April 1975, see Summers, *On Strategy*, p. 1.

22. See Sarkesian's analysis of the revolutionary's total war versus the United States' limited war in Sarkesian, 'Low Intensity Conflict: Concepts, Principles, and Policy Guidelines', *Air University Review*, Vol. XXXVI, No. 2 (January–February 1985), p. 3.

23. Sarah Miles, 'The Real War: Low Intensity Conflict in Central America', *NACLA*, Vol. XX, No.2 (April/May 1986), p. 29.

24. See Statement of General Paul Gorman, US Army (ret.), Chairman, Regional Conflict Working Group, Commission on Integrated Long-Term Strategy, 28 January 1987, in *Hearings 1*, p. 755.

25. The military funded many studies and forums on low intensity conflict, see for example, Department of Defense, *Proceedings of the Low-Intensity Warfare Conference, January 14–15, 1986*, as cited in Klare, 'The Interventionist Impulse' U.S. Military Doctrine for Low-Intensity Warfare', in Klare and Kornbluh, *Low Intensity Warfare*, p. 50. Much of the military's appraisal of LIW was ultimately synthesised in Army manuals, which of most particular note was Field Circular 100–20, *Low Intensity Conflict*, published in 1986 by the United States Army Command and General Staff College.

26. See Statement of Admiral William Crowe, Jr, US Navy, Chairman, Joint Chiefs of Staff, in *Hearings 1*, p. 422.

27. For an example, see the dispute between the Defense and State Departments over the pursuit of elements of LIC in Angola, see *Hearings 1*, p. 64.

28. See Nayan Chanda, 'Here Comes The Spies', *Far Eastern Economic Review* (9 April 1987), p. 19.

29. Bob Woodward, *Veil: The Secret Wars of the CIA 1981–87* (London: Simon & Schuster, 1987), p. 137.

30. Robert Pastor, *Condemned to Repetition – The United States and Nicaragua* (Princeton: Princeton University Press, 1987), p. 237.

31. Sarkesian, 'Low Intensity Conflict', p. 9.

32. *Hearings 2*, p. 3632 (for full *Hearings 2* reference, see Chapter 1, note 4).

33. See *Hearings 1*, p. 773.

34. Cited in Miles, 'The Real War', p. 27.

35. See Statement of General Gorman in *Hearings 1*, p. 765.

36. In a speech central to this debate, Secretary of State Shultz argued that the US needed a more coherent strategy with which to combat what he termed 'ambiguous warfare'. See George Shultz, Secretary of State, 'Low-Intensity Warfare: The

Challenge of Ambiguity', Address before the Low-Intensity Warfare Conference, National Defense University, Washington, DC, 15 January 1986.

37. See interview with General Wallace H. Nutting, *Newsweek* (6 June 1983), p. 24.
38. See statement of Senator William Cohen, in *Hearings 2*, p. 3635.
39. See John Prados, *President's Secret Wars – CIA and Pentagon Covert Operations from World War II through to Iranscam* (New York: Quill, 1986), pp. 357–86.
40. Executive Order 12333: reprinted in *New York Times*, 5 December 1981.
41. See Summers, *On Strategy*, p. 12.
42. See 'America's Secret Soldiers The Buildup of US Special Operations Forces', *The Defense Monitor* (Washington, DC: Center for Defense Information, 1985), pp. 1, 12.
43. General Gorman gave an outline of the unique role of US Special Forces in LIC in his testimony in *Hearings 1*. See *Hearings 1*, p. 767.
44. Nairn, 'Endgame', p. 43. Also see Prados, *President's Secret Wars*, p. 386.
45. See summary and statement of Assistant Secretary of Defense Armitage in *Hearings 2*, pp. 3645–55. For details of the projected build-up of SOFs between 1986 and 1990, see 'America's Secret Soldiers', p. 5.
46. For SOCOM's mission in preparing and training Army SOFs, see Dr Richard Shultz, 'Low Intensity Conflict and US Policy: Regional Threats, Soviet Involvement, and the American Response', in David Dean, Lt Colonel USAF (ed.), *Low Intensity Conflict and Modern Technology* (Maxwell Air Force Base: Air University Press, Center for Aerospace Doctrine, Research and Education, June 1986), p. 91.
47. Summers, *On Strategy*, p. 8.
48. It is claimed that the Grenada operation in 1983 saw the debut of these revitalised SOFs, see Robinson and Norsworthy, *David and Goliath*, p. 34.
49. See the testimony of General Galvin in *Hearings 1*, p. 911.
50. Zindar had been a Tactical Intelligence Officer in Central America in the mid-1980s.
51. Zindar interview.
52. See Prados, *President's Secret Wars*, p. 386.
53. *Hearings 1*, p. 762.
54. See statement of Assistant Secretary of Defense for International Security Affairs, Richard L. Armitage, in *Hearings 2*, p. 3650, see also pp. 3635–41 for the structure of this position and the subordinate personnel.
55. See statement of Senator Edward Kennedy in *Hearings 1*, p. 3633.
56. Stuart M. Butler, Michael Senera and W. Bruce Weinrod (eds), *Mandate for Leadership II: Continuing the Conservative Revolution* (Washington, DC: Heritage Foundation, 1984), p. 228.
57. The 208 Committee was named after the room number in which the committee met in the Old Executive Office Building. For its members see 'The CIA's War', in *NACLA*, Vol. XX, No. 4 (July/August 1986), pp. 21–2.
58. See 'The CIA's War', pp. 21–2.
59. See 'The Byrne and Whitehall Attacks', unpublished monograph by Peter Brock, 1 May, 1987, p. i.
60. This was published by TRADOC at Fort Monroe, Va. See US Army Training and Doctrine Command, 1986.
61. See Bello, *Creating the Third Force: US Sponsored Low Intensity Conflict in the Philippines* (San Francisco: Institute for Food and Development Policy, 1987), pp. 53–67.
62. See Sarkesian, 'Low Intensity Conflict', p. 12.
63. See Miles' position in 'The Real War', p. 25.

CHAPTER 4

1. For an outline of the Kennedy counterinsurgency doctrine which combined military means with political and economic means (the 'other war') later abandoned in Vietnam, see Michael Klare, *Beyond The Vietnam Syndrome: US Interventionism in the 1980s* (Washington, DC: Institute for Policy Studies, 1982), pp. 87–8.

2. Jeane Kirkpatrick claimed the Reagan Doctrine lacked clarity because it sanctioned covert activity, which the Administration's spokespeople did not normally defend. Rosenfeld claimed it was because the President failed to clarify it, see Stephen Rosenfeld, 'The Guns of July', *Foreign Affairs*, Vol. 64, No. 4 (Spring 1986), p. 702.

3. Charles Krauthammer, 'The Poverty of Realism', *New Republic* (17 February 1986), p. 15.

4. This address is entitled: 'Secretary of State George P. Shultz: America and the Struggle for Freedom' (February 1985), and is cited in full in Robert Leiken and Barry Rubin (eds), *The Central American Crisis Reader* (New York: Summit Books, 1987), pp. 583–90. The address is hereafter cited as 'Shultz: America'.

5. See William Bode, 'The Reagan Doctrine', *Strategic Review* (Winter 1986), p. 22. Bode was named in the Christic Papers as being involved with the Enterprise and its activities in Central America (see Chapter 6, note 10, this volume).

6. 'Shultz: America'.

7. 'The State of the Union Address by the President of the United States' (4 February 1986), Congressional Record–House, 99th Congress, 2nd Session, p. H323. See also USIS release: 'America Growing Stronger Each Day' (5 February 1986), p. 6.

8. 'The State of the Union Address' (4 February 1986).

9. The White House, *National Security Strategy of the United States* (January 1988), p. 10.

10. Interview with Charles Salmon, Director of the Philippines Department, Bureau of East Asian and Public Affairs, State Department, Washington, DC, 26 May 1988.

11. *National Security*, p. 10.

12. President Reagan's 1985 State of the Union Address, see Bode, 'The Reagan Doctrine', p. 22.

13. See for example Richard Pipes, *Survival is not Enough: Soviet Realities and America's Future* (New York: Simon & Schuster, 1986), pp. 37–44, 222–3. For more on the extreme right's view of Soviet expansionism in the Third World, particularly in Nicaragua and Cuba, see David Horowitz, 'Nicaragua: A Speech to my Former Comrades on the Left', *Commentary* (June 1986), pp. 28–30.

14. See Raymond Copson and Richard Cronin, 'The Reagan Doctrine and its Prospects', *Survival* IISS (January/February 1987), pp. 46–7.

15. See Larry Pratt, 'The Reagan Doctrine and the Third World', *Socialist Register* (London: Merlin Press, 1987), p. 89.

16. Bode, 'The Reagan Doctrine', p. 24.

17. For an analysis of this resistance see also Maggie Gallagher and Charles Bork, 'The New Freedom Fighters', *Commentary* (September 1985), p. 61.

18. See Gallagher and Bork, 'The New Freedom Fighters', p. 59.

19. Bode, 'The Reagan Doctrine', p. 24.

20. For other neo-conservative analyses of the nature and intentions of the Soviet Union and the desired responses that favoured the Reagan Doctrine, see Michael Leeden, 'Fighting Back', *Commentary*, Vol. 80, No. 2 (August 1985), pp. 28–31, and Krauthammer, 'The Poverty of Realism', pp. 14–22.

21. Pratt, 'The Reagan Doctrine', p. 69.

22. For an account of the feelings within inner Administration circles at the time the doctrine was emerging, see Bob Woodward, *Veil: The Secret Wars of the CIA 1981–87* (London: Simon & Schuster, 1987), see also Bode, 'The Reagan Doctrine', p. 25.

23. See Michael Klare, 'The New US Strategic Doctrine', *Nation* (28 December 1985/4 January 1986), p. 715.

24. Reagan also added: 'None of these struggles is a purely internal affair.' Message from the President, 'Freedom, Regional Security, and Global Peace', 14 March 1986, Congressional Record – Senate, 99th Congress, 2nd Session, p. S2852.

25. Interview with Richard Fisher, Heritage Foundation, Washington, DC, 1 June 1988, hereafter cited as 'Fisher interview'.

26. See Viron Vaky, 'Positive Containment of Nicaragua', *Foreign Policy*, No. 68 (Fall 1987), p. 58.

27. See Stephen Rosenfeld, 'The Guns of July', *Foreign Affairs*, Vol. 64, No. 4 (Spring 1986), p. 702.

28. The CIA's covert activities in support of the Contras began to be fully exposed by the press in 1982 and most publicly by *Newsweek*, see 'America's Secret War-Target: Nicaragua', *Newsweek* (8 November 1982).

29. These positions ranged from think tanks, key positions in the Pentagon, the State Department, the National Security Council, the Central Intelligence Agency and US missions abroad. See Jerry Sanders, *Peddlers of Crisis* (Boston: Southend Press, 1983), pp. 287–8, 341–2.

30. See Pratt, 'The Reagan Doctrine', p. 69, see also Joshua Muravchik, 'The Reagan Doctrine After Iranamok – Maximum Feasible Containment', *New Republic* (1 June 1987), p. 25.

31. See Pratt, 'The Reagan Doctrine', p. 68. For the entire message see 'Freedom, Regional Security, and Global Peace'.

32. See Secretary of State, George P. Shultz, 'America and the Struggle for Freedom' (February 1985) in Leiken & Rubin, *Crisis Reader*, pp. 583–4; also see pp. 586–9.

33. For an overview of how combating 'international terrorism' became the new guideline for US foreign policy see Saul Landau, *The Dangerous Doctrine – National Security and U.S. Foreign Policy* (London: Westview Press, 1988), p. 139.

34. For Shultz on terrorism, see George Shultz, 'New Realities and New Ways of Thinking', *Foreign Affairs*, Vol. 63, No. 4 (Spring 1985), pp. 717–18.

35. Cited in Klare, 'The New US Strategic Doctrine', pp. 714–15.

36. 'Official Text of Reagan State of the Union Address' (issued 5 February 1986), USIS, p. 6.

37. See extract from Committee of Santa Fe, 'A New Inter-American Policy for the Eighties' (Santa Fe: New Mexico, Council for Interamerican Security, May 1980), p. 20.

38. See 'The Reagan Doctrine and Counterrevolution', *NACLA*, Vol. XX, No. 4 (July/August 1986), p. 16.

39. See Copson and Cronin, 'The Reagan Doctrine', pp. 42–3.

40. See Krauthammer, 'The Poverty of Realism'.

41. See for example a January 1986 Heritage Foundation paper entitled 'Rhetoric vs Reality: How the State Department Betrays the Reagan Vision', cited in Copson and Cronin, 'The Reagan Doctrine', p. 46. Also see Winsor, 'From Reagan Doctrine to Détente', *Global Affairs* (Winter 1988), pp. 52–5.

42. For some of the debate within the Administration, particularly on the question of aid to Angola in 1985, see Christopher Thomas, 'Anxious State Department seeks to avoid Angola tangle', *The Times* (19 October 1985), p. 32. For Shultz actually opposing US aid to the right-wing UNITA guerrillas in Angola in October 1985, see Doyle McManus, 'Rightists Fight Shultz on Aid to Angolan Rebels', *The Age* (25 October 1985).

43. McManus, 'Rightists Fight Shultz'.

44. See Winsor, 'From Reagan Doctrine to Detente', pp. 54–5.

45. See Gallagher and Bork, 'The New Freedom Fighters', pp. 58–9.

46. For the impact of this exposure and then the threat it posed to continued Reagan foreign policy, see Michael Klare and Peter Kornbluh (eds), *Low Intensity Warfare* (New York: Pantheon, 1988), pp. 156–7.

CHAPTER 5

1. For a detailed background of the revolution in El Salvador see Tommie Sue Montgomery, *Revolution in El Salvador* (Boulder, Colorado: Westview Press, 1982).

2. For an analysis of many of Central America's revolutionary movements at this time, see James Levy (ed.), *Crisis in Central America* (The University of New South Wales: The School of Spanish and Latin American Studies, 1984), pp. 42–53.

3. For a comprehensive description of these moves and the internal debates within the Administration, see Holly Sklar, *Washington's War on Nicaragua* (Boston: South End Press, 1988), pp. 57–73.

4. Raymond Bonner, *Weakness and Deceit* (New York: Times Books, 1984), pp. 224–9. Some US aid was suspended after the assassination of three US nuns and a lay missionary on 2 December 1980 but was restored again after the beginning of the FMLN's offensive in January 1981.

5. See Karen DeYoung, 'El Salvador: Where Reagan Draws the Line', *Washington Post* (8 March 1981), p. 1.

6. See Viron Vaky, 'The Positive Containment of Nicaraua', *Foreign Policy*, No. 68 (Fall 1987), pp. 42–3.

7. These claims were made, among others, in a publication known as the 'White Paper', see 'Communist Interference in El Salvador', Special Report No. 80, United States Department of State, Bureau of Public Affairs, Washington, DC (23 February 1981). For a full survey of the question of Nicaraguan aid to El Salvador which seriously questions the US claim of Sandinista arms for the FMLN, see John Lamperti, *What Are We Afraid Of?* (Boston: South End Press, 1988), pp. 55–69.

8. For increased US aid levels to El Salvador in March 1981 see Michael McClintock, *The American Connection Volume One: State Terror and Resistance in El Salvador* (London: Zed Books, 1985), pp. 288, 326–53.

9. See, for example, the February 1981 State Department 'White Paper' that Haig used to justify his stance, see 'Communist Interference in El Salvador,' Special Report No. 80, United States Department of State, Bureau of Public Affairs (Washington, DC, 23 February 1981), p. 3, hereafter cited as 'Communist Interference'.

10. See *Hearings 1*, p. 712 (for full *Hearings 1* reference, see Chapter 1, Note 2).

11. See the estimates of the US State Department where it quotes US economic and military aid to El Salvador to be $76.8 million in 1980, in The U.S. Department of State, Congressional Presentation, Security Assistance Programs: fiscal years 1981–1983, Washington, DC, cited in Alan White, *The Morass* (New York: Harper & Row, 1984), p. 183.

12. This was the position of Secretary of State Al Haig, and Under-Secretary of Defense for Policy Fred Ikle. It was also supported by such studies as that undertaken by the Kissinger Commission, for an extract see Kissinger Commission; 'Report on Central America' (January 1984) in Robert Leiken and Barry Rubin (eds), *The Central American Crisis Reader* (New York: Summit Books, 1987), pp. 557–62.

13. The question of the actual amounts of military and other aid supplied to the FMLN by Nicaragua and indeed Cuba has been strongly debated as noted, see Allan Nairn, 'Endgame – A Special Report on US Military Strategy in Central America', *NACLA Report on the Americas*, Vol. XVIII, No. 3 (May/June 1984), p. 38.

14. For some observations on the reasons for the growth of the US peace and anti-nuclear movement see Fred Halliday, *The Making of the Second Cold War* (London: Verso, 1986), pp. 255–7.

15. For evidence that the majority of the US public supported the Administration but remained opposed to direct intervention in Central America, see poll evidence in John Rielly (ed.), *American Public Opinion And US Foreign Policy 1983* (Chicago: The Chicago Council On Foreign Relations, 1983).

16. In March 1981, Reagan authorised covert action against Nicaragua by approving a Presidential finding that an operation was desirable to halt the claimed flow of arms from Nicaragua to the guerrillas in El Salvador.

17. For one account see Gregory Treverton, 'US Strategy in Central America', *Survival* (March/April 1986), p. 138.

18. Many writings of the Heritage Foundation provided vivid examples of the tone of this campaign. The State Department's White paper on Communist Interference in El Salvador, also formed part of this campaign.

19. See Sklar, *Washington's War on Nicaragua*, pp. 50–54 for US support and organisation of ORDEN, a rural paramilitary and intelligence network in El Salvador from which the notorious 'death squads' of the far right grew.

20. There are many detailed accounts of US covert action in El Salvador since the Second World War and even earlier. For example, see McClintock, *The American Connection...El Salvador*, particularly pp. 147–372. For origins of the death squads see Craig Pyes, 'Roots of the Salvadoran Right: Origins of the Death Squads', in Marvin Gettleman, Patrick Lacefield, Louis Menashe and David Mermelstein (eds), *El Salvador: Central America in the New Cold War* (New York: Grove Press, 1986), pp. 86–9.

21. The Reagan Administration allowed the Sandinistas to draw their own conclusions about the US willingness to use direct military force in Grenada. Consequently in the weeks and months that followed the invasion, the Nicaraguans feared the worst and began to intensify their preparations for an American invasion – interview with Father Miguel D'Escoto, Foreign Minister, Government of Nicaragua, Managua, 14 February 1985.

22. See Remarks of the Hon. Fred C. Ikle, Under Secretary of Defense for Policy to Baltimore Council on Foreign Affairs, Monday, 12 September 1983, News Release No. 450–83, Office of Assistant Secretary of Defense for Public Affairs, Washington, DC, p. 4. For a comprehensive and detailed analysis of the Grenada invasion see William Blum, *The CIA: a Forgotten History* (London: Zed Books, 1988), pp. 306–15.

23. See Phillip Berryman, *Inside Central America* (New York: Pantheon Books, 1985), p. 87.

24. Berryman, *Inside Central America*, p. 91. See also Theodore Moran, 'The Cost of Alternative U.S. Policies Toward El Salvador: 1984–1989', in Robert S. Leiken (ed.), *Central America: Anatomy of Conflict* (New York: Pergamon Press, 1984).

25. See 'The Objectives and Costs of U.S. Military Operations Against Nicaragua: An Interview with Lt. Colonel John Buchanan', Memo Central America, Commission on United States-Central American Relations, Washington, DC (15 October 1984).

26. ARDE is the acronym for Alianza Revolucionaria Democratica.

27. As reported in Nairn, 'Endgame', p. 48.

28. The prospect of a protracted conflict also meant the possibility that Congress could force the Administration to withdraw US forces from the conflict after 60 days due to the War Powers Act. The Administration would therefore be under the added pressure to win the conflict quickly or at best give the appearance of not being bogged down in Nicaragua.

29. See Nairn, 'Endgame', p. 48.

30. For example see Leiken and Rubin, *Crisis Reader*, p. 609.

31. Sklar, *Washington's War in Nicaragua*, p. 192.

32. See William M. LeoGrande, *Central America and the Polls: A Study of U.S. Public Opinion Polls on U.S. Foreign Policy Toward El Salvador and Nicaragua under the Reagan Administration* (Washington DC: Washington Office on Latin America, 1984). For the public's 2 to 1 opposition to aid to the Contras from the years from 1983–86 and an analysis of this opposition, see Robert Pastor, *Condemned to Repetition – The United States and Nicaragua* (Princeton: Princeton University Press, 1987), p. 260.

33. Sklar, *Washington's War in Nicaragua*, p. 192.

34. Berryman, *Inside Central America*, p. 64.

35. See Treverton, 'U.S. Strategy in Central America', p. 129.

36. Reagan viewed the threat posed by the Sandinistas and others as 'pervasive, immediate, and dire'. Pastor, *Condemned to Repetition*, p. 231. See also 'United States

Central American Policy', USIS Press Release, (700) 11/25/87, and (701) 'Central American Negotiations', hereafter cited as 'Negotiations'.

37. Weekly Compilation of Presidential Documents (Friday, 13 November 1981), p. 1242.

38. See *New York Times*, 3 October 1985.

39. The US claimed that Nicaragua called for the export of its revolution. This was derived from a statement attributed to a 19 July 1981 speech by Nicaraguan Interior Minister Tomas Borge Martinez. See Wayne Smith, 'Lies About Nicaragua', *Foreign Policy*, No. 67, Summer 1987, p. 89.

40. D'Escoto interview.

41. For Nicaraguan claims of CIA interference before 1981, see Pastor, *Condemned to Repetition*, pp. 211–38. See also President Reagan, *New York Times* (6 June 1986), p. 5.

42. This was particularly with the onset of the 'Big Pine' exercises in Honduras. For one account see Manlio Tirado, 'The United States and the Sandinista Revolution', in Richard Harris and Carlos Vilas (eds.), *Nicaragua: A Revolution Under Siege* (London: Zed Books, 1985), pp. 206–10.

43. For an example of some of the Congressional debate over the question of US intervention into Nicaragua, see the debate concerning Republican Lee Hamilton and Republican Robert Michel: Debate on Contra Funding (April 1985), Congressional Record, 23 April 1985.

44. The Hon. Zbigniew Brzezinski, Assistant to President Carter for National Security Affairs, in *Hearings 1*, p. 103.

45. The primary objective of the Contras of the Nicaraguan Democratic Front (FDN) (Frente Democratico Nicaraguense), based in Honduras, from the outset was always to overthrow the Sandinista government. Interviews with multiple Contra prisoners in Esteli, Nicaragua, on 15 February 1985, hereafter cited as 'Esteli interviews'.

46. For former CIA agent David MacMichael's elaboration on this ruse see Blum, *The CIA*, pp. 336–7.

47. This was at a public press conference, see Curtin Winsor, 'From Reagan Doctrine to Détente', *Global Affairs* (Winter 1988), p. 78.

48. For a published version of the manual see Tayacan, 'Psychological Operations in Guerrilla Warfare', in Tayacan (ed.), *Psychological Operations in Guerrilla Warfare – The CIA's Nicaragua Manual* (New York: Vintage Books, 1985).

49. See the excellent summary *U.S. Military Intervention in Central America* (Washington, DC: The Commission on United States-Central American Relations, 8 May 1984).

50. For some views on the Boland Amendment see John Prados, *President's Secret Wars – CIA and Pentagon Covert Operations From World War II through to Iranscam* (New York: Quill, 1986), pp. 413–37. The last of the CIA money for the Contras was spent in March 1984 and the last CIA agents had reportedly officially left the operation in May.

51. The role of the NSC was made abundantly clear in the Iran-Contra investigations. For one in-depth overview of North's major role see Bob Woodward, *Veil: The Secret Wars of the CIA 1981–87* (London: Simon Schuster, 1987), pp. 459–69, 496–501.

52. The 208 Committee was created in 1985. After Casey's death and the onset of the 'Irangate' controversy, this committee was dissolved and was replaced by a new 'Board of Low Intensity Conflict' set up within the NSC. In June 1987, Reagan signed an authorisation for a new comprehensive LIC.

53. See the testimony of Colonel Oliver L. North, *Taking the Stand* (New York: Pocket Books, 1987), p. 373. National Security Adviser Robert McFarlane also testified that Reagan authorised various operations, see 'Reagan "approved rifle drop"', in *Weekend Australian* (18–19 March 1989), p. 16.

54. For further discussion, see Noam Chomsky, *Turning the Tide: U.S. Intervention in Central America and the Struggle for Peace* (Boston: South End Press, 1985), p. 131.

55. These included Woody Kepner Associates, International Business Communications, the Richard Mellon Scaife group, the Citizens for America group and publisher Rupert Murdoch's media interests.

56. See Stephen Rosenfeld, 'The Guns of July', *Foreign Affairs*, Vol. 64, No. 4 (Spring 1986), pp. 705–6.

57. See 'Marines Killed in San Salvador: New Stage in the Salvadoran War', in Gettleman et al. (eds), *El Salvador*, pp. 268–9.

58. See Rosenfeld, 'The Guns of July', pp. 705–6.

59. See John Muravchik, 'The Nicaragua Debate', *Foreign Affairs*, Vol. 65, No. 2 (1986), p. 371.

60. See Maggie Gallagher and Charles Bork, 'The New Freedom Fighters', *Commentary* (September 1985) p. 60. For what were regarded as the 'swing Democrats' see R. Pardo-Maurer, *The Contras, 1980–1989* (London, Praeger, 1990), pp. 26–8, 51–5.

61. See Saul Landau, *The Dangerous Doctrine – National Security and U.S. Foreign Policy* (London: Westview Press, 1988), p. 5.

62. See 'The Contras Need Our Help', *Washington Post* (5 March 1986).

63. See Larry Pratt, 'The Reagan Doctrine and the Third World', *Socialist Register* (London: Merlin Press, 1987), pp. 86–7.

64. For an account of some liberal intellectuals and politicians changing their opinions and beginning to support the Contras in April 1986, see Jill Smolowe, 'Conversion of a Timely Kind', *Time* (21 April 1986), p. 38.

65. For Nicaragua taking the US to the World Court on 27 June 1986, a case in which it won, see Pastor, *Condemned to Repetition*, p. 257.

66. As early as 1979 ex-national guardsmen of the Somoza regime had already organised themselves into insurgent forces to combat the Sandinistas, see Pastor, *Condemned to Repetition*, pp. 21–6.

67. See for example the establishment of trade unions, such as the Sandinista Workers Federation and the Sandinista Defense Committees, among other organisations, in Gary Ruchwarger, 'The Sandinista Mass Organizations and the Revolutionary Process', in Harris and Vilas, *Nicaragua*, pp. 88–119.

68. COSEP is the acronym for an umbrella organisation of business and employer groups who formed the 'Superior (or High) Council of Private Enterprise', which formed in 1974. For an account of where the FSLN determined that COSEP was opposed to the government, see Carlos M. Vilas, 'The Workers' Movement in the Sandinista Revolution', in Harris and Vilas, *Nicaragua*, p. 129. For an overview of the Nicaraguan domestic opposition in the context of the 1984 elections, see Latin American Studies Association, 'The Electoral Process in Nicaragua: Domestic and International Influences', in Peter Rosset and John Vandermeer (eds), *Nicaragua: Unfinished Revolution* (New York: Grove Press, 1986), pp. 76–81.

69. COSEP effectively placed itself in opposition to the Sandinista government and in return the government prohibited COSEP from receiving a $5.1 million grant from USAID in 1982. The government believed that the grant was to be used to finance movements trying to destabilise the new regime. FUNDE – the Nicaraguan Development Foundation which was established by USAID-funded programmes designed to compete directly with the government's campaign to win the support of small agricultural producers. For an overview of COSEP and its affiliate FUNDE, see Tom Barry, Beth Wood and Deb Preusch, *Dollars and Dictators* (London: Zed Press, 1982), pp. 90, 95, 220.

70. For one analysis of this struggle see Patricia Hynds, 'The Ideological Struggle Within the Catholic Church in Nicaragua', *Covert Action Information Bulletin*, No. 18 (Winter 1983), pp. 16–20. For the Pope's criticism of the popular church, see Margaret Crahan, *The Church and Revolution: Cuba and Nicaragua* (Melbourne: La Trobe University Institute of Latin American Studies 1987), p. 25.

71. Four priests figured at the centre of the dispute over the Church's role in the revolution. Miguel D'Escoto and Ernesto Cardenal became Foreign Minister and Minister of Culture respectively. Fernando Cardenal was appointed Minister of Education on 13 July 1984. And there was Adgar Parrales who served as Minister of Social Welfare and Ambassador to the Organization of American States. See Andrew Bradstock, *Saints and Sandinistas* (London: Epworth Press, 1987), pp. 59–69.

72. For the conservative bishops' arguments that the Sandinista government was anti-Church and no less than a pro-Soviet, pro-Cuban dictatorship, see Luis Serra, 'Ideology, Religion and the Class Struggle in the Nicaraguan Revolution', in Harris and Vilas, *Nicaragua*, pp. 160–1.

73. For one overview of the ideological conflict within the Nicaraguan Church, see the Michigan Interchurch Committee on Central American Human Rights, 'Ideological Struggle in the Nicaraguan Church', pp. 434–7, in Rosset and Vandermeer, *Nicaragua: Unfinished Revolution*.

74. At the grassroots level and not belonging to any pro-Somoza elites, a small number of Protestant groups (particularly Pentecostals) were similarly alienated from the regime. For a brief but concise account of these religious cleavages, see Crahan, *The Church and Revolution*, pp. 20–9.

75. Serra, 'Ideology, Religion', pp. 161–2.

76. See Carlos M. Vilas, *State, Class & Ethnicity in Nicaragua* (London: Lynne Rienner Publishers, 1989), pp. 1–95; see pp. 102–113 for the Sandinista programme to spread the revolution to the Atlantic coast.

77. For a more extensive coverage of the role of the Morovian Church, see Vilas, *State, Class & Ethnicity*, particularly pp. 116–17.

78. The Sandinistas later admitted that they had mishandled the operation and subsequently allowed the Mesquitos to return to the area in 1985. For the earlier relationship of the Mesquitos with the Sandinistas see George Black, *Triumph of the People* (London: Zed Press, 1981), pp. 247–8.

79. Interview with Roger Mayaga, Lieutenant Commander, State Security Head, 1st Region (MINT), Esteli, Nicaragua, 1985. Between 1980 and 1985 as much as one quarter of the Nicaraguan rebels came from the Atlantic coast and minority ethnic groups. These 'rebels' strongly opposed the Sandinista land and other reforms.

CHAPTER 6

1. For example see The White House, *National Security Strategy of the United States*, January 1988, pp. 5–6, 7. Both Reagan's State of the Union addresses (1985 and 1986) were also typical of this campaign.

2. This group were identified as the 'Contadora' group because their negotiations were conducted on the Mexican holiday resort island of Contadora.

3. For one example of this continued strategy, see *National Security*, p. 25. For the US attempts to discredit the elections of 1984, see J. Spence, 'Color it Undemocratic – Nicaragua Election Coverage', in *NACLA*, Vol. XIX, No. 1 (January/February 1985).

4. Interview with Charles Silver, United States Information Agency, Washington, DC, 24 May 1988.

5. For one account of the Enders–Ortega 1981 correspondence and the conditions for strengthening relations with the United States which the Nicaraguans rejected and America followed by terminating negotiations, see Robert Pastor, *Condemned to Repetition – the United States and Nicaragua* (Princeton: Princeton University Press, 1987), p. 235.

6. Yet another example of Washington's diplomatic manoeuvrings was the US objection to the negotiation initiative proposed by Costa Rican President Oscar Arias Sanchez in August 1987. For details see Viron Vaky, 'Positive Containment', *Foreign Policy*, No. 68 (Fall 1987) pp. 48–9.

7. Bermudez was a former Somoza Defense Attaché to Washington. For details of its leaders see R. Pardo-Maurer, *The Contras, 1980–1989* (London: Praeger, 1990), pp. 14, 24. On 9 March 1981, President Reagan signed a 'Presidential Finding' authorising the CIA, who were assisted by the Argentinean military, to organise the Contras of this group into the FDN.

8. For the statement of the goals and intentions of the FDN, see 'Nicaraguan Democratic Force: Principles', (February 1983) in Robert Leiken and Barry Rubin (eds), *The Central American Crisis Reader* (New York: Summit Books, 1987), pp. 261–3. The FDN expanded from 600 men in 1982 to upwards of 5,000 men in 1985.

9. Pastora, a charismatic former Sandinista leader, abandoned the Sandinista cause in 1981 complaining about the 'Cubanisation' of the revolution. In April 1982, he moved to Costa Rica where he formed the Alianza Revolucionaria Democratican (ARDE).

10. The ARDE also included members of the former Tercerista faction of the Sandinistas led by Alfonso Robelo, a millionaire agri-businessman from Nicaragua and former member of the Sandinista government. For notes on Robelo and the MDN, see Pardo-Maurer, *The Contras*. See also Christic Institute Papers, United States District Court Southern District of Florida, Civil Action No. 86–1146-CIV-KING and Civil Action No. 87–1545-CIV-KING, p. 78, hereafter cited as 'Christic Papers'. Two American reporters in Costa Rica joined with the Christic Institute in a civil lawsuit filed in Miami against those they claimed were involved in the probable US-directed La Penca bombing of Eden Pastora of ARDE. Pastora wanted to negotiate with the Sandinistas but was violently opposed by the FDN. The defendants included Adolfo Calero, Oliver North, Robert Owen, John Singlaub, Richard Secord and Theodore Shackley, formerly of the CIA.

11. For MISURA – an acronym taken from the first letters of the tribes' names and the later splinter group MISURASATA; see George Black, *Triumph of the People* (London: Zed Press, 1981), pp. 210–12, 247–8. For a short account of the origins of the MISURASATA involvement with the Contras see Roxanne Dunbar Ortiz, 'Miskitus in Nicaragua: Who is Violating Human Rights?', in Stanford Central America Action Network (eds), *Revolution in Central America* (Boulder: Westview Press, 1983), pp. 466–70.

12. See 'Christic Papers', pp. 78–80.

13. In 1984 the Reagan Administration upgraded the White House Office of Public Liaison to the Office of Public Diplomacy to wage psychological warfare within the United States. For one view, see for example W. Robinson and K. Norsworthy, *David and Goliath: Washington's War Against Nicaragua* (London: Zed Books, 1987), pp. 36–7.

14. This group's operations were described in the *Washington Post* (17 June and 24 September 1983).

15. See Report of the National Bipartisan Commission on Central America – January 1984.

16. Singlaub created the USCWF on 22 November 1981. For extensive notes on Singlaub's involvement, see Holly Sklar, *Washington's War on Nicaragua* (Boston: South End Press, 1988), pp. 233–42.

17. These groups were formed by Alabama National Guardsmen in July 1983.

18. See Reagan's speech to the American Bar Association, reported in the *New York Times* (9 July 1985), p. A1.

19. In 1985, President Reagan claimed that 'Support for freedom fighters is self-defense, and totally consistent with the OAS (Organization of American States) and UN charters', *New York Times* (25 January 1985).

20. Other private agencies that assisted in promoting the terrorist theme included the Soldier of Fortune, PRODEMCA, the American Security Council, the Council for

Inter-American Security and influential individuals such as Jeane Kirkpatrick and Henry Kissinger. For some comments on Reagan's 'founding fathers' speech, see Pardo-Maurer, *The Contras*, p. 29.

21. Also included among many of these groups were Gospel Crusade and Christian Retreat. For an extensive study and analysis of fundamentalist groups involved in the pursuit of US foreign policy, see 'Special Issue on the Religious Right', *Covert Action Information Bulletin*, No. 27 (Spring 1987).

22. Jerry Falwell often spoke of America's mission for 'world evangelization' with Central America its first target and Nicaragua the foremost testing ground for the defeat of 'atheistic communism'.

23. The IRD was claimed to be a 'shady New Right Outfit' with ties to the CIA. It was formed in 1981 by members of the Heritage Foundation, the Coalition for a Democratic Majority and others as an organisation to combat the 'evils' of liberation theology. For one account see Patricia Hynds, 'The Ideological Struggle Within the Catholic Church in Nicaragua', *Covert Action Information Bulletin*, No. 18 (Winter 1983), p. 16.

24. For an overview see Samuel T. Francis, *Smuggling Revolution: The Sanctuary Movement in America* (Washington, DC: Capital Research Center, 1986).

25. *The Committee of Santa Fe Report*, which provided much of the intellectual justification for the foreign policies of the incoming Reagan Administration in 1981, claimed the US had to seize the ideological initiative against liberation theology as utilised in Latin America. See 'U.S. Military Intervention in Central America', The Commission on United States–Central American Relations (8 May 1984).

26. See 'Franchising Aggression', *NACLA*, Vol. XX, No.4 (July/August 1986) p. 29.

27. Regarding non-lethal aid, groups that actively supplied the Contras included 'refugee' organizations such as Friends of the Americas (FOA). The FOA received funds and supplies from many other interrelated groups with direct ties to the Contras. These included the WACL, Americares and the Christian Broadcasting Network. The Soldier of Fortune, the Enterprise and the CMA were all involved in supplying arms and training. Also, John Singlaub and some Contra leaders were prominent in fund-raising activities, for details and other groups see 'Franchising Aggression', pp. 30–1, and 'Network Profiles' *NACLA*, Vol. XX, No.4 (July/August 1986), pp. 32–3.

28. Often claimed to be represented by figures such as Eden Pastora (former Commandante Zero) and Chamorro.

29. See Michael Klare and Peter Kornbluh (eds), *Low Intensity Warfare* (New York: Pantheon, 1988), p. 140.

30. To stimulate potential sponsors for this group, President Reagan granted interviews with those with significant funding or other aid to offer.

31. For members of the Nicaraguan right-wing opposition, see Robert Leiken, 'The Battle for Nicaragua', *New York Review of Books* (13 March 1986), p. 44.

32. For a brief overview of the election of 1984, see Carlos Vilas and Richard Harris, 'National Liberation, Popular Democracy and the Transition to Socialism', in Richard Harris and Carlos Vilas (eds), *Nicaragua: A Revolution Under Siege* (London: Zed Books, 1985), pp. 230–4.

33. See William Blum, *The CIA: a Forgotten History* (London: Zed Books, 1988), p. 332.

34. For some details on the AIFLD, including its ties with the CIA and the claim that it received 95 per cent funding by USAID see Tom Barry, Beth Wood and Deb Preusch, *Dollars and Dictators* (London: Zed Press, 1982), pp. 103–14.

35. See 'US Policy and the Marxist Threat to Central America,' Heritage Foundation, *Backgrounder 128* (Washington, DC: 15 October 1980).

36. Martin Walker, 'Veil lifted on Washington's genteel CIA surrogate', *The Age* (20 April 1990), p. 9. The NED claimed to be a non-profit organisation and received Congressional funding channelled through the United States Information Agency.

After 1984 over 95 per cent of its income of $114 million came from the US government. NED has a history of financially backing movements, organisations and governments favoured by the US Administration at any one particular time as demonstrated by its backing and funding of the Noriega election campaign in 1984, and then its support of the 1989 anti-Noriega campaign in Panama. See *The Washington Post* (19 March 1986).

37. See Walker, 'Veil lifted...'. The opposition in 1990 was in the form of the broad UNO alliance.

38. 'Network Profiles', p. 32.

39. The Administration supported PRODEMCA via funding from the NED, see Christopher Hitchins, 'A Modern Medieval Family', *Mother Jones* (July/August 1986), p. 74.

40. See *Washington Post* (21 March 1986).

41. USAID termed pro-American groups in Nicaragua, 'Private Voluntary Organizations', see US Army, *Guide for the Planning of Counterinsurgency* (Washington DC: Department of the Army, 1975), pp. 26–7.

42. Margaret Crahan, *The Church and Revolution: Cuba and Nicaragua* (Melbourne: La Trobe University Institute of Latin American Studies, 1987), p. 26.

43. For example, in July 1982, Nicaragua prevented USAID from giving $5 million to the Catholic Church which it believed would be used to undermine government programmes. See Crahan, 'The Church', p. 23.

44. This manual was revealed for the first time in the US press in October 1984, see *Washington Post* (24 October 1984) and *Newsweek* (26 November 1984), p. 42. The manual directly conflicted with Executive Order 12333 signed by President Reagan in 1981 that prohibited political assassinations. For CIA/Contra assassination plots against Foreign Minister Miguel D'Escoto and the nine members of the Sandinista National Directorate, see Blum, *The CIA*, pp. 335–6.

45. See Tayacan, 'Psychological Operations in Guerilla Warfare' in Tayacan (ed.), *Psychological Operations in Guerilla Warfare – the CIA's Nicaragua Manual* (New York: Vintage Books, 1985). I inspected copies of this manual taken from Contra prisoners in Esteli in Northern Nicaragua on 15 February 1985. The Soldier of Fortune organisation also distributed the manual in Honduras. For extensive notes on the former Green Beret and CIA contract employee with the pseudonym 'John Kirkpatrick' who was attributed with writing the manual, see John Prados, *President's Secret Wars – CIA and Pentagon Covert Operations from World War II through to Iranscam* (New York: Quill, 1986), p. 406.

46. This was in particular regard to the military or guerrilla strategy of 'people's war', see for example Mao Tse Tung, *Selected Military Writings of Mao Tse Tung* (Peking: Foreign Language Press, 1963), particularly pp. 187–262.

47. Interviews with multiple Contra prisoners in Esteli, Nicaragua, 15 February 1985.

48. See Tayacan, 'Psychological Operations', p. 83.

49. This was confirmed in my interviews with captured Contras in Esteli on 15 February 1985. The Contras also used some of the Sandinistas' own actions against them in their propaganda campaigns among the campesinos. The Contras argued that the 'communist atheists' will come and destroy their religion and this appeared confirmed by the EPS in some regions where they occupied the churches to use as their bases, which were usually on a hill and well fortified. As a consequence these churches were often destroyed. Interview with Maria Lopez Vigil, Journalist, *ENVIO*, Instituto Historico Centroamericano, Managua, Nicaragua, 13 February 1985.

50. For example, see Tayacan, 'Psychological Operations', p. 57. For one stark example of the Contras using Christian symbolism for political effect, see Andrew Bradstock, *Saints and Sandinistas* (London: Epworth Press, 1987), p. 39.

51. Tayacan, 'Psychological Operations', p. 62.

52. This provided simplistic instructions on how to carry out sabotage operations on such regionally inappropriate targets as telephone boxes and other amenities more associated with the First World. I inspected a copy of this booklet in Esteli on February 15 1985.

53. Interview with Lietenant Commander Roger Mayaga, Nicaragua State Security Head, 1st Region (MINT), Esteli, Nicaragua (15 February 1985), hereafter cited as 'Mayaga interview'.

54. Between 1981 and 1987, the Reagan Administration conducted at least 14 major military exercises in Honduras and significantly increased its military presence in Central America. In conjunction with these exercises, it also constructed new military bases and other facilities in Honduras that the Contras were able to use. Under cover of these exercises, the US was able to supply further arms and training to the Contras and its Honduran and Salvadoran allies.

55. This was particularly so in 1987 when the 'Solid Shield' manoeuvres saw the participation of over 50,000 US troops in Honduras, causing the Sandinista government to react with such alarm that it declared that an invasion was imminent. For one view see Alan White, *The Morass* (New York: Harper & Row, 1984), pp. 64–5.

56. One particular example of intentional US tactics to induce fear in the Nicaraguan population was the frequent practice of high- speed US flyovers to create sonic booms to unnerve the population. This was reportedly an idea of Oliver North, see Prados, *President's Secret Wars*, p. 412.

57. D'Escoto interview. By 1985, the financial burden of defence had forced the Nicaraguan government to raise taxes and limit funding for education and other social programmes. The policy of subsidising basic consumer goods was also abandoned resulting in stiff price increases and an annual inflation rate of over 200 per cent.

58. Interview with Father Miguel D'Escoto, Foreign Minister, Government of Nicaragua, Managua, 14 February 1985. My own observations also verified this. One particular problem such war scares induced was the disruption of streets in urban areas due to the movement and positioning of armoured vehicles and other preparations for a military assault, particularly on Managua. For one estimation of the economic costs to Nicaragua due to the US-backed war, see Richard Harris, 'Epilogue: Revolution Under Siege', in Richard Harris and Carlos Vilas (eds), *Nicaragua: A Revolution Under Siege* (London: Zed Books, 1985), pp. 242–4.

59. General Paul Gorman, a member of the restricted Interagency Group is accredited with formulating this psyops strategy, see *Washington Post*, 6 August 1983.

60. American psychologist Fred Landis received his PhD from the University of Illinois for his thesis 'Psychological Warfare and Media Operations in Chile, 1970–1973'. Landis served as a consultant for the Church Committee's Subcommittee on CIA Covert Action in Chile. See Fred Landis, 'CIA Media Operations in Chile, Jamaica, and Nicaragua'. *Covert Action Information Bulletin*, No. 16 (March 1982), pp. 32–43.

61. This was carried out, for example, in other parts of Central America and even as far afield as India, see Landis, 'CIA Media Operations', pp. 35–6.

62. Landis further claimed that this propaganda campaign essentially replicated the blueprint for psychological warfare outlined in the US Army Field Manual of Psychological Operations. Landis drew strong parallels with CIA campaigns waged in Chile and Jamaica, which were revealed in the investigations of the Church Committee, see Landis, 'CIA Media Operations', pp. 32–43.

63. Esteli interviews.

64. In March 1985, the State Department's Office of Public Diplomacy published a booklet entitled 'Misconceptions About US Policy Toward Nicaragua', in which it denied imposing any sort of economic boycott on Nicaragua and denied trying to strangle Nicaragua economically.

65. For the later formulation of an embargo policy based on the recognition of Nicaragua's dependence on imports and in particular Soviet weapons and foreign oil in 1983, which also led to the decision to mine Nicaraguan harbours, see the testimony of Robert McFarlane on 13 May 1987 in 'U.S. Congress, Testimony of Robert C. McFarlane, Gaston J. Sigur, Jr., and Robert W. Owen, Joint Hearings before the House Select Committee to Investigate Covert Arms Transactions with Iran and Senate Select Committee on Secret Military Assistance to Iran and the Nicaraguan Opposition', May 1987, hereafter cited as *Hearings 4*.

66. This was relatively easy to do as many of these agencies were dependent on US funds for their lending programs. See *Washington Post* (8 March 1985).

67. Between 1979 and 1982, Nicaragua obtained 34 per cent of its external financial assistance from these bodies. Until 1985, Mexico was also a major supplier of petroleum to Nicaragua on credit. For one summary see Peter Kornbluh, 'Uncle Sam's Money, *Washington Post*, C1, C4 (27 August 1989)'.

68. For one account, see Pastor, *Condemned to Repetition*, p. 242.

69. See Abraham Lowenthall, 'Threat and Opportunity in the Americas', *Foreign Affairs*, Vol. 64, No. 3 (1986), pp. 554–5. The reason for the long delay in imposing a full trade embargo was because of basic differences of opinion between the State Department and the NSC over the use of such embargoes.

70. The CIA was not the only US agency behind these sabotage missions. The Pentagon's Special Operations Division and Army Intelligence Support Activity (ISA) also played a critical role. The Special Operations Division operated 'in the black', under strict cover within the Office of the Army's deputy chief of staff for operations (DCSOPS). The Special Operations Forces helped CIA operatives in Honduras train specially recruited Honduran troops for hit-and-run operations in Nicaragua.

71. Interview with Christian Pichardo, Commandante, FSLN, Zone 1, Ministry of Interior, Nuevo Segovia, Esteli, Nicaragua, 15 February 1985, hereafter cited as 'Pichardo interview'. One example of the serious impact these operations had was in October 1982 when the Standard Fruit Company suspended its banana operations in Nicaragua leaving four thousand workers unemployed and approximately six million cases of bananas rotting with no transport or market, 'Pichardo interview'.

72. See Bob Woodward, *Veil: The Secret Wars of the CIA 1981–87* (London: Simon & Schuster, 1987), p. 281.

73. Over 25 per cent of Nicaragua's factories suffered damage to plant inventory during the revolution and over 90 per cent closed in its final stage. An estimate of the cost of the war to Nicaragua had the country losing $500 million in physical damage, $200 million in lost cotton exports, and $700 million in capital flight, as well as suffering a 25 per cent reduction in cattle. At the time of the Sandinista victory, unemployment was estimated to be 40 per cent and inflation 80 per cent. The Somoza family had plundered the national banks, leaving only $3.5 million in the national treasury and a national debt of approximately $1.6 billion. For one account see Barry et al., *Dollars and Dictators*, p. 217.

74. For one view see Scott Whiteford & Terry Hoops, 'Labor Organization and Participation in the Mixed Economy: The Case of Sugar Production', in Michael E. Conroy (ed.), *Nicaragua: Profiles of the Revolutionary Public Sector* (Boulder: Westview Press, 1987), pp. 171–99.

75. D'Escoto interview.

76. Interview with Rigos Law Downs, Mesquito Indian in Managua, Nicaragua, 9 February 1985, hereafter cited as 'Downs interview'.

77. See Klare and Kornbluh, *Low Intensity Warfare*, p. 138.

78. Interview with former Captain John Zindar, School of Army Intelligence, Center for Defense Information, Washington, DC, 25 May 1988. See also *Washington Post*, 8 May 1983. For Pastor's analysis of the 'nation building' of the Contras, an operation

to which Secretary of State Haig was opposed, see Pastor, *Condemned to Repetition*, pp. 236–7.

79. Pastor, *Condemned to Repetition*, p. 246.

80. Historically this sort of action is not commonly pursued by insurgent movements for fear of alienating local support. For example, in the Philippines the NPA abandoned economic sabotage in rural areas because of the disruptive effects and hardship this inflicted on the local peasantry, interview with members of General Staff, New People's Army (aliases 'Rich' and 'George'), Manila, Philippines, 29–30 May 1987, hereafter cited as 'Rich and George interview'.

81. The CIA's timetable calling for Contra 'liberated zones' to be established before the end of 1983 had gone badly awry with their failure to capture and hold towns.

82. For an in-depth cover and analysis of the US secret wars/covert operations in Nicaragua see Sklar, *Washington's War*, pp. 75–392. For a series of Contra interviews which virtually chronicles the US-Contra campaign against the Sandinistas from a 'grassroots' combatants perspective, see Dieter Eich and Carlos Rincon, *The Contras* (San Francisco: Synthesis Publications, 1985).

83. Esteli interviews. It is estimated that between 1981 and November 1984, the Contras had assassinated 910 state officials and killed 8,000 civilians, see Blum, *The CIA*, p. 334.

84. Downs interview.

85. Downs interview.

86. The Sandinistas were displaying 143 people recovered from the Contras in one way or another. Most were '*secuestrados*' (kidnapped people), peasants originally kidnapped by the Contras in Neuva Segovia and Madrid department and forced into armed service. While some claimed to have joined voluntarily, others were bribed with money. Most claimed to have been in the pay of the CIA.

87. See Americas Watch Committee, *The Miskitos in Nicaragua 1981–1984* (Washington, DC: Americas Watch Report, November 1984), p. 7.

88. For an overview of the Sandinista agrarian reform programme both implemented and proposed, see Eduardo Baumeister, 'The Structure of Nicaraguan Agriculture and the Sandinista Agrarian Reform', in Harris and Vilas, *Nicaragua*, pp. 10–35.

89. Maria Frenkel, 'Evolution of Food and Agricultural Policies During Economic Crisis and War', in Conroy, *Nicaragua*, pp. 220–21.

90. Special Operations Forces were used most extensively in Military Training Teams (MTTs) to train the Contras, as well as transport and supply. For the role of the Alabama National Guard, see Leslie Cockburn, *Out of Control* (New York: Atlantic Monthly Press, 1987), pp. 90–3. For Alabama Police Force and Atlanta National Guard cooperation in assisting the Contras see also Colonel Harry Summers, *On Strategy: The Vietnam War in Context* (US Army War College, Carlisle Barracks, Pennsylvania: Strategic Studies Institute, November 1983), p. 14.

91. 'Unilaterally Controlled Latino Assets' was first quoted in the *Washington Post* (18 April 1984). They were trained and supported by the Pentagon and the CIA, see 'The CIA's War', *NACLA*, Vol. XX, No. 4 (July/August 1986) p. 25, see also *Los Angeles Times* (4 March 1985).

92. Zindar interview. For one account of the activities of the UCLAS, see Edgar Chamorro, 'World Court Affidavit', in Rosset and Vandermeer, *Nicaragua: Unfinished Revolution*, pp. 235–46.

93. See *Newsweek*, 16 April 1984, and 'Chimera' in *First Principles Center for National Security Studies*, Vol. 11, No. 1 (Washington, DC: September–October 1985), p. 7. In 1984 the CIA, apart from other actions, was involved in the destruction of the oil storage facility at Corinto.

94. Esteli interviews.

95. Downs interview.

96. For the economic impact caused by the CIA mining and sabotage operations see *Select Committee on Intelligence (94/2) Report, 1 January 1983 to 31 December 1984* (Washington DC: Government Printing Office, 1985), pp. 7–10.

97. For a detailed analysis of Israel's role in assisting the Contras, see Jane Hunter, *Israeli Foreign Policy* (Boston, Spokesman for the Bertrand Russell Peace Foundation, South End Press, 1987), pp. 145–68.

98. Indicating this, the embassy in Honduras was upgraded and Ambassador John Negroponte assumed the role of 'theatre commander'. CIA and Special Forces were based in both Honduras and El Salvador.

99. See Sklar, *Washington's War*, pp. 223–5.

100. See Michael McClintock, *The American Connection Volume Two: State Terror and Popular Resistance in Guatemala* (London: Zed Press, 1985), pp. 187–96. Such claims were substantiated by the Tower Commission Report of 26 February 1987.

101. See also Samuel Segev, *The Iranian Triangle* (New York: The Free Press, 1988), pp. 149–52, for Segev's observation of joint US–Israeli policy in the Middle East which involved the redirection of aid to the Contras, see p. 214.

102. For further reading on this topic one should consult Peter Dale Scott and Jonathan Marshall, *Cocaine Politics* (University of California Press, 1991).

103. For more detail see for example: *Taking the Stand: The Testimony of Lieutenant Oliver L. North* (New York: Pocket Books, 1987).

104. Secretary of Defense Caspar Weinberger, testimony, 31 July 1987, before the Iran-Contra committee, cited in Saul Landau, *The Dangerous Doctrine – National Security and U.S. Foreign Policy* (London: Westview Press, 1988), p. 173.

105. Richard Secord is accredited with calling this loose organisation the 'Enterprise'. It has also been termed the 'Cabal'.

106. For some accounts of these activities see Cockburn, *Out of Control*; Jonathan Marshall, Peter Scott and Jane Hunter, *The Iran Contra Connection* (Boston: South End Press, 1987).

107. Included within the Enterprise were such 'front' companies as Lake Resources, Gulf Marketing, and Udall Research.

108. Sklar infers that the Enterprise was a recently formed organisation to circumvent Congressional scrutiny, see Sklar, *Washington's War*, pp. 236–51.

109. Retired General Secord played a prominent role in directing this organisation. He was recommended by Casey as a person who could assist 'us' outside the Government to comply with the Boland proscriptions. See Sklar, *Washington's War* p. 253. From January 1984 to August 1986, he served as a member of the Special Operations Policy Advisory Group (SOPAG). In this time, Secord was enlisted by North to help run the Contra Program under the supervision of Casey and North.

110. For a definition of sheepdipping, see 'Right Wing Vigilantes and US Involvement', *Report of a US-Philippines Fact Finding Mission to the Philippines, May 20–30, 1987* (Manila: Philippine Alliance of Human Rights Advocates, July, 1987), also known as the 'Ramsay Clarke Report', p. 42. Other individuals involved with the Enterprise included ex-members of US armed or intelligence services. Eugene Hasanfus was one such example, he had worked with the CIA in air operations in Laos.

111. Zindar interview.

112. For one in-depth coverage of this private war and the connections between Administration officials, the Enterprise and drug trafficking for arms funding, as well as the other operations of the secret war, including activities of the Medellin Cartel, see Leslie Cockburn, *Out of Control* (New York:Atlantic Monthly Press, 1987).

113. The Contra support plan also involved weapons being funnelled through inflated sales of equipment to other countries, including Honduras, Guatemala, Brazil and Argentina, the establishment of offshore bank accounts, and Special Operations Forces building airstrips in Costa Rica.

114. This was according to a plan presented by National Security Adviser Robert McFarlane to President Reagan who approved it. See the *Washington Post* (11 August 1985).

115. The WACL was created by the intelligence organisations of Taiwan and South Korea to provide an outlet for anti-communist propaganda.

116. For Singlaub's activities within the US raising money and weapons for the FDN, see also 'Reagan "Approved Rifle Drop"', *Weekend Australian* (18 March 1989), p. 16.

117. See John Dillion and Jon Lee Anderson, 'Who's Behind Aid to the Contras?', *Nation* (6 October 1984). For extensive details of CAUSA and the WACL see *Covert Action Information Bulletin*, No. 27 (Spring 1987), particularly pp. 36–46.

118. *New York Times* (13 December 1984).

119. Oliver North, for example, directed a secret army unit called the Intelligence Support Activity, a helicopter assault group and a navy unit that had engaged the Nicaraguan military.

120. The White House Office of Public Liaison also participated in generating sponsors. Oliver North was the White House liaison to the CIA on the Contra issue. He was instructed by McFarlane to maintain the faith and spirit of the Contras until the Administration could win new funding for the conflict.

121. These were named after George Patton, Jeane Kirkpatrick and other 'heroes'.

122. In this campaign the activities of NEPL were critical and significant. See for example, Klare and Kornbluh, *Low Intensity Warfare*, pp. 155–6. For Casey's actions lobbying support for the Contras during the period after the amendment, see Prados, *President's Secret Wars*, pp. 431–63.

123. Also involved in fund raising activities were Daniel Graham of 'High Frontier', the Star Wars lobby, fundamentalists and evangelists such as the Reverend Sun Myung Moon, Pat Boone, Jerry Falwell, Pat Robertson, and many associated groups such as Gospel Crusade and Christian Retreat.

124. See 'Franchising Aggression', p. 33.

125. Esteli interviews. This selective elimination of Sandinista representatives and other activities in the rural areas was reminiscent of 'Operation Phoenix' in Vietnam and was designed to separate the Sandinistas from the civilians (and primarily the *campesinos*) and thereby isolate the regime.

126. Downs interview.

127. The USWCF was the US branch of the WACL. Formed in 1967 it has been reportedly associated with 'European fascists, Nazis and Latin American death squads'. See 'Franchising Aggression', pp. 30–1.

128. See statement of the Administration on p. v of *National Security*, where it indicates it is applying the Reagan Doctrine in Afghanistan, Nicaragua, Cambodia and the Philippines.

CHAPTER 7

1. This agreement was originally scheduled to terminate on 13 March 2046, but was later altered to 16 September 1991. For some of the rights given to the United States under the Military Bases Agreement see 'The U.S Bases in the Philippines: Assets or Liabilities?', *Defense Monitor*, Vol. XV, No. 4 (Washington, DC: Center For Defense Information, 1986).

2. For a description of the operational facilities of the five major bases (especially Clark and Subic), see Niksch report in *Insurgency and Counterinsurgency in the Philippines*, Prepared for the Committee on Foreign Relations United States Senate by the Foreign Affairs and National Defense Division, Congressional Research Service, Library of Congress, November 1985, (Washington, DC: U.S. Government Printing Office, 1985), p. 6, hereafter cited as *Insurgency and Counterinsurgency*.

3. In 1984, at least 15 per cent of the top thousand Philippine companies were American, see *Right Wing Vigilantes and US Involvement, Report of a US-Philippines*

Fact Finding Mission to the Philippines, May 20–30, 1987 (Manila: Philippine Alliance of Human Rights Advocates, July 1987), pp. 10–11 (within this publication the 'Clarke Report', named after US Attorney General Ramsay Clarke, is cited in full). By 1983 US firms in the Philippines had a book value of $1.3 billion and had absorbed 33 per cent of Philippine exports; for other figures, see Juvenal L. Angel, compiler, *American Firms Operating In the Philippines* (New York: World Trade Academy Press, Inc. 1984).

4. For one overview of the importance of the Philippines see Christopher Madison, 'Rare White House-Congress Consensus on Policy Toward Philippines', *National Journal* (11 November 1985), pp. 2708–10.

5. Waldon Bello, for example, considered this insurgency to be merely 'round four' of the long confrontation between the United States and Philippine nationalism which dated back to 1898, see Walden Bello, *Creating The Third Force: US Sponsored Low Intensity Conflict in the Philippines* (San Francisco: Institute for Food and Development Policy, 1987), p. 3.

6. In 1986, the NPA was claimed to number about 23,000 members and was still growing, see *Hearings 1*, pp. 501–2 (for full *Hearings 1* reference, see Chapter 1, note 2). For other estimates see Statement of Richard L. Armitage, Assistant Secretary of Defense for International Security Affairs in 'Preparation for February 1986 Philippine Presidential Election', *Hearing Before the Committee on Foreign Relations*, United States Senate, 99th Congress, First Session, December 18, 1985 (Washington, DC: U.S. Government Printing Office, 1986), p. 46, hereafter cited as *Hearings 3*.

7. See *Hearings 3*, pp. 18–26, 46–7. For one analysis of the NPA's rapid growth see the testimony of Karl Lande in Richard Armitage, 'Situation in the Philippines and Implications for US Policy', *Statement to the Subcommittee on Asian and Pacific Affairs*, Committee on Foreign Affairs, House of Representatives, Washington, DC (12 March 1985), pp. 14–18, hereafter cited as 'Armitage Report'.

8. 'Armitage Report', pp. 3–4.

9. The serious ramifications for the United States of the loss of the Philippines at this time was underscored by former National Security Adviser Zbigniew Brzezinski. See statement of Hon. Zbigniew Brzezinski, Assistant to President Carter for National Security Affairs, in *Hearings 1*, pp. 105–6.

10. For one account of the loss of support of the Filipino middle class see the Statement of Carle H. Lande, Professor of Political Science, University of Kansas, in the 'Armitage Report', p. 3. Also see pp. 147–63.

11. Larry Niksch, of the Congressional Library Research Service, outlined these and other key factors contributing to the growth of the communist insurgency. For an extensive elaboration of these points, see *Insurgency and Counterinsurgency*, p. 8.

12. See Bello, *Creating the Third Force*, pp. 39–42.

13. Marcos's direct control of the military was facilitated with the formation of the Metropolitan Command (METROCOM) for the Manila area in 1967, see Bello, *Creating the Third Force*, pp. 30–1.

14. Marcos had a particular obsession with the number seven. For accounts of such superstitions see Raymond Bonner, *Waltzing With a Dictator* (New York: Times Books, 1987).

15. By 1985, the NPA insurgency had grown to the point where it was operational in most provinces of the Philippines archipelago; for one in-depth account of the growth and fortunes of the CPP/NPA insurgency, see Gregg R. Jones, *Red Revolution* (London: Westview Press, 1989).

16. I witnessed some of these actions, see also Bello, *Creating the Third Force*, pp. 36–9, and Enrique Delacruz, Aida Jordan and Jorge Emmanual (eds), *Death Squads in the Philippines* (Manila: Alliance for Philippine Concerns, September 1987), p. 7.

17. A US Senate Foreign Relations Committee report also concluded that the AFP used violence indiscriminately and without regard to political consequences of waging war against the people, see the US Senate Foreign Relations Committee Staff, 'The Situation in the Philippines', Washington, DC: US Senate (September 1984), p. 15.

18. This was admitted by Brigadier General Jose Magno Jr, Commanding Officer, Central Mindanao Command (CEMCOM), in an interview with myself in Cotabato City on 5 August 1983. A further case illustrating this was the destruction by the AFP of the town of Jolo in the Sulu Archipelago to eject the Moro National Liberation Front and in effect 'destroying the town to save it': interview with Rear Admiral (Former Commander in Chief, Philippines Southern Command) and Minister of Muslim Affairs, Romulo Espaldon, Manila, 11 August 1983.

19. *Insurgency and Counterinsurgency*, p. 3. For an elaboration of the government's strategy, see pp. 30–2. The estimates of CHDF strength usually ranged from 65,000 to 70,000, whereas the Constabulary or Integrated National Police (INP) numbered around 43,500.

20. See *Hearings 3*, p. 21.

21. For example, see 'Armitage Report', pp. 135–43.

22. The Philippine Constabulary were in effect the military police of the AFP, a rural police force established during the US colonial rule to combat insurgency.

23. See *Insurgency and Counterinsurgency*, pp. 4–5, 36–40. For some reported abuses of the military under Marcos see also Amnesty International, *Philippines, Unlawful Killings by Military and Paramilitary Forces* (New York: Amnesty International Publications, 1988).

24. For some reported and recorded abuses of the CHDF, see *Human Rights in the Philippines, Report of an Australian Fact-Finding Mission To The Philippines, 28 November–5 December 1987*, edited by Shirley Randell (Melbourne: Philippines Resources Centre, February 1988), pp. 42–3, hereafter cited as *Human Rights*.

25. See Amnesty International, *Philippines, Unlawful Killings*, p. 8. Good examples of these 'warlords' were Ali Dimaporo (a Muslim) in Lanao del Sur, Mindanao, and Jose Durano in Cebu: see Bello, *Creating the Third Force*, p. 29. Marcos also often legitimised his cronies' private armies by giving them official CHDF status. The CHDF were soon discredited for their involvement in numerous political murders, or salvagings, disappearances and massacres and other notorious human rights violations.

26. 'Armitage Report', p. 2.

27. This compromise was part of the process whereby the LIC approach was gaining conceptual coherence within the US Administration.

28. This was apparent when the Department of State indicated that the Marcos government still relied primarily on military actions to combat the insurgency virtually ignoring civic action. See 'Armitage Report', p. 231, for other recognised shortcomings within the Philippine military such as poor equipment, training and discipline, see also pp. 255–7.

29. Interview with Brigadier General Jose Magno, Jr, Commanding Officer, Central Mindanao Command (CENCOM), Cotabato City, Philippines (5 August 1983), hereafter cited as 'Magno interview'.

30. In November 1984, in the wake of the Aquino assassination, General Ramos became Acting Chief of Staff of the Armed Forces. Supported by the group of AFP officers who formed the Reform the Armed Forces Movement (RAM), Ramos tried to implement some military reforms in 1985. For a list of recommendations, and the moves that Ramos did make, including ordering civic action programmes, see *Insurgency and Counterinsurgency*, pp. 48–55.

31. The Congressional report urged reform of the leadership and the adoption of more civic action and other political approaches. It also stressed the need for reforming the CHDF and retraining the AFP with an emphasis on discipline, morale and better relations with the civilian population.

32. USAID has a long history of operations in the Philippines. For USAID operations in 1984 see Statement of Hon. Charles W. Greenleaf, Jr, Assistant Administrator, Bureau for Asia, Agency for International Development in 'Armitage Report', pp. 163–74.

33. The CPP charged that the CIA carried out many covert operations including propaganda manipulation, economic destabilisation, counterinsurgency activities, the formation of paramilitary groups and outright political assassinations of leftist leaders, see *Ang Bayan*, Vol. XX1, No. 8 (October 1989), p. 12.

34. Other agencies, though not necessarily involved in Central America, included the Asian Development Bank, the Free Trade Union Institute, the Wycliffe Bible Translators, the Asia Foundation, the Christian Anti-Communist Crusade, the Asian American Free Labor Institute (AAFLI), an arm of the AFL-CIO also operative in Central America.

35. Cline, like Singlaub, was a long-time CIA asset, see *Right Wing Vigilantes*, p. 38.

36. For comprehensive list of these vigilante groups see Delacruz et al., *Death Squads*, pp. 46–8.

37. Interview with members of the NPA 'Sparrow' squad of the Alex Boncayao Brigade, New People's Army, Navotas, Manila, 29 May 1987, hereafter known as 'Sparrow interview'.

38. By virtue of the simple logic that any challenge to the status quo meant communism, reform organisations were often deemed subversive and therefore were to be eliminated, see *Right Wing Vigilantes*, p. 1.

39. This was recognised by the Department of State in its response to the Subcommittee on Asian and Pacific Affairs in 1984, see 'Armitage Report', p. 265.

40. Considered an accompanying document to the US–RP bases agreement, the MAA was signed on 21 March 1947. In June 1953, it was updated and renamed the 'Mutual Defense Assistance Pact'.

41. The most important forms of this US assistance were the Military Advisory Group, logistics assistance, the training of military students in the US and shared intelligence, for an overview see Roland Simbulan, *The Bases of our Insecurity* (Metro Manila: Balai Fellowship, 1985), pp. 80–1.

42. This was argued as early as April 1967 by the Chairman of the Committee on National Defense in the Philippines House of Representatives, Carmelo Barbero, see William J. Pomeroy, 'The Philippines: A Case History of Neocolonialism', in *Remaking Asia*, at p. 165 as cited in 'The U.S. Bases in the Philippines: Assets or Liabilities?', *Defense Monitor*, Vol. XV, No. 4 (Washington, DC: Center for Defense Information, 1986).

43. It was claimed that Washington signed this treaty strictly to get the Philippines to agree with the Japanese Peace Treaty, see Stephen Shalom, *The United States and the Philippines* (Quezon City: New Day Publishers, 1986), p. 75.

44. In the mid-1980s the largest US Peace Corps programme was in the Philippines, see *Hearings 2*, p. 5 (for full *Hearings 2* reference, see Chapter 1, note 4).

45. This form of leverage was inferred in a Department of State statement to the Subcommittee on Asian and Pacific Affairs, see 'Armitage Report', p. 265.

46. The military and the vigilantes often used intimidation and terror tactics to force the local population in contested areas into joining these groups.

47. See Delacruz et al., *Death Squads*, pp. 13–14. The military and government backing of the vigilante groups was also claimed by the Philippine Senate Committee on

Justice and Human Rights, see 'Report of the Committee on Justice and Human Rights on Vigilante Groups', Philippine Senate Committee on Justice and Human Rights, 1988, pp. 16–17.

48. Note that the Ramsay Clarke team were the authors of *Right Wing Vigilantes*. The other human rights groups also included the Australian Fact Finding Team, the Philippine Alliance of Human Rights Advocates, the Ecumenical Partnership for International Concerns (EPIC) and many other organisations and individual researchers including the author.

49. For some testimonies of local government officials among others, see *Right Wing Vigilantes*, p. 16, and Amnesty International, *Philippines, Unlawful Killings*, pp. 26–41.

50. I attained a copy of a Calida memo in which the extent of the Constabulary's control over the Alsa Masa is revealed. In this Memorandum of Lt Colonel Franco Calida to the Davao Metropolitan District Command, Camp Captain Domingo & Leonor, Intelligence Division, Davao City, dated 15 December 1986.

51. President Aquino in October 1987 and Cardinal Sin in November 1987 also endorsed the formation of the vigilante groups, see *Philippines Daily Inquirer* (8 November 1987).

52. See Sheila Coronel, 'Dangers Aired in Arming Untrained Civilians', in *Manila Chronicle* (28 March 1987).

53. See Mark Tran, 'CIA Sweep in Philippines', *Manchester Guardian Weekly* (2 March 1987).

54. See Peter Tarr, 'Philippine Vigilantes Reflect U.S. Strategy for Low Intensity Conflict', *Los Angeles Times* (10 November 1987), pp. 2, 6. Tarr claims that Aquino's backdown was also linked to the bomb attempt on her life at the Philippine Military Academy on 13 March 1987.

55. As reported in Delacruz et al., *Death Squads*, p. 39.

56. 'Rich and George interview'. Members of a NPA 'Sparrow' unit also claimed that the US formed vigilante groups by recruiting criminals and religious fanatics, Sparrow interview. Also, a leading Filipino businessman Enrique Zobel de Ayala was reportedly identified as a CIA operative in funding and forming the vigilante groups, see *Ang Bayan*, Vol. XX1, No. 8 (October 1989), pp. 12–13.

57. Interview with Arnel De Guzman, Director of Philippine Alliance of Human Rights Advocates (PAHRA), Manila, Philippines, 27 May 1987.

58. US personnel had visited Lt Colonel Calida and other key officials in Davao and Davao del Sur associated with the Alsa Masa and the Nakasaka vigilante movements. Money and ideas reportedly changed hands. See *Right Wing Vigilantes*, pp. 16–17, see also pp. 39–41.

59. See *Ang Bayan*, Vol. XIX, No. 2 (April 1987), p. 4, hereafter cited as *Ang Bayan 2*, see also Delacruz et al., *Death Squads*, p. 45.

60. Delacruz et al., *Death Squads*, p. 4.

61. The NPA general staff claimed that US private organisations were involved, including the Moonies and CAUSA. They also claimed the vigilantes were supported by USAID in Davao, Rich and George interview.

62. Zindar interview.

63. Interview with Bimboy Penaranda, PARUD, Manila, 28 May 1987, hereafter cited as 'Bimboy interview.'

64. See *Right Wing Vigilantes*, p. 41.

65. These included death squad operations and training AFP officers and troops in techniques of terrorism, torture and assassination, as reported in *Ang Bayan 2*, p. 4, also recorded in the Bimboy interview. There has a been a long tradition of 'former' Special Force personnel involving themselves in CIA operations, see *Right Wing Vigilantes*, pp. 41–2.

CHAPTER 8

1. For the article upon which this assessment was based see Ross Munro, 'The New Khmer Rouge', *Commentary*, Vol. 80 (December 1985), pp. 19–38.

2. See Statement of Richard Armitage, Assistant Secretary of Defense for International Security Affairs in 'Preparations for February 1986 Philippine Presidential Election', *Hearing Before the Committee on Foreign Relations*, United States Senate, 99th Congress, First Session, 18 December 1985 (Washington DC: U.S. Government Printing Office, 1986), p. 45, hereafter cited as *Hearings 3*.

3. Statement of Richard Armitage in *Hearings 3*, pp. 25–6. See also the Executive Summary of a Report to the Committee on Foreign Relations, United States Senate by the Center for Democracy, Boston University: 'The Presidential Election Process in the Philippines' in *Hearings 3*, p. 76.

4. Statement of Richard Armitage in *Hearings 3*, pp. 25–6.

5. Marcos was particularly pressured to get rid of General Ver who was implicated in the Aquino assassination. It was also thought he would make the conduct of fair and free elections extremely difficult, see *Hearings 3*, p. 39.

6. See Christopher Madison, 'Rare White House-Congress Consensus on Policy Toward Philippines', *National Journal* (11 November 1985), p. 2711.

7. Enrile in particular also had his own presidential ambitions. Enrile was fired by Aquino as Defence Minister in November 1986 after she was provoked by rumours of an imminent Enrile-led coup.

8. Statement of Richard Armitage in *Hearings 2*, pp. 94–5 (for full *Hearings 2* reference, see Chapter 1, note 4).

9. See statement of Richard Armitage in *Hearings 2*, p. 103.

10. In this process, Ambassador Bosworth was accredited with much success in getting Aquino to move closer to the US position, see Delacruz et al., *Death Squads*, p. 38.

11. See *Right Wing Vigilantes and US Involvement, Report of a US-Philippines Fact Finding Mission to the Philippines, May 20–30, 1987* (Manila: Philippines Alliance of Human Rights Advocates) (July 1987), p. 38.

12. For the Committee's account of some atrocities inflicted by the military, CHDF and the vigilantes see 'Report of the Committee', pp. 10–13.

13. This was probably more Aquino's own initiative as it was against the advice of the military. For details on the number of prisoners released see Amnesty International, *Philippines, Unlawful Killings*, by Military and Paramilitary Forces (New York: Amnesty International Publications, 1988), p. 11.

14. The NDF cited this incident as the reason for its withdrawal from the ceasefire – interview with General Staff members, New People's Army (aliases 'Rich' and 'George'), Manila, Philippines, 29–30 May 1987.

15. Interview with members of the NPA 'Sparrow' squad of the Alex Boncayao Brigade, Navotas, Manila, 29 May 1987.

16. Three members of the Sparrow squad that I interviewed were involved in the demonstration on the Mendiola Bridge and claimed that the military action was premeditated. It was also the reason they claimed they had joined the NPA.

17. This was most apparent in the different views of Gaston Sigur, the Assistant Secretary of State for East Asian and Pacific Affairs, and Richard Armitage, the Assistant Secretary of Defense.

18. For the breakdown of the peace negotiations and ceasefire, see *Human Rights in the Philippines, Report of an Australian Fact-Finding Mission to the Philippines, 28 November–5 December 1987*, edited by Shirley Randell (Melbourne: Philippines Resources Centre, February 1988) pp. 51–3.

19. See Statement of Charles D. Gray, Director of the Asian American Free Labour Institute in *Hearings and Markup Before The Committee on Foreign Affairs and its Sub-committee on Asian and Pacific Affairs*, House of Representatives, 99th Congress, April

29–July 23, 1986 (Washington DC: US Government Printing Office, 1986), pp. 166–9, hereafter cited as *Hearings* 5.

20. For an outline of their programmes which included low-interest loans, training and health programmes in order to keep farmers and others in work thereby preventing them from joining the insurgency, see *Hearings 2*, pp. 167–85.

21. *Hearings* 5, pp. 174–6.

22. *Hearings* 5, p. 176. The AAFLI was also identified as pursuing psyops activities in communist areas to undercut the revolution's support base. See Weldon Bello, *Creating the Third Force: US Sponsored Low Intensity Conflict in the Philippines* (San Francisco: Institute for Food and Development Policy, 1987), p. 91.

23. The White House, *National Security Strategy of the United State*s (January 1988), p. 31.

24. Interview with Richard Fisher, Heritage Foundation, Washington, DC, 1 June 1988.

25. Fisher interview.

26. This uprising was named 'EDSA' after the main street in Manila in which the February people's power revolution was centered.

27. The NPA itself claimed that disinformation was central to these anti-communist propaganda campaigns. The NPA general staff claimed such propaganda accused them of atrocities and overtaxing the people, whereas they claimed: 'It's long been the practice of the military in the Philippines to demand tribute from the people. The P.C. are known as "Squeezer" or "Karakao" and the army also tax', Rich and George interview.

28. This was claimed in Bello, *Creating the Third Force*, p. 96.

29. See *Right Wing Vigilantes*, pp. 38–48. For an extract of the Christic Institute's account of Singlaub's activities in the Philippines see 'Christic Papers', pp. 299–300 (for full 'Christic Papers' reference, see Chapter 6, note 10).

30. See Roland Simbulan, *The Bases of our Insecurity* (Metro Manila: Balai Fellowship, 1985), p. 186.

31. Silver interview. For the CPP/NPA view see also *Ang Bayan*, Vol. XXI, No. 8 (October 1989), p. 12.

32. Representatives of student groups told the Clarke team that these activities had been going on since 1984, see *Right Wing Vigilantes*, pp. 20–30.

33. *Right Wing Vigilantes*, pp. 21, 41, 50.

34. For military disinformation as well as media campaigns, see Delacruz et al., *Death Squads*, pp. 3, 32–3. For some reported examples of the military abuses see Amnesty International, *Philippines, Unlawful Killings*, pp. 5–26.

35. For Pala's and other radio commentators' pro-vigilante activities in Davao, see Enrique Delacruz, Aida Jordan and Jorge Emmanuel (eds), *Death Squads in the Philippines* (Manila: Alliance for Philippine Concerns, September 1987), pp. 30–1.

36. See *Right Wing Vigilantes*, pp. 44–51. The Clarke Report was strongly supported by other human rights groups also investigating the CIA role in the Philippines including the Philippine Alliance of Human Rights Advocates and the Ecumenical Partnership for International Concerns.

37. As admitted by Under-secretary of State Armacost, see Delacruz et al., *Death Squads*, pp. 39–40.

38. *Bulletin Today* (4 May 1987), pp. 1, 21.

39. The fanatically religious nature of the vast majority of these groups was so often reflected in their names.

40. Interview with Bimboy Penaranda, PARUD, Manila, 28 May 1987.

41. Sparrow interview.

42. This was often undertaken by a bizarre and brutal fanatical religious sect called 'Lord of the Sacred Heart'. Its members were also dubbed 'TadTad' (Filipino for 'chop-chop'), because of the ritual in which they used machetes to chop up their enemies (author's own observations). For more details of these human rights abuses

committed by the vigilantes and the military, see Amnesty International, *Philippines, Unlawful Killings*, pp. 26–37, *Human Rights*.

43. See 'Report of the Committee', p. 25.

44. 'Armed Civilian Vigilantes – Right Wing Death Squads?', *Philippine Issues*, Vol. 1, No. 8, p. 2.

45. 'Surrenderees' is a term commonly used by both the Philippine military and press to denote those fighters who have surrendered or 'returned' to the government side.

46. As claimed by Lt Colonel Calida, the Davao City Military Commander, see Delacruz et al., *Death Squads*, p. 18. For further examples noted by the Clarke team, see *Right Wing Vigilantes*, p. 15.

47. I inspected a poster, sanctioned by the AFP, that encouraged the capture of certain rebels 'dead or alive'. Also for claims that the military were using vigilantes to kill civilians, see Delacruz et al., *Death Squads*, pp. 15–16.

48. These claims were made by members of both PAHRA and EPIC. Members of the NPA also made these claims.

49. By the end of December 1987, Aquino had been challenged by five attempted coups waged by the right wing of the military and the RAM group.

50. General Ileto was forced to retire in January 1988, see Alfred McCoy, 'Low Intensity Conflict in the Philippines' in Barry Carr and Elaine McKay (eds), Low Intensity Conflict: Theory and Practice in Central America and South-East Asia (Melbourne: La Trobe University Institute of Latin American Studies and Monash University Centre for South-East Asian Studies, 1989), p. 61. Both Ileto and Ramos, however, were pro-US, see Bello, *Creating the Third Force*, p. 71.

51. Falling living standards were highlighted as a prominent factor in the growth of the communist insurgency in the Philippines by a Congressional Research Service report, see Madison, 'Rare White House-Congress Consensus', p. 2710.

52. See Prepared Statement of John C. Monjo, Deputy Assistant Secretary of State for East Asia and Pacific Affairs in 'United States Policy toward the Philippines And The Proposed Supplemental Aid Package', in *Hearings* 5, p. 89.

53. Monjo in *Hearings* 5, pp. 77–89.

54. See Monjo in *Hearings* 5, p. 118.

55. This aid programme was based on an assessment of Philippine economic and military needs by a US assistance team headed by a USAID administrator and including senior Treasury, State, and Defense Department officials, see statement of John Monjo in *Hearings* 5, pp. 89–90. For details of the USAID report and details of the bilateral economic assistance package for the Philippines in 1986, see Statement of the Hon. Charles Greenleaf, Assistant Administrator, Asia Bureau, Agency for International Development in *Hearings* 5, pp. 112–27.

56. For this and other economic measures designed to assist the Philippines, see *Hearings* 5, pp. 114–17.

57. Armitage Statement to the US Senate Foreign Relations Committee Hearings, 3 June 1986, p. 10, as reported in Delacruz et al., *Death Squads*, p. 40.

58. 'Armitage Report', pp. 6–10 (for complete 'Armitage Report' reference, see Chapter 7, note 7).

59. For one account, see 'America's Secret Soldiers: The Buildup of U.S. Special Operations Forces', *Defense Monitor*, Vol. XIV, No. 2 (Washington, DC: Center for Defense Information, 1985), pp. 6–7.

60. Statement of Richard L. Armitage, Assistant Secretary of Defense for International Security Affairs, 'Situation in the Philippines and Implications for US Policy', Statement to the Subcommittee on Asian and Pacific Affairs, Committee on Foreign Affairs, House of Representatives, 12 March 1985, p. 9, hereafter cited as Armitage, 'Situation in the Philippines'.

61. See Armitage testimony in *Hearings* 5, p. 100.

62. Armitage Statement in *Hearings* 5, pp. 105–6.

63. Delacruz et al., *Death Squads*, p. 40.

64. This was the equivalent of six battalions, previously used for the security of the Marcos regime, see Armitage Statement in *Hearings* 5, pp. 96–7.

65. There is considerable evidence that Aquino succumbed to pressure from the NAFP and sectors within her government to adopt this hard-line approach long advocated by the military, see *Right Wing Vigilantes*, p. 7.

66. Simbulan argued that US Special Operations teams operated in Zamboanga province in Mindanao, a focus of the Muslim insurgency, see Simbulan, *The Bases*, pp. 178–9. This was also claimed by Rear Admiral and Minister of Muslim Affairs (former Commander in Chief, Philippines Southern Command) Romulo Espaldon in an interview I had with the Rear Admiral in Manila on 11 August 1983, hereafter cited as 'Espaldon interview'.

67. For example, the US military participated in the bombing of Jolo against Muslim rebels in 1974, according to Rear Admiral Espaldon. This was also claimed by Hadji Morad Ibrahim, Commander Overall Kotabato Revolutionary Committee Chairman (former Commander of the Moro National Liberation Front (MNLF) in an interview I had with him in Cotabato, August 14, 1983, and Abo Kalil Yahiya, Vice Chairman (MNLF) Sultan Kuderat (former member of Cease-fire Committee, Tripoli, 1976) whom I also interviewed at Sultan Kuderat, 7 August 1983. For another account of US involvement see Simbulan, *The Bases*, pp. 169–82.

68. See Nayan Chanda, 'Here Comes the Spies', *Far Eastern Economic Review* (9 April 1987), p. 19.

69. Ralph McGehee, a former CIA agent in Vietnam, argued that these would most likely be used in the area of intelligence gathering, computerising military and police files, as cited in Bello, *Creating the Third Force*, p. 90.

70. *Right Wing Vigilantes*, p. 4.

71. A 'Finding' allows an agency to undertake actions recommended in the document that might otherwise be prohibited. It was also suggested that the Finding removed restrictions on CIA operatives visiting field commands and liaising with military officers below the level of Chief of Staff, see Phil Bronstein, 'Reagan OKs CIA Aid for Philippines', *San Francisco Examiner* (22 March 1987).

72. Key agencies coordinated by NISA included the Military Intelligence Groups of the AFP, the Constabulary's Intelligence Service, Metrocom Intelligence and Security Group, the Constabulary's Criminal Investigation Service and Army Intelligence Units (G2).

73. In Davao, DPAs strongly infiltrated all levels of the NPA causing a decimating and bloody fratricidal reaction within the organization. The Davao front thus collapsed and many genuine NPA cadre sought refuge with the military or even the vigilantes, 'Rich and George interview'.

74. General Lim in Manila even labelled his own anti-Sparrow, vigilante 'hit-squad' creations as 'Eagle' units.

75. See Candy Quimpo, 'The Vigilantes', *Asia Magazine, Sunday Morning Post* (7 August 1988), p. 12.

76. A common explanation for such outrages as the beheading of labour leaders or communists was that they were carried out by the Filipino people who were reacting against the terrorism of communism by taking justice into their own hands.

77. Arnel De Guzman claimed for example: 'LIC blurs the distinction of the responsibilities between the civilian and the military ... and so it's a very good excuse for the killings because the military can wash their hands and say this is the people – Alsa Masa is the people', De Guzman interview.

78. See Bello, *Creating the Third Force*, p. 92.

79. Ma. Socorro Diokno argued that approximately US$6 million was spent by the US bases on civic action annually. Diokno cited a Presidential Cabinet Committee, RP-US Military and Security Relations, 1985, at Annex. pp. 10–11 (unpublished paper located at PAHRA, Manila, 23 May 1987).

80. As recorded in Bello, *Creating the Third Force*, p. 92.

81. Many projects were funded out of the 'Economic Support Funds' (ESF) provided for under the Bases Agreement of 1983. See Gaston Sigur, Assistant Secretary of State for East Asia and Pacific Affairs, 'The Philippines: Recent Developments and US Assistance', Statement to the Sub-Committee for Asian and Pacific Affairs (17 March 1987), pp. 3–4.

82. As reported at the Philippine International Forum, USNS hospital ship Mercy on Medical Mission to Davao, International Civic Action for Philippine Counterinsurgency, 1987. The mission was a combined United States–Philippines military manoeuvre coordinated by the JUSMAG.

83. Diokno's unpublished paper, pp. 11–12.

84. The Clarke Report came to a similar conclusion arguing that the activities of CAUSA and Singlaub, for example, indicated the kind of 'privatizing' of US foreign policy that the Tower Commission warned specifically against. See *Right Wing Vigilantes*, p. 38.

85. 'Rich and George interview'.

86. 'Rich and George interview'. See also Gregg R. Jones, *Red Revolution* (London: Westview Press, 1989), pp. 157–9.

87. See for example the Monjo Statement in *Hearings* 5, pp. 84–5.

88. There were six frustrated coups in Aquino's first 18 months proving that right-wing elements of the AFP were also obstacles to LIC.

89. Bello, *Creating the Third Force*, p. 78.

90. Salmon interview.

91. For an indication of these divergent views see the differences between Assistant Secretary of State for East Asia and the Pacific, Gaston Sigur, and Assistant Secretary of Defense, Richard Armitage, in Chanda, 'Here Come the Spies', p. 19. Secretary of State Shultz also agreed with Armitage.

92. For example, see Armitage, 'Situation in the Philippines', p. 19.

CHAPTER 9

1. Operation Desert Storm was the term used to describe the war waged by the United States with the support of its major European allies (under the auspices of the United Nations) against Iraq in 1990–91.

2. See Raymond Copson and Richard Cronin, 'The Reagan Doctrine and its Prospects', *Survival* IISS (January/February 1987).

3. See Copson and Cronin, 'The Reagan Doctrine', pp. 40–5.

4. The long military conflict continued however, as the victorious US-backed 'freedom fighters' immediately began to fight among themselves.

5. The intense socioeconomic crisis that Cuba endured was labelled by Castro in March 1990 as the 'Special Period in Time of Peace', or in other words – an economic and political state of emergency. See 'Ending the Cold War', *Defense Monitor* Vol. XXIII, No. 1 (Washington DC: Center for Defense Information), p. 3.

6. See 'Ending the Cold War', p. 3.

7. Major among these efforts has been the use of the electronic media beamed in from the US mainland. Interview with Nancy Mason, Deputy Coordinator, Office of Cuban Affairs, Department of State, Washington, DC, February 1995.

8. Interview with Wayne Smith, former Head of Mission, US Interests Section in Cuba (1979–82), Washington, DC, 3 February 1995.

9. Perhaps the most stark example of recent US attempts to further impose its will on Cuba was Washington's implementation of the Cuban Democracy Act (CDA), also known as the Torrecelli Amendment of 1992. This draconian act further tightened the embargo to the extent that even the most basic commodities were rationed or no longer available in Cuba. For details of the embargo, see 'What You Need to Know About the US Embargo' (Washington, DC: Office of Foreign Assets Control, US Department of Treasury, 26 August 1994).

INDEX